STECK-VAUGHN
PRE-GED
WRITING

REVIEWERS

Jim Barlow
Retired Vice-Principal
of Adult Education
Waterloo Region
District School Board
Educational Consultant
and Author
Kitchener, Ontario

William Burns
Instructor
San Mateo County
Office of Education
Palo Alto, California

Sherri Claiborne
Literacy Coordinator
Claiborne County
Adult Reading Experience
(CCARE)
Tazewell, Tennessee

Bill Freeland
Almonte Adult School
Almonte, California

Joanie Griffin-Rethlake
Adult Education Division
Harris County
Department of Education
Houston, Texas

Jim Scheil
Jersey City Adult Education Center
Jersey City, New Jersey

STECK-VAUGHN
C O M P A N Y

A Division of Harcourt Brace & Company

www.steck-vaughn.com

Acknowledgments

Executive Editor: Ellen Northcutt

Project Editor: Julie Higgins

Senior Editor: Donna Townsend

Design Manager: Jim Cauthron

Cover Design: Jim Cauthron

Cover Production: Donna Neal and Alan Klemp

Media Researchers: Claudette Landry, Christina Berry

Electronic Production: PC&F, Inc.

Photograph Credits: Cover, p. i and title page, p. ii © Telegraph Colour Library/FPG International; p. 13 © Gary A. Conner/PhotoEdit; p. 72 © PhotoDisc; pp. 81,146 © Superstock; p. 155 © Spencer Grant/PhotoEdit; p. 202 © Tony Freeman/PhotoEdit; p. 210 © PhotoDisc

Literary Credits

p. 26	Reprinted with the permission of Simon & Schuster Books for Young Readers, an imprint of Simon & Schuster Children's Publishing Division from *My Grandmother's Journey* by John Cech. Text copyright © 1991 John Cech.
p. 36	"The Voice from the Wall" from *The Joy Luck Club* by Amy Tan. Copyright © 1989 by Amy Tan. Used by permission of Putnam Berkley, a division of Penguin Putnam Inc.
p. 48	From "On Becoming A Scientist" by Dr. Mae C. Jemison, as appeared in *Odyssey*, January 1996. Reprinted by permission of the author.
pp. 113, 121	© 1994–1998 Federal Express Corporation. All Rights Reserved. Reprinted by permission.

ISBN 0-7398-0981-4

1 2 3 4 5 6 7 8 9 10 PO 03 02 01 00 99

Contents

UNIT 1

• Steps in the Process • Step 1: Prewriting, Define Your Topic, Generate Ideas, Organize Your Ideas • Step 2: Writing the First Draft, Writing Topic Sentences, Developing Supporting Details, Organizing Details, Writing the Conclusion • Step 3: Editing and Revising, Editing Checklist • Step 4: Writing the Final Draft, Proofreading Checklist • Step 5: Publishing (Sharing the Final Draft)

• Elements of Narrative Writing • Time Order • Point of View • Supporting Details • Apply Your Writing Skills: Write a Narrative Essay • Grammar Links: Pronouns • Subjects and Predicates • Complete Sentences and Fragments

• Elements of Descriptive Writing • Descriptive Details • Sensory Details • Figurative Language • Apply Your Writing Skills: Write a Descriptive Essay • Grammar Links: Adjectives and Adverbs • Compound Sentences • Complex Sentences • Words in Series

• Elements of Expository Writing • Connecting Words and Phrases • Connecting Words for Style • Expanding Your Vocabulary with Synonyms • Choosing the Best Synonym • Point of View • Polishing Your Work • Apply Your Writing Skills: Write an Expository Essay • Grammar Links: Active and Passive Voice • Changing Voice • Sentence Revision

• Elements of Persuasive Writing • Using Connecting Words • Writing Compare and Contrast Sentences • Using Specific and Fresh Language • Supporting the Main Idea • Apply Your Writing Skills: Write a Persuasive Essay • Grammar Links: Subject-Verb Agreement • Compound Subjects • Singular and Plural Words

UNIT 2

• Personal Letters • Business Letters • Writing Style • Personal Letter Format • Business Letter Format • Organizing Business Letters • Apply Your Writing Skills: Write a Letter Requesting Information • Write Letters for a Job Interview • Grammar Links: Capitalization • Punctuation

• Resumes • Personal Data Sheet • Job Application Forms • Apply Your Writing Skills: Write Your Resume • Complete a Job Application Form • Grammar Link: Action Verbs and Phrases

• Formats and Uses • Forms • Order Forms • Invoices • Shipping Forms • Messages • Fax Messages • E-mail Messages • Memos • Apply Your Writing Skills: Completing a Form • Writing a Memo • Grammar Links: Plurals • Possessives • Contractions

To the Student

How to Use This Book

Writing, like speaking, is a form of expression and communication. When you speak clearly, other people can understand what you are saying. Likewise, when you write well, your words express your ideas so the reader can understand them.

In this book you will learn many types of writing that you can use in your everyday life. You will also learn to use the Writing Process. In addition, you can review and practice grammar skills to help you write more clearly and effectively.

THE WRITING PROCESS

Writing is a process, a series of steps. This five-step process is presented in the first section of the book so you can apply it immediately to all your writing. The Writing Process will help you generate ideas and organize them before you begin writing. Then you will follow the other steps in the Writing Process to write, edit, revise, polish, and publish—or share—your work.

WRITING SKILLS

Each section in Unit 1: Essay and Creative Writing and Unit 2: Workplace and Personal Writing, covers one type of writing. You will learn the skills and elements that are unique to that type of writing. As you work through each section, you will practice by doing several writing activities. There are three main kinds of writing activities in this book:

Practice. Practice activities are short writing exercises that you can usually complete in this book. You will write on the lines provided. Then you can check your answers in the **Answers and Explanations** on pages 231–260.

Write. These are longer writing activities that give you a chance to use the skills you've worked on in the practice activities. You will usually use a separate piece of paper. Then you can compare your writing to sample answers given in the Answers and Explanations.

Apply Your Writing Skills. This is the last activity in each section. Here you will use all of the skills you learned in the lesson to produce a piece of writing. These application pages guide you through each step of the Writing Process for a given topic. At the end of the activity, you can include your final draft in your **Writing Portfolio,** a special folder or notebook where you collect your best pieces of writing.

GRAMMAR LINK

Grammar skills are also presented in each section of Unit 1 and Unit 2 (except Section 1: The Writing Process) on pages titled *Grammar Link*. These grammar skills are the ones most often used with the type of writing covered in that section. Grammar Exercises allow you to practice the grammar skills. If you need further practice in a grammar skill, the colored box next to the Grammar Exercise directs you to specific grammar lessons in Unit 3: Grammar Guide.

HANDBOOKS

Unit 3 is a **Grammar Handbook** that includes instruction and practice on important topics in mechanics, usage, and sentence structure. Unit 4 is a **Writing Handbook.** It includes model essays that illustrate the steps in the Writing Process. It also includes an Editing Checklist and a Proofreading Checklist. These handbooks are good references to consult if you have a question while you are writing.

WRITING AT WORK

Writing at Work is a two-page feature included in each unit. Each Writing at Work introduces a specific job, describes the writing skills the job requires, and includes comprehension and writing activities related to it. It also gives information about other jobs in the same career area.

WRITING CONNECTION

Writing Connection is an interdisciplinary feature included in each unit that shows how writing is related to another content area. It provides information about the relationship, an exercise to check comprehension, and a writing activity.

UNIT REVIEWS

Units 1, 2, and 3 include a Unit Review that lets you see how well you have learned the grammar and writing skills covered in the unit. Each Unit Review also includes a **Writing Extension** activity that provides an opportunity for further practice with the writing skills for the unit.

INVENTORY AND POSTTEST

The Inventory is a self-check to see which skills you already know. When you complete all the items in the Inventory, check your work in the Answers and Explanations section in the back of the book. Then fill out the Inventory Correlation Chart. This chart tells you where each skill is taught in this book. When you complete this book, you will take a Posttest. Compare your Posttest score to your Inventory score to see that your skills have improved.

Inventory

Use this Inventory before you begin Section 1. Don't worry if you can't easily answer all the questions. The Inventory will help you determine which writing skills you are already strong in and which skills you need to practice further.

Read and answer the questions that follow. Check your answers on pages 231–233. Then enter your scores on the chart on page 11.

Capitalization and Punctuation

Read each sentence. If the underlined part is correct, write *C* in the blank. If the part is wrong, write *W* in the blank.

_____ 1. Joe DiMaggio was born in 1914 in <u>Martinez California</u>.

_____ 2. In 1932 he got his start in baseball as a shortstop for a minor league <u>team.</u>

_____ 3. After only two years, he joined the <u>new york yankees</u>.

_____ 4. His first game was attended by 25,000 <u>Italian Americans</u>.

_____ 5. The fans <u>clapped cheered and shouted</u> when he came out on the field.

_____ 6. In the 1941 <u>season;</u> he hit safely in 56 consecutive games.

_____ 7. Many fans wonder if anyone will ever break that <u>record?</u>

_____ 8. During <u>World War II</u>, he took a break from baseball to serve in the Army.

_____ 9. When he returned, he made <u>Summer</u> an exciting time for fans once again.

_____ 10. He had health <u>problems; and</u> he retired from baseball in 1951.

_____ 11. He married movie star Marilyn Monroe in <u>1954; they</u> were divorced soon after.

_____ 12. <u>however,</u> when she died, he brought flowers to her grave.

_____ 13. Later in his life, he appeared on TV as the spokesman for <u>Mr. Coffee</u>.

_____ 14. DiMaggio died on <u>march 8, 1999</u>, of lung cancer at his home in Florida.

Plurals and Possessives

Complete each sentence by writing the correct word in the blank.

15. Sometimes _____ cannot get their children to behave.

    parents   **parents'**   **parent's**

16. They appreciate getting an _____ advice.

    experts   **experts'**   **expert's**

17. Experts say it is wise to show _____ an example of good behavior.

    childrens   **children's**   **children**

18. Mothers and fathers are the most important role models in their children's _____ .

    lifes   **lives**   **life's**

19. Also, be consistent, and make sure your _____ rules do not change.

    familys   **family's**   **families**

20. Remind children to show good manners when they go to a _____ house to play.

    friends   **friends'**   **friend's**

Spelling, Homonyms, and Contractions

Complete each sentence by writing the correct word in the blank.

Did you _____ that diamonds are the hardest
       (21) no   know

substance on Earth? You can _____ a diamond only with a
       (22) break   brake

sharp blow in a certain spot. The diamond will then split,

_____ pieces with flat, even surfaces. A diamond's value is
(23) produceing   producing

based on its clearness, color, and _____ . Diamonds are
       (24) weight   wieght

used to make _____ jewelry, but they can also be used to
      (25) beautiful   beautifull

drill a _____ through metal. That is because
     (26) hole   whole

_____ so very hard. In fact, _____
   (27) their   they're   (28) its   it's

difficult to think of anything that a diamond _____ cut.
                        (29) ca'nt   can't

Go on to the next page.

Nouns and Pronouns

Read each sentence. If the underlined part is correct, write *C* in the blank. If the part is wrong, write it correctly in the blank.

_____ 30. A thousand years ago, only the people living around the city of Kiev called themselves <u>Russians</u>.

_____ 31. In the 1200s, the warlike Mongols conquered <u>they</u>.

_____ 32. By the 1500s, one prince had the <u>strengths</u> to proclaim himself czar, or king.

_____ 33. This prince was named <u>ivan</u>.

_____ 34. In 1556, he made his own city, <u>moscow</u>, the capital of Russia.

_____ 35. Over the next three <u>Centuries</u>, Russia's empire grew across Asia.

_____ 36. There were many different people in the country, and <u>they</u> spoke many different languages.

_____ 37. Many poor peasants farmed land owned by the rich, and <u>their's</u> was a hard life.

_____ 38. Then in 1917, the czar was overthrown, and <u>him</u> and his family were later killed.

_____ 39. The Communists took over and divided the country into 15 separate republics, each with <u>their</u> own capital city.

_____ 40. All <u>them</u> republics together formed the Soviet Union.

_____ 41. Under the Communists, the <u>Government</u> ran the economy.

_____ 42. The people were told that the factories and farms belonged to the state, not to <u>them</u>.

_____ 43. In the 1980s, the Soviet Union broke up, and Russia became a smaller, democratic country whose people vote for leaders to govern <u>them</u>.

Subject-Verb Agreement, Tenses, and Irregular Verbs

Complete each sentence by writing the correct verb in the blank.

44. In the past, recovery from an operation _____ a slow process.

    is   **was**

45. No one _____ expected to go home quickly after an operation.

    was   **were**

46. Today, medical students are _____ that people should resume activity quickly.

    teached   **taught**

47. Now we know that the sooner patients _____ back to their normal activities, the better their health will be.

    go   **went**

48. Patients who _____ an exercise program will recover even more quickly.

    begin   **begun**

49. New medicines _____ the danger of infection.

    reduce   **reduces**

50. Wounds _____ faster, too, thanks to better bandage materials.

    heal   **healed**

51. Some recent drugs _____ blood clots from forming.

    prevent   **prevents**

52. Researchers have _____ that sharp rises in blood pressure can be controlled by fluids and exercise.

    found   **finded**

53. In the past ten years, we have _____ big advances in other medical methods, too.

    saw   **seen**

54. For example, doctors _____ some hearing problems with sharp beams of light.

    repair   **repairs**

55. Plastics _____ used to repair noses, ears, and chins.

    are   **is**

Adjectives and Adverbs

Complete each sentence by writing the correct word in the blank.

56. It is a fact that widows and widowers do not live as

    _____ as married people.

    well   good   best

57. Their illnesses are _____ than those of married
    people.

    worse   worst   bad

58. They often recover from illnesses more _____.

    slow   slowly   slower

59. They are even likely to die _____ than married
    people, too.

    soon   sooner   soonest

60. Research has shown that people tend to do _____ if
    they do not have social ties.

    bad   badly   worst

61. Those who are alone have death rates two to three times

    _____ than those with many friends.

    higher   more high   highest

62. Even having a pet is _____ than being completely
    alone.

    better   best   good

63. Perhaps the _____ life is the lonely one.

    difficult   difficultest   most difficult

64. Loneliness can be the _____ condition of all to bear.

    harder   hardest   most hardest

Sentences, Fragments, and Run-ons

Below are six sentences (complete thoughts), five fragments (incomplete thoughts), and four run-on sentences (two complete thoughts run together without correct punctuation).

Put an *S* next to each complete sentence. Put an *F* next to each fragment. Put an *R* next to each run-on.

_____ 65. One good way to save money.

_____ 66. Is to perform minor car repairs yourself.

_____ 67. Begin by reading through the owner's manual.

_____ 68. Buy some simple supplies get everything you need.

_____ 69. Buying spark plugs, coolant, and oil at a discount store.

_____ 70. You will spend less money there, try it and see.

_____ 71. Be sure to have your owner's manual handy.

_____ 72. If you read it over while you are working on the car.

_____ 73. Your job will be much easier.

_____ 74. Don't skip any steps you might make mistakes.

_____ 75. Work slowly and carefully; there's no need to rush.

_____ 76. You can ask a friend to help, don't be afraid to ask.

_____ 77. Someone who has worked on cars before is best.

_____ 78. Dispose of all waste products carefully.

_____ 79. Washing your hands with a good cleaner, too.

Compound and Complex Sentences

In each blank write the correct word from the list below.

Word List

80. so that	while	because	**83.** yet	so	and
81. or	but	for	**84.** but	and	so
82. and	so	but	**85.** even though	since	when

People used to avoid the sun ——————— 80 ——————— they wanted to keep their skin untanned. They wore hats, ——————— 81 ——————— they stayed inside on sunny days. Women even wore gloves,

——————— 82 ——————— they carried small umbrellas.

Today, doctors warn people about the sun, ——————— 83 ——————— many people still want to get a tan. They go to beaches, pools, and suntan parlors to "catch some rays," ——————— 84 ——————— they smear on gobs of suntan lotion. People do not see how harmful the sun's rays are,

——————— 85 ——————— doctors warn us that too much sun can cause skin cancer.

Combine each pair of sentences to make a compound sentence. Use the connecting word in parentheses.

86. **(and)** The sun dries out your skin. It affects the growth of skin cells.

_____

87. **(but)** The sun feels good. It's not good for you.

_____

Combine each pair of sentences to make a complex sentence. Make the second sentence a dependent thought. Use the connecting word in parentheses.

88. **(if)** You should see your doctor. A mole changes shape or color.

_____

89. **(because)** Changes in a mole can be dangerous. They can be a warning sign of skin cancer.

_____

Parallelism, Modifiers, and Clarity

Underline the word or phrase that best completes each sentence.

90. A rap singer recites rhyming verses while instrumental music
_____ in the background.

    plays   playing   to play

91. _____ African Americans, rap music was first heard in the 1970s.

    Having been developed by   Developed by   Being the creation of

92. A DJ would create the background by mixing parts of different songs and _____ scratching sounds.

    adding   to add   added

93. _____, the background music might be created by synthesizers or drum machines.

    Today   In these present times   In the current situation

94. Rap artists might also include street sounds _____ it more interesting.

    **in the desire to be making   to make
    with the intention of making**

95. When rap music first started, you would _____ in nightclubs.

    only hear it   hear only it   hear it only

96. Now, by listening to the radio, _____ every day.

    rap is heard   you can hear rap   DJs play rap

97. Many teenagers _____.

    **use rap slang who like the music   use rap slang, liking the music
    who like the music use rap slang**

98. Rap music often deals with difficult topics such as gangs, crime, and

    _____.

    drugs   drug addiction   being on drugs

99. By showing violence against women in a positive light,

    _____.

    **some people criticized male rappers
    some criticism of rappers occurred
    some male rappers opened themselves to criticism**

100. Queen Latifah was a female rap singer in the 1990s who was talented, popular, and _____.

    was a big success   successful   she successfully sang

Essay Writing

This part of the Inventory will help you determine how well you write. You will write about something that happened to you. To write clearly, follow these steps.

- ❏ 1. Read the topic carefully.

- ❏ 2. Get your thoughts flowing. On a separate sheet of paper, write down all your ideas that relate to the topic.

- ❏ 3. Plan what you will say before you start to write. Choose the details of your story that will be the most interesting. Decide the order in which you will tell them.

- ❏ 4. Write your first draft on a separate sheet of paper.

- ❏ 5. Review what you have written, and make any changes that will improve your work.

- ❏ 6. Read over your essay for correct sentence structure, spelling, punctuation, capitalization, and usage.

- ❏ 7. Copy your final draft on a separate sheet of paper.

TOPIC

Sometimes a decision that seems unimportant can change the course of our future: where we will live, what kind of career we will have, who we will settle down with. Other times, it is clear to us that our decisions will have a huge impact on us, and the choice is even harder to make.

Write about a decision that changed your life. Tell about the events leading up to the decision, how you eventually decided, and the consequences of your choice. Write at least three paragraphs.

When you have finished your essay, give it to your instructor or a person you know with good writing skills. You may also give the person the checklist on page 10 to help him or her evaluate your essay.

Inventory

Essay Evaluation Guide

If an area is checked *NO*, turn to these pages for practice: 17–23, 27, 32–33, 49, 61, 68–69;

pages 22–23, 45, 50, 51–52, 55, 64–65, 140–141, 193–194, 197–201;

pages 22–25.

See also the Correlation Chart on page 11 for pages to practice specific topics.

	YES	NO
Content		
Is the main idea stated clearly?	❏	❏
Does each paragraph have a topic sentence?	❏	❏
Are topic sentences supported by details?	❏	❏
Are details written in a logical order?	❏	❏
Is the right amount of information included?	❏	❏
(Check for details that are missing or not needed.)		
Style		
Did the writing hold your interest?	❏	❏
Are thoughts and ideas expressed clearly?	❏	❏
Are any ideas repeated?	❏	❏
Are some words used too many times?	❏	❏
Grammar		
Are all sentences complete sentences?	❏	❏
Are any sentences too long and hard to understand?	❏	❏
Are any sentences too short and choppy?	❏	❏
Are nouns and pronouns used correctly?	❏	❏
Are verbs used correctly?	❏	❏
Are adjectives and adverbs used correctly?	❏	❏
Is correct punctuation used in every sentence?	❏	❏
Is correct capitalization used in every sentence?	❏	❏
Are all words spelled correctly?	❏	❏

Overall, on a scale of 1 to 6, how would you rate this essay?

_____

Inventory Correlation Chart

The chart below will help you determine your strengths and weaknesses in grammar and writing skills.

Directions

Circle the number of each item you answered correctly on the Inventory. Count the number of items you answered correctly in each row. Write the amount in the Total Correct space in each row. (For example, in the Capitalization and Punctuation row, write the number correct in the blank before *out of 14*.) Complete this process for the remaining rows. Then add the nine totals to get your TOTAL CORRECT for the Inventory.

Skill Areas	Item Numbers	Total Correct	Pages
Capitalization and Punctuation	1, 2, 3, 4, 5, 6, 7, 8, 9, 10, 11, 12, 13, 14	13 out of 14	50, 87–89, 156–160
Plurals and Possessives	15, 16, 17, 18, 19, 20	5 out of 6	116–117, 161–162
Spelling, Homonyms, and Contractions	21, 22, 23, 24, 25, 26, 27, 28, 29	9 out of 9	118, 163–167
Nouns and Pronouns	30, 31, 32, 33, 34, 35, 36, 37, 38, 39, 40, 41, 42, 43	11 out of 14	28, 169–175
Subject-Verb Agreement, Tenses, and Irregular Verbs	44, 45, 46, 47, 48, 49, 50, 51, 52, 53, 54, 55	11 out of 12	30, 66–67, 140–141, 180–184
Adjectives and Adverbs	56, 57, 58, 59, 60, 61, 62, 63, 64	9 out of 9	38–39, 176–179
Sentences, Fragments, and Run-ons	65, 66, 67, 68, 69, 70, 71, 72, 73, 74, 75, 76, 77, 78, 79	11 out of 15	30–31, 187–190
Compound and Complex Sentences	80, 81, 82, 83, 84, 85, 86, 87, 88, 89	10 out of 10	42–44, 191–192, 195–196
Parallelism, Modifiers, and Clarity	90, 91, 92, 93, 94, 95, 96, 97, 98, 99, 100	8 out of 11	45, 55, 128–129, 193–194, 197–201

TOTAL CORRECT FOR INVENTORY 82 **out of 100**

If you answered fewer than 95 items correctly, look at the skill areas listed above. In which areas do you need more practice? Page numbers for practice are given in the right-hand column above.

Essay and Creative Writing

Writing is an important basic skill—as important as reading. You need to write well for school and for most good jobs. You can also write for personal development or enjoyment. This unit will help you learn how to use a writing process with different types of writing.

Essays are writings about real things—people, places, objects, events, or ideas. You write them from your personal viewpoint. Short stories, plays, and poetry are all examples of creative writing. These writings are usually about people or events that you make up, or create, but sometimes they also include things that really happened. You will get an opportunity to write essays and creative pieces as you work in this unit.

○ If something unusual happened to you, would you choose to write an essay about it or a short story?

○ If you had to write about prejudice, would you choose to write an essay about it or a short story?

SECTIONS

❶ **The Writing Process**

❷ **Narrative Writing**
Grammar Link: **pronouns, subjects and predicates, complete sentences and fragments**

❸ **Descriptive Writing**
Grammar Link: **adjectives and adverbs, compound sentences, complex sentences, words in series**

❹ **Expository Writing**
Grammar Link: **active and passive voice, changing voice, sentence revision**

❺ **Persuasive Writing**
Grammar Link: **subject-verb agreement, compound subjects, singular and plural words**

The Writing Process

Steps in the Process

In this section you will be introduced to the five steps of the Writing Process:

Step 1: Prewriting
Step 2: Writing the First Draft
Step 3: Editing and Revising
Step 4: Writing the Final Draft
Step 5: Publishing (Sharing the Final Draft)

Step 1: Prewriting

Prewriting means planning before you begin to write. This first step in the writing process involves defining your topic, generating ideas about it, and organizing those ideas.

Define Your Topic

To define your topic, first define your **purpose** for writing and the **audience** for whom you are writing.

- **Identify Your Purpose** Ask, *Why am I writing?* Possible answers are to tell a story, to describe, to explain, or to persuade.
- **Identify Your Audience** Ask, *Who will read what I am writing?* Possible answers are a friend, a coworker, a teacher, or a potential employer.

EXAMPLE Melissa Sanchez attended a class at a community college. Her English instructor asked the students to write an essay on a topic that would help fellow students do well in the class. Melissa thought about what might help the other students. First Melissa defined her purpose and audience.

Purpose: To explain   **Audience:** Students in my English class

Then she made the following list of possible topics:

1. Finding your way around the library
2. Good study habits
3. How to use the library
4. Places to study on campus

Melissa selected "how to use the library" as her topic.

Choose a topic that is not either too general or too limited. For example, suppose you are asked to write a two-page essay on hobbies. This is a general topic that could fill a book. But some topics that you could cover in a brief essay are "refinishing old furniture" or "getting started in photography."

A topic that is too narrow or limited is also hard to write about because you may run out of things to say. For example, the topic of "wood-refinishing tools" is too limited for a two-page essay on hobbies.

Choose a topic that you already know something about or one that you find interesting. This will make your writing task easier.

PRACTICE

Below each general subject, list two topics that you could write about. The first one is started for you.

1 Subject: Sports
   Purpose: To explain
   Audience: A group of children
   Topic 1: _How to Play Soccer_
   Topic 2: _____

2 Subject: Jobs
   Purpose: To describe
   Audience: Your friends
   Topic 1: _____
   Topic 2: _____

3 Subject: Movies
   Purpose: To describe
   Audience: Your friends
   Topic 1: _____
   Topic 2: _____

4 Subject: Animals
   Purpose: To persuade
   Audience: Fellow students
   Topic 1: _____
   Topic 2: _____

Generate Ideas

After your purpose, audience, and topic are clear in your mind, you are ready to generate ideas about your topic.

- **Explore your thoughts about the topic.** What interests you about the topic? Do you already have information, or will you need to do research?
- **Brainstorm ideas.** Ask yourself questions about the topic to get your ideas flowing. Ask, *Who? What? Where? When? How? Why?* to help you focus on your topic.
- **Talk to other people.** If you have strong opinions on a topic, you might want to discuss the topic with someone whose views are different. If you are unfamiliar with a topic, ask an expert or talk to several people to collect information.
- **Do research.** Read books or articles, watch videotapes, or do online searches on the Internet. You can get help with all these research resources at the library.

Organize Your Ideas

While you are generating ideas, write them down. You can refer to them when you begin to write. First, make a list of your ideas. Next, organize the ideas in the order that you want to write about them. Writing an **outline** and drawing an **idea map** are two ways to organize your ideas.

EXAMPLE   Melissa asked the librarian some questions. She also talked with some other students. Then, she made notes for her essay.

Topic: How to Use the Library

Main Desk   *Services*

staff, pamphlets   *books, periodicals, references*

Next, she wrote an outline to organize her ideas.

I. Main desk   III. Periodicals
     a. Staff — librarians   a. Locating magazine articles
     B. Pamphlets   B. Locating newspaper articles

II. Finding books   IV. Reference section
     a. Card catalog   a. Types of reference materials
     B. Electronic catalog   B. How to use them
     C. Books on shelves

Melissa could have written this idea map instead of writing an outline.

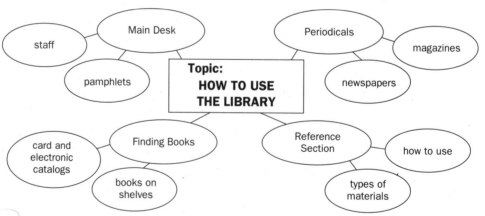

PRACTICE

Brainstorm and list your ideas for this topic: What are the advantages (or disadvantages) of a small (or large) family? Write an outline to organize your ideas. Then make an idea map. Which way of organizing ideas works best for you? Use a separate piece of paper.

Step 2: Writing the First Draft

In Step 1 of the Writing Process, you created a plan for what you are going to write. In Step 2 you will follow your plan and write the first draft. A **first draft** is the first version of your piece. Sometimes you'll need to write two or three drafts before a piece is final. With each draft you will improve the piece.

When writing the first draft, the main goal is to get your ideas on paper in an organized way. Choose words and develop sentences that best express your ideas. Don't worry about perfect word choice, spelling, and punctuation at this stage.

The first draft of the essay will have several paragraphs. Each paragraph will have a topic sentence and supporting details. The **topic sentence** states the main idea that you will develop in the paragraph. The **supporting details** are sentences that relate to the main idea.

Writing Topic Sentences

The first topic sentence you write is an opening statement that tells the **main idea** of the entire piece. It tells the reader your purpose for writing the essay. If you write a good opening statement, you can refer back to it as you continue writing to make sure you have not drifted away from your point.

A good opening statement should be a clearly written summary of the main idea. It should be general enough to introduce the points you will cover in the rest of the piece. Avoid making opening statements that are vague (unclear) or statements that simply announce the topic.

EXAMPLE Melissa reviewed her outline. Then she wrote her main idea:

Students will feel comfortable using the library if they understand how its services work.

Melissa wrote three possible opening statements:

1 *This essay is about how to use the library.*

2 *Using the library is not as hard as you may think.*

3 *The library can be a scary place until you get to know how to use its many services.*

Sentence 1 just announces what the essay is about in general terms. Sentence 2 states the main idea, but it is vague. Since Melissa's goal was to make students feel comfortable using the library by explaining how library services work, she decided that the third sentence was the best opening statement.

Each topic below is followed by three opening statements. Put an X in front of the best statement to introduce each topic.

1 Topic: The Case Against Gun Control

    _____ A.   Owning guns is a constitutional right of all Americans.

    _____ B.   Some people want gun control, but many others don't.

    _____ C.   I am going to write about gun control.

2 Topic: Every Citizen Should Vote

    _____ A.   Voting is not a right; it is a duty of every citizen.

    _____ B.   Voting has been expanded to include almost all adults.

    _____ C.   Some people don't believe in voting.

3 Topic: Avoiding Sun Exposure

    _____ A.   Many people like to spend hot summer days outside.

    _____ B.   You don't have to stay inside to avoid the danger of too much sun.

    _____ C.   There are all kinds of sunscreens on the market.

Developing Supporting Details

Your outline or idea map will guide you through the main points of the essay. As you get to each main point, begin a new paragraph. Each paragraph in an essay has a topic sentence and other sentences that support the topic sentence. You can write several types of detail sentences to support a topic sentence.

Details may:
- be statements of **facts** or **reasons** that prove or disprove a point.
- be **examples** that explain or prove a main idea.
- be listed in **time order,** according to the order in which they occur.
- be listed in **order of importance,** from the most important to the least important or from the least important to the most important.
- show **cause and effect,** how one thing causes another thing to happen.
- **compare or contrast** to show how things are alike or different.

As you write paragraphs, use several types of details to support your topic sentences.

Here are the first three paragraphs of Melissa's essay. Compare these paragraphs to the outline and map of Melissa's essay. Notice that she wrote a topic sentence for each main point and then wrote supporting details to explain those statements.

EXAMPLE **Paragraph 1** The library can be a scary place until you get to know how to use its many services. The basic services in the Central Community College Library are the main information desk, the card catalog, the electronic catalog, the periodical section, and the reference section.

Paragraph 2 The main information desk is staffed by a professional librarian and an assistant librarian. They will answer any questions you have about how to use the library. They also have pamphlets that explain how to use all the library services.

Paragraph 3 The card catalog and the electronic catalog are the basic tools for finding library books. These catalogs list all the books in the library. Books are listed in alphabetical order by subject, title, and author. In the card catalog, the entries are on small cards arranged in drawers. The electronic catalog lists each entry on a computer. Instructions on how to use the electronic catalog are usually posted next to each computer.

PRACTICE

Circle the type of detail used in each supporting sentence.

Paragraph 1 Topic Sentence: Spectator sports are the great American pastime.

1. Many Americans never seem to get enough of the excitement of sports.

    time order   **fact/reason**

2. Some people think football is the most popular of all sports, but soccer is gaining new fans every day.

    compare/contrast   **cause/effect**

3. Another sport that has become more popular is tennis. It used to be the sport of the rich, but now people everywhere are playing and watching.

    cause/effect   **examples**

Paragraph 2 Topic Sentence: Rap music began on the street corner, but it soon entered the musical mainstream.

1. Rap music began topping the charts on almost every major rock radio station.

    fact/reason   **examples**

2. When rap first began, most of the artists dressed in sneakers and sweat suits. It wasn't long before they were wearing expensive clothes and jewelry.

    compare/contrast   **examples**

3. Rap artists began to be featured in major motion pictures. They got recording contracts with major record labels. The Grammy Awards even created a special category to honor rap music artists.

    compare/contrast   **order of importance**

Organizing Details

When you write supporting details, organize them in the clearest, most logical order. This way, the reader can easily follow your train of thought.

PRACTICE

A. Each set of sentences below has a topic sentence and supporting details. Find the topic sentence and write 1 by it. Then number the details in the clearest, most logical order. The first paragraph is started for you.

Paragraph 1

_____1_____ Good study skills take time to develop.

_____ The last rule is turn off the telephone, the TV, and the headphones.

_____ Next, find a quiet place where you can avoid distractions.

_____ First, set aside enough time to get all your assignments done.

_____ Make sure you have all the books and supplies you need.

Paragraph 2

_____ If you don't eat before an interview, you might feel weak and less talkative.

_____ Don't let nervousness spoil your appetite.

_____ Your physical condition can be important to a job interview.

_____ Otherwise you might not be alert during the interview.

_____ Go to bed early the night before.

B. Circle the type of supporting details used in Practice A.

Paragraph 1	examples	time order	cause/effect
Paragraph 2	facts/reasons	compare/contrast	cause/effect

WRITE Write a paragraph on one of the topics below. Use a separate piece of paper.

❶ Morning people and night people are very different. (compare/contrast)

❷ Learning to organize your time will change your life. (time order)

❸ Friendship is one of the most important things in life. (facts/reasons)

Prewrite: List supporting details. Use the type of details shown in parentheses after the topic sentence.

Write: Write the topic sentence and then sentences for your supporting details.

Writing the Conclusion

The last paragraph of your essay is the **conclusion.** The topic sentence of the last paragraph should signal that the essay is drawing to a close. The supporting details should highlight what you want the reader to remember.

Certain words and phrases signal a conclusion. The most commonly used are *in conclusion, to conclude, finally, last, as a result, consequently,* and *therefore.* Here are four methods for writing conclusions.

- **End with a summary and a final thought.**

EXAMPLE Therefore, the facts speak for themselves. The campus library has the greatest number of resources to help you with your studies. And there is one last feature of the library that should be mentioned. It is the quietest and most comfortable place on campus to study.

- **End with a prediction for the future.**

EXAMPLE Once you visit the library and get to know how to use its many services, you will wonder how you ever lived without it.

- **End with a recommendation.**

EXAMPLE Finally, I recommend that you visit the library as soon as possible. If you don't, you will be cheating yourself out of a chance to get to know the best friend a student can have on this campus.

- **End with a question.**

EXAMPLE Now that you have heard all about what the library has to offer, are you still feeling a little insecure about using it? If so, consider talking with one of the librarians. Their job is to make you feel at ease.

PRACTICE

Write the method of conclusion used in each paragraph below.

1 In conclusion, I ask, how many more people will die needlessly before our lawmakers ban the sale or ownership of handguns and automatic weapons?

_____

2 Sadly, it seems that Congress will continue to focus on getting rid of guns instead of getting rid of the drug dealers and other criminals who use guns.

_____

3 To conclude, we must keep the gun control issue alive. Write to your representative and support gun control laws.

_____

Step 3: Editing and Revising

The next step of the writing process is to review and evaluate your work. This is your chance to polish your draft before writing the final version. When you edit, look at **content, style,** and **grammar.** The following checklist contains questions to ask yourself as you edit your work. Read the questions, then read your work. If your answer to a question is *no,* change or **revise** that part of the work. This checklist is also on page 218.

Editing Checklist	YES	NO
Content Does the content reflect your original purpose?	❏	❏
Is the content right for your intended audience?	❏	❏
Is the main idea stated clearly?	❏	❏
Does each paragraph have a topic sentence?	❏	❏
Are topic sentences supported by details?	❏	❏
Are details written in a logical order?	❏	❏
Is the right amount of information included?	❏	❏
(Check for details that are missing or not needed.)		
Style Will the writing hold the reader's interest?	❏	❏
Are thoughts and ideas expressed clearly?	❏	❏
Are any ideas repeated?	❏	❏
Are some words used too many times?	❏	❏
Grammar Are all sentences complete sentences?	❏	❏
Are any sentences too long and hard to understand?	❏	❏
Are any sentences too short and choppy?	❏	❏
Are nouns and pronouns used correctly?	❏	❏
Are verbs used correctly?	❏	❏
Are adjectives and adverbs used correctly?	❏	❏

EXAMPLE This is the first draft of Paragraph 3 of Melissa's essay. You will see some mistakes in it.

The card and electronic catalogs list all the books in the library. You will not find books listed if they don't have them. For example, if you want to find books on the subject of education, look in *E* drawer of the subject index. You will find all the books on education listed by author and title. If you use the electronic catalog you will type in the word *education* on the computer. You will get a list of all the books on education.

Melissa read her draft and used the checklist questions. She found four mistakes in the third paragraph. Her edited and revised versions are on the next page. As Melissa edited her draft, she used the Proofreader's Marks shown on page 24.

Edited Version

The card and el^ectronic catalogs list all the books in ~~the library. You will not find books listed if they don't have them.~~ For example, if you want to find books on the

add detail subject of education, look in *E* drawer of the subject index. You will find all the books on education *are* listed *alphabetically* by author and title. If you use the electronic catalog, you will type in the word *education*. ~~You will get a list of all the books on education.~~

delete unnecessary detail

place details in logical order

delete repeated idea

Revised Version

The card and electronic catalogs list all the books in the library. For example, if you want to find books on the subject of education, look in *E* drawer of the subject index. If you use the electronic catalog you will type in the word *education*. All the books on education are listed alphabetically by author and title.

PRACTICE

Read each sentence to see if it contains an error. Then look at the Editing Checklist. Write the letter for the type of error by the number of the sentence.

(1) There are far fewer smokers today than there were in the past. (2) The time has come to outlaw smoking in all public places. (3) Smoke is a hazard to the healthy nonsmoker. (4) In public places pollutes the air, irritates the eyes. (5) Nonsmokers should stand up and be counted. (6) Since nonsmokers is the majority, they must push for laws that protect their rights.

Sentences

1 _____

2 _____

3 _____

4 _____

5 _____

6 _____

Editing Checklist

a. content error—supporting detail out of order

b. grammar error—wrong verb

c. content error—topic sentence out of order

d. style error—idea not clearly expressed

e. grammar error—incomplete sentence

f. no error

WRITE Now that you have found the mistakes, edit and revise the paragraph on a separate sheet of paper.

Step 4: Writing the Final Draft

After editing and revising your work, prepare a **final draft.** Proofread the revised version to make sure that you did not miss any errors, such as misspelled words, incorrect punctuation, or missing paragraph indentation. To **proofread,** look at each word and punctuation mark to make sure it is correct. Use the following checklist when preparing your final draft. This checklist is also on page 219.

Proofreading Checklist	YES	NO
Is the content right for your intended audience?	❏	❏
Is correct punctuation used in every sentence?	❏	❏
Is correct capitalization used in every sentence?	❏	❏
Are all words spelled correctly?	❏	❏
Are new paragraphs clearly shown?	❏	❏
(Check to see if paragraphs either are indented or have an extra line space in between.)		
If handwritten, is the handwriting as neat as possible?	❏	❏
Is there enough space between words and lines?	❏	❏
If typed on a computer or word processor, are the type font and size appropriate?	❏	❏
Are the margins adequate?	❏	❏

There are special symbols you can use to mark mistakes when you are proofreading. These marks help you spot the errors to fix when you rewrite or retype your final draft. Some basic proofreader's marks are shown below.

Proofreader's Marks

b̲ B	change to a capital letter
B̸ b	change to a lowercase letter
red, white ⌃ and blue ⊙	insert a comma or period
Will you go ?	insert a question mark
Will you go? (and Sue)	insert word(s)
Sp (there) car	check spelling
end. ¶ We will	insert a paragraph indent
go on away	delete a word
and a half	add a space between words

Melissa proofread her essay. Then, she wrote the final version. Compare the two paragraphs on the next page.

Proofread Version

The card and ~~eltronic~~ *electronic* catalogs list all the books in the library. For example, if you want to find books on the subject of education, look in the *E* drawer of the subject index. If you use the electronic catalog, you will type in the word *education* on the computer. All the books on education are listed alphabetically by author and title.

Final Version

The card and electronic catalogs list all the books in the library. For example, if you want to find books on the subject of education, look in the *E* drawer of the subject index. If you use the electronic catalog, you will type in the word *education* on the computer. All the books on education are listed alphabetically by author and title.

PRACTICE

Below is a paragraph from a cover letter to a job application. Use proofreader's marks to make corrections for nine errors.

I am enclosing copy of my resume in resonse to your ad in the *Boston Journal* on June 26, 1999. I hope you will find my my exereience and skills inline with the qualifications for the telemarketing sales position I available to come to your office for a job interview please call me at 555-6242.

WRITE On a separate sheet of paper, rewrite the final version of the paragraph from the exercise above.

Step 5: Publishing (Sharing the Final Draft)

The final step in the Writing Process is **publishing** or **sharing the final draft.** Before sharing the entire piece, if you wish, read it aloud to yourself. As you read, think about what you enjoyed most about doing the writing and what you found to be the hardest part. Make notes.

Then read your essay to a partner or have your partner read it. Ask, *Is the writing clear? Is the piece interesting to read? Is the message clear? What parts need improvement?* Make notes. Use the notes to help you improve your writing.

Date your final draft and notes and keep them in a special folder or notebook. Keep an ongoing record of everything you write. Review your work weekly and add the best pieces to your **writing portfolio.**

For more practice on the Writing Process, turn to pages 212–217 of the Writing Handbook.

Narrative Writing

Elements of Narrative Writing

Narrative writing is a form of writing in which you tell a story about yourself or someone else. If you are writing about yourself, the piece is called a **personal narrative.** This might be an anecdote, a brief story about something that happened to you. Or it could be an autobiography, the story of your life.

Writing a personal narrative in a diary or journal is a good way to think about things that you have done or that have happened to you. It is also a good way to help you consider what you might do differently. Writing a personal narrative in a letter can connect you with a family member or friend.

A narrative essay is a way for you to tell a story about real people—yourself or someone you know. A fictional story is a kind of narrative writing, too. In a fictional story, you make up the people and the events that happen to them.

EXAMPLE Below is an example of a personal narrative. The narrator is the Russian grandmother of writer John Cech, to whom she is telling her story. She survived wars and troubles in Eastern Europe before she came to the United States.

Then came World War II. The enemy marched through our country and took everything—our animals, our crops, our young people. Again we tried to escape to somewhere safe, but soldiers were everywhere, ours and theirs. Both would shoot you if they caught you—they thought you might be a spy.

We hid in a forest while the fighting raged around us. That's where your mother was born, by the banks of a river on a cold March day. When she slept in my arms, I remember thinking that there must still be angels.

WRITE As you read in the narrative, John Cech's grandmother realized something from her story. She learned that there is hope and goodness even in times of war and fear.

On a piece of paper, write a personal narrative paragraph about an event in your life that taught you something important.

You might choose the birth or death of a loved one. You might write about your wedding day or a day that was ordinary until something unusual happened. Tell the events that led up to the moment when you learned an important lesson. Follow the Writing Process you learned in Section 1.

Time Order

When you write a narrative, you can tell about the events in the order in which they happened. This is called **time order**. Time order is one good way to organize a narrative. It makes the story easy to understand.

EXAMPLE Below is an example of a narrative written in time order:

When Sam moved to a new apartment, he had to make lots of arrangements. First he had to call the water and electric company to turn on the utilities. Then he had to get his cousin Vincent to help him move his furniture. Finally, when he moved into the apartment and found that the stove was broken, he had to call the building manager to get the stove fixed.

Some words you can use to show time order are *first, then,* and *finally.*

PRACTICE

Put each list of events in time order. Number the first event 1, the second event 2, and so on. The first list is started for you.

1 _____ a. Griffin swatted wildly at the wasp.

_____ b. The car jumped the curb and knocked over a hot dog cart.

_____ c. Fortunately, no one was hurt.

___1___ d. Griffin carefully backed his car out of the driveway.

_____ e. As Griffin drove out, a large wasp flew into the car.

2 _____ a. A week later she called on the telephone to follow up on her letter.

_____ b. Rosa looked for a job in the Help Wanted section of the newspaper.

_____ c. First she wrote a letter of application and mailed it with her resume.

_____ d. Next she went to the library to research the company.

_____ e. She saw an ad in the paper for a job opening at Blakely Insurance.

WRITE Write a paragraph about a recent experience. Use time order to tell the story.

Prewrite: List the events of the experience. Number them in the order in which they occurred.

Write: Write sentences about the events. Use time order words to make your narrative clearer.

Grammar Link
Pronouns

The personal narrative by John Cech's grandmother on page 26 used **pronouns** such as *we, us,* and *our.* Pronouns are words that can replace nouns in a sentence. We use pronouns in our writing to keep from repeating the same noun over and over again.

EXAMPLE

<u>Janice</u> is getting a new job.   <u>She</u> starts training next week.
noun   *pronoun*

A pronoun can be used as a subject, as an object, or to show possession.

EXAMPLE

<u>He</u> bought <u>me</u> a wallet for <u>my</u> birthday.   <u>She</u> drove <u>him</u> to <u>his</u> job every day.
subject   *object*   *possessive*   *subject*   *object*   *possessive*

Grammar Exercise A

Write pronouns to take the place of the underlined words. The first one has been done for you.

❶ On New Year's Day, <u>Sam</u> will marry <u>Alice</u>.   *he* _____ _____

   he   him   her   them

❷ <u>Paolo</u> will be going to <u>Sam and Alice's</u> wedding.   _____ _____

   he   they   their   my

❸ Invitations should go to <u>Sally, Keisha, and Corinne</u>. _____

   him   them   they   her

❹ The bills for the wedding will be sent to <u>Diego</u>.   _____

   them   he   him   his

For more work with pronouns, turn to pages 171–175 of the Grammar Guide.

❺ <u>Sam and Alice</u> are going on a honeymoon.   _____

   Them   They   Their   My

Grammar Exercise B

Choose the correct pronoun. Write it in the blank.

The apartment belongs to Terri and _____ **(I, me)**. _____ **(Us, We)** can both
                                        1   2

save money by sharing the rent. This tiny bedroom is _____ **(my, mine)**. The
                                                          3

furniture was loaned to _____ **(we, us)**. Last week _____ **(I, me)** painted
                             4   5

the living room, and tomorrow _____ **(we, us)** will paint the halls.
                                    6

_____ **(Their, Our)** goal is to paint all the rooms by Friday.
   7

Point of View

You can write a narrative from different **points of view.** When you write a personal narrative, use the **first-person point of view.** This means that you refer to yourself by using the pronouns *I, me, my,* or *mine.*

EXAMPLE   Below is a diary entry. The writer uses first-person point of view.

Today was the happiest day of my life. Today, Tina and I got married! When she finally agreed to marry me, I could not believe my luck. I thought it might never happen—especially when I dropped her ring! Now Tina is mine and I am hers.

When you write a narrative about someone else, use the **third-person point of view.** This means that you refer to the people in the narrative by using the pronouns *she, her,* and *hers; he, him,* and *his;* and *they, them,* and *theirs.*

EXAMPLE   Below is a brief story. The writer uses third-person point of view.

Hal and Tina were married today. They stood in front of family and friends and exchanged vows. He was nervous and dropped her ring as he put it on her finger. She, on the other hand, was very confident and had no trouble with his ring. They were obviously in love. The crowd cheered for them when the ceremony ended.

PRACTICE

A.   **Write the correct pronouns to complete this paragraph from the <u>first</u>-person point of view.**

_____ **(I, He)** left in September for overseas duty knowing that _____
    1   2
(her, my) wife was going to have twins. Imagine _____ **(my, their)** surprise
                                                                                            3
when the telegram came telling _____ **(her, me)** that _____ **(she, I)** was
                                                                              4   5
the proud father of triplets!

B.   **Now rewrite the paragraph above on a separate sheet of paper. Begin the first sentence with, "Ray left in September . . ." Then write the rest of the paragraph from the <u>third</u>-person point of view.**

WRITE   **Write a paragraph about an event that turned out differently or better than you or someone else first thought it might.**

Prewrite: Think of an event you can write about. Use an outline or an idea map to organize ideas about it. Decide which point of view to use.
Write: Write a draft narrative of the event. Be sure that your pronouns show the correct point of view.

Grammar Link
Subjects and Predicates

When you write a narrative, you tell the story in sentences. A **sentence** is a group of words that expresses a complete thought. It contains a **subject**, which is the person or thing that the sentence is about. It also contains a **predicate,** which tells what the subject does or is, or what is being done to the subject.

The simple subject is a noun or a pronoun. The simple predicate is a verb.

EXAMPLE   Shelly started her own business.

The **complete subject** may be one word or several words. The **complete predicate** may also be one or more words.

EXAMPLE

My friend Cheryl cooks.   Alvin and I took a vacation.

Grammar Exercise

Put one line under the complete subject and two lines under the complete predicate in each sentence.

1. My niece Alicia plans to be a track star.

2. She runs and exercises every day.

3. Her father trains and coaches her for track meets.

4. My sister and I attend and give our support.

5. Alicia runs for the high school track team.

6. The team won a meet against the state champs last week.

7. My niece competed in three events.

8. She got first place in two events.

For more work with subjects and predicates, turn to pages 183–184 of the Grammar Guide.

Complete Sentences and Fragments

Remember that a sentence expresses a complete thought in addition to having a subject and predicate. To make your narrative essays—and all your writing—clear, you will generally want to write in complete sentences and avoid sentence fragments. A **sentence fragment** is a group of words that does not express a complete thought. It may *look* like a sentence—it may begin with a capital letter and end with a punctuation mark; it may even have a subject and a predicate. But if it does not express a complete thought, it is a sentence fragment.

EXAMPLE

Sentence: The A-1 Software Company on 6th Street hired me today.
Fragment: The A-1 Software Company on 6th Street. (needs a predicate)

Sentence: I will have two weeks of vacation each year.
Fragment: Will have two weeks of vacation each year. (needs a subject)

Sentence: The company offers a health plan for everyone on the payroll.
Fragment: For everyone on the payroll. (needs a subject and a predicate)

Grammar Exercise A

Write *S* by each complete sentence and *F* by each fragment.

_____ **1** Judy plays practical jokes all the time.

_____ **2** Was not so funny.

_____ **3** Told us the wrong place to meet.

_____ **4** For two hours before leaving.

_____ **5** She was sorry and embarrassed.

Grammar Exercise B

Circle what each fragment needs to become a sentence—a subject or a predicate.

1 Went to a surprise party last night.   subject   predicate

2 The host and hostess.   subject   predicate

3 At seven o'clock, Li Ling.   subject   predicate

4 Was the funniest thing ever.   subject   predicate

For more work with writing complete sentences, turn to pages 187–188 of the Grammar Guide.

On a separate sheet of paper, rewrite fragments 2–4 above to make each one a complete sentence.

EXAMPLE *1. Sly and I went to a surprise party last night.*

Supporting Details

A piece of narrative writing has one or more paragraphs. Each paragraph has a **topic sentence** that states the main idea. Other sentences in the paragraph contain **supporting details** that relate to the main idea.

Good supporting details make your narrative clearer and more interesting. They can help your reader picture what happened. They can help your reader understand why things happened and how you feel about them. Supporting details do this by answering the questions *Who? What happened? Where? When? Why?* and *How?*

EXAMPLE The following personal narrative contains a topic sentence followed by several detail sentences. Notice how the detail sentences relate to the main idea and answer *Who? What happened? Where? When? Why?* or *How?*

My hockey team gets together every Saturday morning before practice. We meet at 8 A.M. at a local coffee shop. Gino, Bo, and Paul eat a big breakfast. The rest of us eat donuts and drink coffee. We like to talk about sports, especially professional hockey. This weekly breakfast is a great time for us to socialize before we head off to the rink.

PRACTICE

Match each supporting detail with the question it answers. Write the letter.

Topic Sentence: Going camping was a humbling experience.

_____ ❶ I went as one of the parent leaders for my son's school camping trip.

_____ ❷ We left the city at noon on Friday.

_____ ❸ The campground near the lake was called Whispering Pines.

_____ ❹ That night I could not sleep. The sounds of trees and animals "whispering" kept this city boy awake all night.

_____ ❺ I was so tired the next day that all the other boys made fun of me.

a.   *Where did you go?*

b.   *Why was this a humbling experience?*

c.   *Why did you go camping?*

d.   *What happened on the camping trip?*

e.   *When did you go camping?*

Check your answers on page 236.

WRITE A Use your imagination to write fictional narratives. Complete each paragraph below by writing 3 or 4 sentences with details that support the topic sentence. Remember, your details should tell the reader *Who? What happened? Where? When? Why?* and *How?*

1 Topic Sentence: Carlos came to the United States to improve his life, but he never dreamed he would become such a success.

_____

_____

_____

_____

_____

_____

_____

_____

2 Topic Sentence: Patricia has learned that hard times can make you stronger.

_____

_____

_____

_____

_____

_____

_____

_____

WRITE B Choose one of these topics and write a personal narrative about it. Use a separate piece of paper.

a childhood memory   an unforgettable experience   a hard decision

Prewrite: List as many ideas about your topic as you can. Use an outline or an idea map to organize the most important ideas.

Write: Write one or more paragraphs about your topic. Remember to support your topic sentence(s) with details that add interest and answer questions such as *Where?* and *What happened?*

Apply Your Writing Skills

Write a Narrative Essay

Now you are ready to apply what you have learned by writing a narrative essay. As you write, follow the steps in the writing process.

A narrative essay:
- is a form of writing in which you tell a story about yourself or someone else.
- may be told in the order in which events happened, using time order organization and words.
- can be written in first-person or third-person point of view.

ASSIGNMENT Write a three-paragraph essay about an important event in your life.

Prewriting

1 List some possible events to write about.

_____

_____

_____

2 Choose one event to write about. List the event and some interesting details about it.

Event: _____

Details: _____

_____

_____

3 Organize your ideas in an outline or on an idea map like the one below.

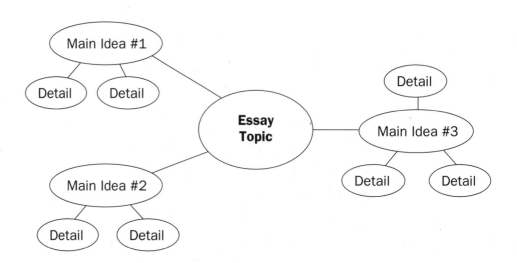

Writing the First Draft

Write a topic sentence. Your first topic sentence will state the main idea of the essay. Try writing the topic sentence several different ways until you think it will be interesting to a reader. Write your final version below.

_____

On a separate piece of paper, write your first draft.

Write an introductory paragraph. Use your topic sentence and supporting sentences to introduce the topic to the reader.

Write the body paragraph. Use the ideas and the details you outlined or mapped to write an interesting paragraph on your topic.
- Each sentence should support the main idea of the essay.
- Use the ideas and supporting details from your outline or idea map to write your sentences.
- Put the sentences in time order to help your reader.

Write the concluding paragraph. Write a concluding sentence to let the reader know that the essay is coming to an end. Use the concluding paragraph to leave the reader with a final viewpoint, a question, or an idea to think about.

Editing and Revising

Review, edit, and revise. Read the entire essay to see if you accomplished what you set out to do.

Then use the editing checklist on page 218 to see how you can improve your writing. Pay special attention to these points that you studied in this section:

❏ Did you organize the narrative details in logical time order? _See page 27._

❏ Did you use supporting details? _See pages 32–33._

❏ Are your sentences complete? _See pages 30–31._

❏ Did you use pronouns correctly? _See page 28._

Writing the Final Draft

Write a final draft. Then proofread it one last time. If necessary, recopy or retype a final draft. Use the proofreading checklist on page 219 to review it.

Sharing the Final Draft

Publish. Let another person read your final draft. Ask if your message was clear. Also ask what else you could do to improve the essay. Make some notes and attach them to a copy of the essay. File the draft in your writing portfolio.

Descriptive Writing

Elements of Descriptive Writing

Descriptive writing is writing that describes a person, place, or thing for a reader. When you write a description, you create a clear picture in the reader's mind. You want your reader to see, hear, feel, smell, or taste exactly what you did. You want your reader to experience what you did. To do that, you use all your senses, your memory, and sometimes your imagination to make a picture with your words.

Descriptive writing often includes feelings about the person, place, or thing that is being described. For example, the feeling you have for a grandmother you loved is different from the feeling you experienced at an accident you saw. You will want to create a different feeling when you describe your grandmother than the feeling you create when you describe an accident.

EXAMPLE   Below is an example of a descriptive paragraph. The author, Amy Tan, describes smells, sights, and sounds to create a picture of her childhood home.

The apartment building was three stories high, two apartments per floor. It had a renovated facade, a recent layer of white stucco topped with connected rows of metal fire-escape ladders. But inside it was old. The front door with its narrow glass panes opened into a musty lobby that smelled of everybody's life mixed together. Everybody meant the names on the front door next to their little buzzers: Anderson, Giordino, Hayman, Ricci, Sorci, and our name, St. Clair. We lived on the middle floor, stuck between cooking smells that floated up and feet sounds that drifted down. My bedroom faced the street, and at night, in the dark, I could see in my mind another life. Cars struggling to climb the steep, fog-shrouded hill, gunning their deep engines and spinning their wheels. Loud, happy people, laughing, puffing, gasping, "Are we almost there?" A beagle scrambling to his feet to start his yipping yowl, answered a few seconds later by fire truck sirens and an angry woman hissing, "Sammy! Bad dog! Hush now!". . .

WRITE   **On a separate piece of paper, write a descriptive paragraph about the place where you grew up or where you live now.**

Begin with prewriting. Brainstorm and list specific details you might want to include in your paragraph. Select the details that will help your reader to "see" your home. Next use an outline or an idea map to organize the details in a way that will create a picture of your home when you write. Follow the Writing Process you learned in Section 1.

Descriptive Details

You can create a word picture by including descriptive details when you write. Begin with details you can see, such as shape, color, and size.

EXAMPLE Below is a paragraph about an operating room that includes clear, vivid descriptive details. Picture the operating room as you read about it.

As I was wheeled into the operating room, I was still awake. Everything in the room looked clean and professional—the stainless steel table, the gleaming knives, the bright light, the white walls. But there, not quite tucked away under a pile of linen, was a gauze bandage covered with brown, faded blood.

Precise Words

Writers use precise or exact words to draw a word picture. Vague, general words may have different meanings for different readers. As you write, ask yourself if a more precise word could help your reader see exactly what you mean.

EXAMPLE   *color*—general   *red*—precise   *scarlet*—even more precise

PRACTICE

A. Use descriptive details to create word pictures. Write a sentence that has two details for each item below. The first one is done for you.

1 (a car) *A gray Ford Escort was parked near the door.*

2 (a cake) _____

3 (a tree) _____

4 (a man) _____

B. Find a precise word on the right side that could replace the general word on the left side. Write the letter.

General				Precise	
_____ **1** shirt	_____ **4** eat	a. devour		d. T-shirt	
_____ **2** jump	_____ **5** doctor	b. leap		e. stare	
_____ **3** child	_____ **6** look	c. six-year-old		f. surgeon	

WRITE On a separate piece of paper, write a paragraph about a place that has memories for you.

Prewrite: List as many details as possible. Select those that create a word picture.
Write: Use precise words in your paragraph.

Grammar Link
Adjectives and Adverbs

In Amy Tan's description on page 36, she included details like "musty lobby" and "drifted down." The words *musty* and *down* helped Ms. Tan paint specific word pictures. *Musty* is an adjective, and *down* is an adverb. Adjectives and adverbs will help you create specific word pictures in your descriptive writing too.

- An **adjective** modifies, or helps describe, a noun or a pronoun. Adjectives answer the following questions:

What kind? This <u>large</u> diner has just opened.
How many? I'll have <u>two</u> eggs with toast.
Which one? It is the <u>first</u> item on the menu.

- An **adverb** is a word that modifies a verb, an adjective, or another adverb. Adverbs answer the following questions:

How? He walked <u>quickly</u>.
When? He left <u>early</u>.
Where? He went <u>there</u>.
To what extent? He went to a <u>very</u> popular restaurant.

Be careful not to use an adjective when an adverb is needed. With adjectives and adverbs that are similar, the adverb usually ends in *ly*.

EXAMPLE Correct: Shanna ran to the store <u>quickly</u>.
Incorrect: Shanna ran to the store <u>quick</u>.
Correct: Shanna wanted a <u>quick</u> snack.

The first sentence is correct because the adverb *quickly* describes the verb *ran*. The third sentence is correct because the adjective *quick* describes the noun *snack*.

Grammar Exercise

Write the correct adjective or adverb to complete each sentence.

❶ Lilly's Kitchen is a _____ restaurant.
fine (adj.)   **finely** (adv.)

❷ The bakery's bread is _____ every day.
fresh (adj.)   **freshly** (adv.)

❸ The dining room is lit _____.
bright (adj.)   **brightly** (adv.)

❹ The tables are decorated _____.
beautiful (adj.)   **beautifully** (adv.)

❺ I eat at Lilly's Kitchen _____.
regular (adj.)   **regularly** (adv.)

 Check your answers on page 236.

Comparing with Adjectives and Adverbs

Adjectives and adverbs can show comparison. To compare two things, use the **comparative** form. To compare three or more things, use the **superlative** form.

adjective	comparative	superlative
long	longer than	longest
careful	more careful than	the most careful

adverb	comparative	superlative
fast	faster than	the fastest
quickly	more quickly than	the most quickly

Adjective: This is a <u>long</u> movie.
Comparative: This movie is <u>longer</u> than the one I saw last week.
Superlative: This is the <u>longest</u> movie I have ever seen.

Some adjectives and adverbs change completely in the comparative and superlative forms.

adjective	comparative	superlative
good	better than	the best
bad	worse than	the worst

adverb	comparative	superlative
well	better than	the best
badly	worse than	the worst

Adverb: I bowled <u>badly</u> Friday.
Comparative: I bowled <u>worse on</u> Sunday than on Friday.
Superlative: I bowled the <u>worst</u> today.

Grammar Exercise

Complete each sentence with the correct form of the adjective or adverb.

❶ hot, hotter, hottest

❷ new, newer, newest

❸ quickly, more quickly, most quickly

❹ important, more important, most important

❺ easy, easier, easiest

For more work with adjectives and adverbs, turn to pages 176–179 of the Grammar Guide.

It was the _____ day of summer, and it was my job to
                    1

train the _____ employee in our mailroom. Ramos learned
                  2

_____ than the last person. When the _____
          3   4

job of the day arrived, he made the work seem _____.
                                                           5

Sensory Details

Another way to create word pictures in descriptive writing is to use words that appeal to the five senses: sight, hearing, smell, taste, and touch. Words that help the reader see, hear, smell, taste, or feel exactly what you did are called **sensory details**. Sensory details make descriptions come alive.

smell ——
sight ——
taste ——
sound ——
touch ——

EXAMPLE This morning I ran across a pair of **musty sneakers** in the closet. I wore them the day my grandfather took me to Coney Island. When I look at those **dirt-encrusted, tattered** sneakers, it all comes back to me. I can taste the **salty fries and sweet cotton candy.** My stomach churns at the memory of that **roaring roller coaster,** the Cyclone. I remember grabbing hold of my grandfather's **big, rough hand** so I wouldn't get lost in the crowd.

PRACTICE

A. Write the sense—sight, hearing, smell, taste, or touch—that is affected by the sensory details in the sentence.

_____ **1** The sea shimmered in shades of turquoise.

_____ **2** The waves tickled my toes.

_____ **3** The breeze whispered through the trees.

_____ **4** The sea air carried the scent of salt.

_____ **5** The ice-cold lemonade was delicious.

B. Write a sentence that describes each item. Use specific details that appeal to the sense listed with the topic.

1 (**Sight:** sunset) _____

2 (**Hearing:** factory) _____

3 (**Smell:** baby) _____

4 (**Taste:** hamburger) _____

5 (**Touch:** handshake) _____

WRITE Write a paragraph to describe a meal you once had. It could be a holiday dinner, a fast-food meal, or a picnic.

Prewrite: List as many sensory details under each of the five senses as you can.
Write: Use details that let the reader see, hear, smell, taste, and feel the meal.

Figurative Language

When you describe exactly how something looks, tastes, feels, smells, or sounds, you are using **literal language.** Sometimes you may find it useful to describe something by comparing it to another thing that is very different. This type of comparison is called **figurative language.** It can make your writing more interesting. Here are three ways to make figurative comparisons.

EXAMPLE   **1.** Use *like* or *as.*
Literal: She was upset.
Figurative: She cried like a baby.

2. Say that something is something else.
Literal: The snow covered the field.
Figurative: The snow was a soft white blanket.

3. Give human qualities to things that are not human.
Literal: The rain fell on my face.
Figurative: The rain caressed my face.

PRACTICE

The following sentences are written in literal language. Rewrite each sentence using figurative language that appeals to the sense listed. The first sentence is done for you.

1 (Sight) My apartment is small.

My apartment is the size of a broom closet.

2 (Touch) Scott has soft hair.

_____

3 (Hearing) The wind was loud last night.

_____

4 (Taste) The cold drink was refreshing.

_____

5 (Smell) I could smell her perfume before she opened the door.

_____

WRITE   Write a descriptive paragraph about one of the topics below.

My Favorite Holiday   A Beautiful (or Stormy) Day   A Strange Person

Prewrite: Choose your topic and write the five senses. List sensory details about your topic under each sense.
Write: As you write about the details, use figurative language.

Grammar Link

Good descriptive writing includes a variety of sentences. If all your sentences are short and simple, your writing will also seem simple. If you combine ideas into a variety of sentence structures, your writing will be more interesting. You will also be able to show how your ideas are related by using connecting words. Here are three ways to vary sentence structure by combining ideas.

1 Use compound sentences.

2 Use complex sentences.

3 Combine words and phrases in series.

Compound Sentences

Remember that a sentence is a complete thought. A **compound sentence** has *two* complete thoughts that are closely related. Each of these thoughts could stand alone as a sentence.

EXAMPLE   The job will be hard, but I can do it.

The complete thoughts in a compound sentence can be joined with a **comma** and a connecting word called a **coordinating conjunction.** The most common coordinating conjunctions are *and, but, or,* and *so.* Make sure you use both a comma and a coordinating conjunction. Otherwise you will have a **run-on sentence,** which is a mistake in sentence structure.

EXAMPLES

1 Rosa takes care of stray animals. Rosa finds new homes for strays.

Compound Sentence: Rosa takes care of stray animals, or she finds new homes for them.

2 Rosa's favorite pet is a sad-eyed puppy. Rosa also loves the white alley cat she found.

Compound Sentence: Rosa's favorite pet is a sad-eyed puppy, but she also loves the white alley cat she found.

3 The cat roams all over the house. The parakeet has to be kept in its cage.

Compound Sentence: The cat roams all over the house, so the parakeet has to be kept in its cage.

4 I help Rosa with the animals. She pays me a small amount for my work.

Compound Sentence: I help Rosa with the animals, and she pays me a small amount for my work.

For practice with identifying and correcting run-on sentences, turn to pages 189–190 of the Grammar Guide.

Grammar Exercise A

Combine each pair of sentences to make a compound sentence. Use a comma and one of the coordinating conjunctions *and*, *but*, *or*, or *so*.

1 The skies opened up. Lightning streaked across the clouds.

_____

2 Last year we had floods. This year was not as bad.

_____

3 The storm caused severe damage. Several people were injured.

_____

4 Windows were shattered by the wind. We went into the basement.

_____

5 We read books. Sometimes we played cards.

_____

Grammar Exercise B

Complete each sentence below by adding a related second thought to make a compound sentence. Use the conjunction listed above the sentence. The first sentence is done for you.

1 **but**
The steak was tender,
The steak was tender, but it was too well done.

2 **and**
The street was deserted, _____

3 **so**
The couch was new, _____

4 **but**
The soldiers marched bravely, _____

5 **so**
The sky looked threatening, _____

6 **and**
The fruit was ripe, _____

7 **or**
I should get gas soon, _____

8 **or**
We could see this movie, _____

For more work with compound sentences, turn to pages 191–192 of the Grammar Guide.

Complex Sentences

Another way to vary your writing is to use complex sentences. A **complex sentence** has two parts: one **independent** (or complete) thought and one **dependent** (or incomplete) thought. Each part is called a **clause.** An independent clause has a subject and a predicate and can stand alone as a sentence. A dependent clause has a subject and a predicate, but it cannot stand alone because it is not a complete thought. It depends on the independent clause to complete the thought.

A dependent clause may come either before or after an independent clause.

EXAMPLE   <u>Wherever</u> you go, you will see tall buildings.
You will see tall buildings <u>wherever</u> you go.

A dependent clause begins with a connecting word called a **subordinating conjunction.** Here are some common subordinating conjunctions.

after	as soon as	even if	though	when
although	as though	even though	unless	whenever
as	because	if	until	whichever
as if	before	since	whatever	while

Grammar Exercise

Write appropriate subordinating conjunctions for each sentence. Use the words above.

_____ the weather is still nice, you should take a drive to
₁

the mountains. Go on a sunny day, _____ you can really
₂

appreciate the scenery. _____ you go, don't forget to take your
₃

camera. _____ you go in the fall, you will see the spectacular
₄

autumn colors. The reds and golds light up the forest _____ it
₅

were on fire. Follow the signs _____ they point out the best
₆

route. _____ you get lost, you will still enjoy the day.
₇

_____ you are in a hurry, don't worry about it.
₈

_____ way you go, you can get back to the highway.
₉

_____ you take just one trip, you'll want to go back every year.
₁₀

For more work with complex sentences, turn to pages 195–196 of the Grammar Guide.

Check your answers on page 237.

Words in Series

Still another way to vary sentence structure to make your writing more interesting is to combine a series of adjectives, noun phrases, or verb phrases. If you say the same thing over and over again, you will annoy your reader. When you combine words in a series, you reduce the number of times you repeat an idea.

EXAMPLES

- **Adjectives**   The ballpark was noisy. The ballpark was crowded. The ballpark was hot.

  Series   The ballpark was noisy, crowded, and hot.

- **Nouns**   The living room had a picture window. The living room had wood floors. The living room had a view of the park.

  Series   The living room had a picture window, wood floors, and a view of the park.

- **Verbs**   The car spun around. It hit a tree. The car landed in a ditch.

  Series   The car spun around, hit a tree, and landed in a ditch.

Grammar Exercise   **Revise each group of sentences into one sentence that uses adjectives, nouns, or verbs in a series. Omit the words that are not needed. Use commas between three or more words or phrases in a series.**

1   The bus driver signaled.
She turned into the traffic.
She slowly made her way along the street.

_____

_____

2   Jose has a red car.
It has bucket seats.
It has chrome trim.

_____

_____

3   The sofa was old.
The sofa was plaid.
The sofa had worn-out cushions.

_____

_____

For more work with words in a series, turn to pages 193–194 of the Grammar Guide.

Apply Your Writing Skills

Write a Descriptive Essay

Now you are ready to apply what you have learned about writing a descriptive essay. Remember that a descriptive essay:

- is a form of writing that helps to create a clear picture in the reader's mind.
- comes alive through the use of precise words and sensory details.
- may use figurative language to help describe something.

As you write, follow the steps in the writing process.

ASSIGNMENT Write a three-paragraph essay describing your favorite character in a movie or TV show.

Prewriting

1. Make a list of several characters you like. Then choose one character. Think of things you can describe about the character such as personality, what the character did, and what he or she looked like. Don't limit yourself to these things. Use your imagination in deciding what you want to write about the character.

2. Organize your ideas in an outline or on an idea map like the one below. List descriptive details, precise words, and sensory details about the character that you want to include in your essay.

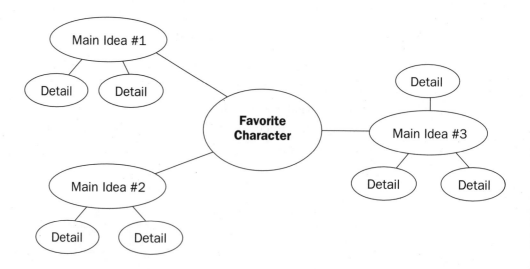

Writing the First Draft

Write a topic sentence. Your first topic sentence will state the main idea of the essay. Try writing the topic sentence several different ways until you think it will be interesting to a reader. Write your final version below.

_____

_____

On a separate piece of paper, write your first draft.

Write an introductory paragraph. Use your topic sentence and supporting sentences to introduce the character to the reader.

Write the body paragraph. From your prewriting, use your details and precise words to write sentences about the character. As you write, you may think of a figurative way to compare the character to something else. You may also think of additional things to say about the character.

Write the concluding paragraph. Write a concluding sentence that lets the reader know the essay is coming to an end. Use the concluding paragraph to leave the reader with a clear picture of what you described in your essay.

Editing and Revising

Review, Edit, and Revise. Read the entire essay to see if you accomplished what you set out to do.

Use the editing checklist on page 218 to see how you can improve your writing. Pay special attention to these points that you studied in this section:

- ❏ Did you use visual details? *See page 37.*
- ❏ Did you use precise words? *See page 37.*
- ❏ Did you use sensory details to appeal to the five senses? *See page 40.*
- ❏ Did you use figurative language? *See page 41.*
- ❏ Did you use adjectives and adverbs to compare items? *See pages 38–39.*
- ❏ Did you vary your sentence structure? *See pages 42–45.*

Writing the Final Draft

Write a final draft. Then proofread it one last time. If necessary, recopy or retype a final draft. Use the proofreading checklist on page 219 to review your final draft.

Sharing the Final Draft

Publish. Let another person read your final draft. Ask if your message was clear. Also ask what else you could do to improve the essay. Make some notes and attach them to a copy of the essay. File the draft in your writing portfolio.

Expository Writing

Elements of Expository Writing

Expository writing informs or explains. You use expository writing to make an idea or situation easier to understand. It is especially useful when you want to explain a complicated idea. Explaining <u>why</u> you believe in something is an example of expository writing. Here are three ways writers explain an idea in an expository essay.

- **Define the word that names the idea.**
  A *friend* is someone who is attached to another by affection.
- **Illustrate an idea by giving a specific example.**
  Calvin's *friend* John drove him to work every morning for eight years.
- **Classify, or group similar types together.**
  Some people are acquaintances, others are good-time buddies, and then there are *friends*.

EXAMPLE Below is a piece of expository writing by Mae Jemison, the first African-American woman in space. She explains what a scientist is and how she came to be one.

As I was growing up, I found a strong source of inspiration in my parents. My mother was a schoolteacher and my father a carpenter and roofer. They also were two of the best scientists and science role models I have ever encountered. . . . They studied and analyzed any issue that came up. When I had a question or a problem they asked me what information I had and what I thought might be a solution. Sometimes they would give me small clues or hints. Then they encouraged me to find my own answer. And when I came up with a solution, they would evaluate it with me and suggest ways to improve it. Isn't that exactly what scientists are supposed to do? Don't they explore the world systematically—review the unknown, develop a hypothesis to answer a question, and then test their hypothesis? I was lucky to have such parents.

WRITE As you read in her expository writing, Mae Jemison's parents had a big impact on her life. Think about some of the role models in your life.

On a piece of paper, write an expository paragraph about someone who has been an important role model for you.

Tell who the person is and define the role this person modeled for you. Give examples that show how this person has been important to you. Follow the Writing Process you learned in Section 1.

Connecting Words and Phrases

Good expository writing moves from one idea to the next in a way that makes sense. If your writing flows smoothly in this way, readers do not have to go back and reread to figure out what you mean. One of the best ways to make your writing flow is to use **connecting words and phrases.**

after a while	first (second, etc.)	however	still
also	for example	in addition	then
as a result	for instance	later	therefore
besides	further	next	what is more

Some of these connecting words are the time-order words you used in narrative writing on page 27. You can also use the coordinating conjunctions *and, but, or,* and *so* to connect ideas, as well as the subordinating conjunctions listed on page 44.

EXAMPLE 1 I had three reasons for not going to work on this dreadful winter day. I slipped on an icy sidewalk and injured my foot. I cannot wear my shoe. My son is not going to school. He has the flu. The heat is off at work. I would not be able to get much done there anyway.

EXAMPLE 2 I had three reasons for not going to work on this dreadful winter day. First, I slipped on an icy sidewalk. As a result, I hurt my foot and cannot wear my shoe. Also, my son is not going to school because he has the flu. Further, the heat is off at work, so I couldn't get much done there anyway.

What does the second example have that the first one does not? Notice the words *first, as a result, and, also, because, further,* and *so* that link ideas.

PRACTICE

Write one connecting word or phrase from the box above to link each set of ideas. The first one is done for you.

1 I am not going out today with my bad cold. ___*Besides*___, it is raining.

2 Mika made dinner. _____, he washed the dishes.

3 Frances studied hard for the GED. _____, she passed the exam.

4 Julio put an ad in the paper. _____, he put signs on the bulletin board at work.

5 The storm damaged the roof. _____, it could have been worse.

6 Hong's mother is ill. _____, he is flying to visit her.

7 Mei Lee worked hard. _____, she got a raise.

Connecting Words for Style

There is no one "right" word or phrase to use when connecting ideas in your expository writing. Pick the one that best joins your ideas and makes your point. The words you choose help create your writing style—your own special way of putting your ideas on paper. Here is the same idea joined three ways:

EXAMPLE   I like living in this building; as a result, I renewed my lease.
I like living in this building; thus, I renewed my lease.
I like living in this building, so I renewed my lease.

Punctuation also helps to show the connection between ideas:
- Use a comma to separate two complete thoughts that are joined by the coordinating conjunctions *and, but, or, nor, yet,* or *so.*
- Use a semicolon to connect two complete thoughts that are not joined by the connecting words *and, but, or, nor, yet,* or *so.*
- Use a comma after connecting words such as *however* and *for example.*

PRACTICE

Rewrite this paragraph to make the ideas flow more smoothly. You can add, take away, or replace words and phrases.

People who win big prizes in the lottery often find that the money does not make them happy. Therefore, they have to deal with lots of people trying to get a piece of the pie. Winners find that their friends expect them to hand over some of the winnings. But they have to be on guard all the time. Lottery winners find that they cannot trust anyone. All this pressure takes the fun out of winning. They can no longer relax and enjoy life. I am willing to give it a try!

_____

_____

_____

_____

_____

_____

WRITE   Someone once said, "There is only one success—to be able to spend your life in your own way."

On a separate sheet of paper, write two paragraphs to explain what you mean by success.

Prewrite: Brainstorm and list specific examples to explain the word *success.*
Write: Write your ideas so that your reader can follow your train of thought. Use connecting words and phrases to link your ideas.

Expanding Your Vocabulary with Synonyms

The purpose of an expository essay is to explain something. When you speak, you have a chance to explain what you meant. But when you write, you do not have a second chance. Therefore, you want to choose words carefully so that your meaning is clear to your readers.

You can choose words more carefully when you know many words. One way to learn new words is to read a newspaper. Another good way is to use a thesaurus.

The word *thesaurus* comes from a Latin word meaning "storehouse of knowledge." Unlike a dictionary, a thesaurus does not give meanings or trace a word's past. Instead, it has lists of **synonyms,** or words that have the same meaning. It also has **antonyms,** or words that have the opposite meaning. For example, look up the word *big* in a thesaurus. Here are just a few of the words you will find under *big*.

EXAMPLE

Synonyms for *big*			Antonyms for *big*		
large	huge	grown	little	small	meek
immense	ample	adult	minute	bantam	cheap
vast	great	head	minor	unknown	young
vital	prime	mature	modest	humble	little

Because a thesaurus has lists of words to choose from, it can help you find new words as well as words whose meanings you may not recall. Using synonyms adds spice to your writing. It can also make your writing more vivid and more precise.

PRACTICE

Use a thesaurus. Write four synonyms for each word.

1. red _____ _____ _____ _____

2. win _____ _____ _____ _____

3. walk _____ _____ _____ _____

4. money _____ _____ _____ _____

WRITE **Write a paragraph explaining what money means to you. Use a separate piece of paper.**

Prewrite: Brainstorm and write down ideas that come to mind when you think of the word *money.*

Write: Use your brainstormed ideas to explain what money means to you. In your paragraph, use at least two of the synonyms you found for *money* in the Practice above.

Choosing the Best Synonym

Words have varied shades of meaning. For instance, there are many words that mean "to hit." Although *bump* and *smash* both mean "to hit," *smash* suggests a harder action that may be more painful. When you write, use the word that says exactly what you want to say.

A. Each line has four words. Three are synonyms; one word does not belong. Write the word that is <u>not</u> a synonym for the others.

_____ **1** careless   hasty   rushed   neat

_____ **2** still   racket   hushed   quiet

_____ **3** mansion   cabin   hut   cottage

_____ **4** decrease   explore   survey   probe

_____ **5** stony   rigid   steely   gentle

_____ **6** yearn   crave   scorn   wish

B. Select the best synonym for the underlined word in each sentence. Write the letter for that word in the blank.

_____ **1** The <u>belligerent</u> dog bit the mail carrier again.

(A) hostile   (B) unfriendly   (C) warlike

_____ **2** That woman is a <u>brilliant</u> research scientist.

(A) glorious   (B) colorful   (C) distinguished

_____ **3** The group was <u>upset</u> when the power went out during the Super Bowl.

(A) overturned   (B) distressed   (C) sad

_____ **4** The ad states that the new cereal is <u>good</u> for you.

(A) nutritious   (B) sufficient   (C) benign

_____ **5** The redhead was made <u>the person in charge</u> of the bowling team.

(A) moderator   (B) ruler   (C) captain

WRITE Write a paragraph explaining the different ways people laugh.

Prewrite: Use a thesaurus to list synonyms for *laugh*.

Write: For each synonym you write about, add details that help a reader picture and hear a person laugh in that way.

Grammar Link
Active and Passive Voice

In good expository writing like Mae Jemison's piece on page 48, verbs like *explore* and *test* tell <u>what</u> actions happen. The **voice** of a verb helps show <u>how</u> an action happens. In the **active voice**, the subject of the sentence does the action. In the **passive voice**, someone or something else does the action to the subject.

EXAMPLE

Active Voice	Passive Voice
Sammy hit the ball.	The ball was hit by Sammy.
Crops need rain.	Rain is needed by crops.
Jen opened the book.	The book was opened by Jen.

Grammar Exercise A

Find the verb in each sentence. On the line, write *active* if the verb is in the active voice or *passive* if the verb is in the passive voice.

_____ **1** The pill was taken by my wife.

_____ **2** We bought a few extra hot dogs for later.

_____ **3** I read the newspaper every night after supper.

_____ **4** New York was reached by the Mexican tourists in a day.

In most cases, use the active voice in your writing. It helps you write crisp, clear sentences. It is strong and direct. It usually saves words. But there are three cases when the passive voice is good to use: (1) when you want to focus on the action, not the actor, (2) when you do not know the name of the actor, or (3) when the actor is not important.

EXAMPLE **Focus on action:** A mistake has been made. (*not* You made a mistake.)

Name unknown: A woman has been charged with theft.

Actor not important: The check was mailed on Tuesday.

Grammar Exercise B

Choose the reason passive voice is used in each sentence. Write 1 (focus is on the action) or 2 (name is not known) or 3 (the actor is not important) on each line below.

> For more practice on the active and passive voice, turn to pages 185–186 of the Grammar Guide.

_____ **1** My friend was struck by a car.

_____ **2** A bad check was passed in the food store.

_____ **3** The phone call was made at 2:00 A.M.

_____ **4** At 10:00 A.M. the doors to the store were unlocked.

Changing Voice

To change a sentence from the active voice to the passive voice, switch the subject and the object. Change the form of the verb, too.

EXAMPLE

Active Voice	to	Passive Voice
The <u>players</u> wore new <u>hats</u>.		New hats were worn by the players.
subject	*object*	

To change a sentence from the passive voice to the active voice, make the subject the object. Make the person or thing that acted the subject.

EXAMPLE

Passive Voice	to	Active Voice
The <u>soda</u> was sold by them.		They sold the <u>soda</u>.
subject		*object*

Grammar Exercise A **Rewrite each of these passive sentences in the active voice.**

❶ passive voice: With great force, the lock was broken by the thief.

active voice: _____

❷ passive voice: The moon was landed on by the crew of *Apollo 11*.

active voice: _____

❸ passive voice: A plaque was left on the moon by them.

active voice: _____

Grammar Exercise B **Choose the best way to write the underlined phrase or sentence. Write the letter.**

_____ ❶ A creature <u>has been seen in Loch Ness</u>.

    (A) Some people who have been to Loch Ness have seen a creature there.

    (B) No change is needed.

_____ ❷ <u>These sightings have been doubted by many</u>.

    (A) Many have doubted these sightings.

    (B) No change is needed.

_____ ❸ <u>Tests were done by experts</u> to see if a monster is in the lake.

    (A) Experts did tests.

    (B) No change is needed.

> For more practice on active and passive voice, turn to pages 185–186 of the Grammar Guide.

Sentence Revision

You can improve your writing by revising sentences to take out unnecessary words. Every word in every sentence should be there for a reason. If a word does not make your writing more vivid or precise, get rid of it. If too many words make it harder for a reader to get to the point, rewrite all or part of the sentence.

EXAMPLE 1   **Too Wordy:** The hikers saw the big, massive, dark, black cloud covering over the sun.

Revised: The hikers saw the big, black cloud covering the sun.

EXAMPLE 2   **Too Wordy:** Mike is of the belief that the death penalty should be allowed.

Revised: Mike believes the death penalty should be allowed.

Grammar Exercise

Rewrite each sentence to get rid of extra words. Be sure not to lose any of the meaning.

1. At the same time that he was driving a taxi, he was also working at a lawn-care type of business.

   _____

2. It goes without saying that in this day and age, many people do not vote.

   _____

3. The dog was very large in size and gave a nasty and fierce growling sound when anyone walked by the yard.

   _____

4. Because of the fact that it took a really very long time to get to his work, Sam quit his job.

   _____

5. Far away in the distance, we could see the little, small ships.

   _____

6. Modern cars of today can be driven faster than the old cars of the past.

   _____

7. I asked the speaker to repeat again what he had said.

   _____

For more practice on revising sentences, turn to pages 199–200 of the Grammar Guide.

Point of View

In expository writing, you can write from different **points of view.** This chart shows how to choose and use points of view:

Point of View

If you are writing . . .	Use . . .
• as yourself or about yourself	• I (I am special.)
• to someone	• you (You are special.)
• about someone	• he, she, or they (He is special.)
• as a member of a group	• we (We are special.)

Be careful not to change your point of view in the middle of a sentence or passage. As you revise your writing, look for errors in point of view.

EXAMPLE **Change in point of view:** Many people say they like to work hard, but when a job is hard, you sometimes get upset.
Revised: Many people say they like to work hard, but when a job is hard, they sometimes get upset.

PRACTICE

Revise the sentences to correct changes in point of view. The sentences can be revised several different ways. If the sentence is correct, write *correct*.

1 I like to read forecasts of the future, but you have to wonder if any of them are true.

_____

2 When a person is treated with respect at work, you feel better about your work.

_____

3 This morning I could not find my keys, so I left the back door unlocked when I left.

_____

4 When one looks for a loan, you find who has the best rate.

_____

WRITE Write a paragraph to define the word *happiness.*

Prewrite: Jot down all the ideas that come to mind when you think of the word *happiness*. Decide how to organize them.
Write: Use your prewriting ideas to write a paragraph defining happiness and giving examples of it. Use the same point of view throughout the paragraph.

Polishing Your Work

Your expository writing does not end with your first draft. If you want to make your writing shine, you must take time to polish your work. Check for correct spelling and punctuation. Be sure no letters or words were left out. To polish your work, ask yourself these questions:

1 Does each sentence begin with a capital letter?

2 Does each proper noun begin with a capital letter?

3 Does each sentence end with a period or question mark?

4 Is each word spelled correctly?

PRACTICE

Read the paragraph. Then circle the best answer to each question.

(1) When I was in school, the teachers did not try to erase our backrounds. (2) they tried to say our real names, even though they did not speak our language. (3) We were never punished for speaking our native langauge in class.

1 Sentence 1: **When I was in school, the teachers did not try to erase our backrounds.** What correction should be made to this sentence?
   (1) Change *backrounds* to *backgrounds*.
   (2) Insert a comma after *teachers*.
   (3) Change *teachers* to *Teachers*.
   (4) Put a question mark at the end of the sentence.
   (5) No correction is necessary.

2 Sentence 2: **they tried to say our real names, even though they did not speak our language.** What correction should be made to this sentence?
   (1) Remove the comma after *names*.
   (2) Insert a comma after *tried*.
   (3) Change *they* to *They*.
   (4) Change *language* to *langauge*.
   (5) No correction is necessary.

3 Sentence 3: **We were never punished for speaking our native langauge in class.** What correction should be made to this sentence?
   (1) Change *were* to *are*.
   (2) Put a question mark at the end of the sentence.
   (3) Change *langauge* to *language*.
   (4) Add a comma after *language*.
   (5) No correction is necessary.

Apply Your Writing Skills

Write an Expository Essay

Now you are ready to apply what you have learned by writing an expository essay. Remember that an expository essay:

- is a form of writing that tells or explains.
- uses specific words and carefully chosen synonyms in clear examples.
- uses active voice to make the essay stronger.
- keeps the same point of view.

ASSIGNMENT

Some people believe that "progress" always means new buildings and roads. Other people believe that "progress" also includes keeping older buildings, parks, and open spaces. Think about something old in your community that has been replaced by something new. Write a four-paragraph expository essay to explain how you feel about this change. Tell whether you think it was an example of progress.

Prewriting

1 List some possible changes to write about.

_____

_____

2 Choose one change to write about. List details—facts, reasons, or examples—and feelings you have about it.

_____

_____

3 Organize your ideas in an outline or on an idea map like the one below.

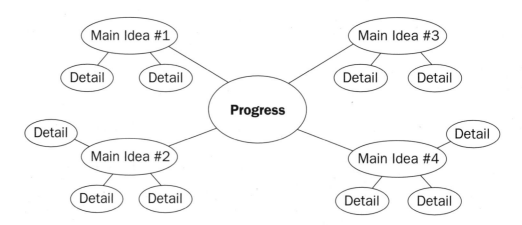

Writing the First Draft

Write the Topic Sentence. Your first topic sentence will state the main idea of the essay. Try writing the topic sentence several different ways until you think it will be interesting to a reader. Write your final version below.

_____

_____

On a separate piece of paper, write your first draft.

Write an introductory paragraph. Use your topic sentence and supporting sentences to introduce your topic to the reader.

Write two body paragraphs. Use the ideas and details you outlined or mapped to write interesting paragraphs.
- Each paragraph should start with a topic sentence.
- Use facts, details, and examples to explain your point to the reader.
- Use connecting words to link your points.
- Use the active voice and cut all extra words from your essay.

Write the concluding paragraph. Write a strong ending that ties up all the points you made. Do not bring up any new issues here.

Editing and Revising

Review, edit, and revise. Read the entire essay to make sure you did what you set out to do.

Then use the editing checklist on page 218 to see how you can improve your writing. Pay special attention to the points that you studied in this section:
- ❏ Did you use good synonyms for overused words? *See pages 51–52.*
- ❏ Did you use connecting words and phrases? *See pages 49–50.*
- ❏ Did you replace the passive voice with the active voice? *See pages 53–54.*
- ❏ Did you revise your work to cut extra words? *See page 55.*
- ❏ Did you revise so there are no changes in point of view? *See page 56.*
- ❏ Did you polish your work? *See page 57.*

Writing the Final Draft

Write a final draft. Then proofread it one last time. If necessary, recopy or retype a final draft. Use the proofreading checklist on page 219 to review your final draft.

Sharing the Final Draft

Publish. Let another person read your final draft. Ask if your message was clear. Discuss what the person sees as the essay's weak and strong points. Make some notes that you attach to a copy of the essay. File the draft in your writing portfolio.

Persuasive Writing

Elements of Persuasive Writing

Persuasive writing shows your readers your side of an issue, why they should agree with it, or why they should take a certain action. First, you state your position clearly. Then you give facts, opinions, or reasons that support it. You must back up your opinion with specific details so the reader knows <u>why</u> you feel the way you do.

Ads and sales messages, letters to the editor, and requests from charities are all forms of persuasive writing. A cover letter to an employer is also a form of persuasive writing that you may need to write.

Persuasive writing may appeal to readers' reason, to their emotions, or to their sense of right and wrong. A good piece of persuasive writing might appeal to all three.

EXAMPLE   Below is part of a letter from the leader of a nonprofit group against family violence. She wants to persuade her readers to support the group's work with a donation.

Your support will help us continue sending our teaching materials, *Safe Homes/Safe Families,* free to teachers across the country. Last year we mailed information to over 350,000 teachers who requested it. The sample lessons, discussion topics, and classroom activities help teachers show their students how to recognize violence in the home, how to work toward solutions, and where to find help.

The problem of family violence is growing. It occurs in all parts of the country—in cities, suburbs, small towns, and rural areas. It occurs in families of all social, economic, and educational levels. Children who grow up in violent homes are often unaware that the behavior they experience is a problem. And, unfortunately, they may grow into violent adults. We believe that getting information into the hands of students and teachers can help break the cycle of family violence.

WRITE   As you read in the letter, the writer believes in a cause. She wants to persuade you to believe in it, too, and to act by supporting her group.

On a piece of paper, write two paragraphs about a cause you believe in. Persuade your reader to believe in it, too, or to take some specific action to help it. Choose an issue that you have a strong opinion about—crime, politics, rights. Give specific facts and examples to support your opinion. Follow the Writing Process you learned in Section 1.

Using Connecting Words

Your opinion will make more sense to your reader if your ideas are connected. As you saw in the previous section on expository writing, connecting words join your ideas and help your writing flow smoothly.

EXAMPLE   **No connecting word:** People have the most energy at 10:00 A.M. You should read and do other memory tasks at that time.
Connecting word: People have the most energy at 10:00 A.M. Therefore, you should read and do other memory tasks at that time.

EXAMPLE   **No connecting word:** Your body goes into an energy slump at 2:00 P.M. You should do easier tasks in the afternoon.
Connecting word: Your body goes into an energy slump at 2:00 P.M., so you should do easier tasks in the afternoon.

Review the list of connecting words on page 49 and the rules for punctuation with connecting words on page 50.

PRACTICE

Fill in each blank with the connecting word that best joins the two thoughts.

❶ Bran cereal is high in fiber. _____, it is a good choice for breakfast.

   In summary   **Finally**   **Therefore**

❷ People react to caffeine in many ways, _____ whether you drink coffee is up to you.

   in summary   **in brief**   **so**

❸ Walking, running, and jogging give you energy. _____, any exercise that speeds up your heart rate is good.

   Finally   **In brief**   **Therefore**

❹ Eat plenty of vegetables and fruits. _____, limit foods high in fat, such as ice cream, peanuts, and cheese.

   In addition   **Finally**   **As a result**

❺ I like to exercise every day; _____, I joined a health club.

   after   **as a result**   **whenever**

WRITE **Write a letter to ask a friend to give up smoking, drinking, overeating, or some other bad habit.**
Prewrite: Choose your topic. Brainstorm to think of facts, examples, and reasons to give up the bad habit.
Write: Use connecting words to join your thoughts and to make your points easier to follow.

Writing Compare and Contrast Sentences

You can help persuade your readers to agree with your opinion by writing sentences that compare and contrast. To **compare** is to show how things are the same. To **contrast** is to show how things are <u>not</u> the same.

EXAMPLE Compare | Contrast
Both political parties have plans for the extra money. | The Republicans want to cut taxes. The Democrats want to pay off part of the debt.

A. Write *compare* if the sentence shows how two things are the same. Write *contrast* if the sentence shows how two things are not the same.

_____ **1** People who walk to work are healthier than those who drive.

_____ **2** A half cup of ice cream has the same fat content as ten peanuts.

_____ **3** Japan exports more cars to the U.S. than France does.

_____ **4** Lake Superior is the largest of the five Great Lakes.

Compare and contrast sentences make your point more clearly when the ideas are smoothly joined. Here are some connecting words and phrases you can use to join ideas that compare and contrast.

> **Words that compare:** and, also, too, same as, as . . . as, like, similarly, in the same way, likewise
> **Words that contrast:** but, yet, than, still, however, likewise, in contrast, on the other hand

EXAMPLE I like to shop on weekends <u>as</u> much <u>as</u> I like to shop during the week.
The stores are crowded<u>;</u> however, I can still buy what I need.

Review the rules for punctuation with connecting words on page 50.

B. Complete each sentence to compare or contrast. The connecting words are in bold type. The first sentence is done for you.

1 I liked the movie, **but** *it wasn't as interesting as the book.*

2 The movie told the ending in the first scene, **in contrast to** _____.

3 I like him as an actor; **however,** _____.

Check your answers on page 239.

Remember these three points when you write sentences that compare and contrast.

1 **Avoid obvious statements.** If you want to compare and contrast two books, for example, it would be pointless to say that both have words.

2 **Stick to two subjects at a time.** You cannot compare and contrast more than two subjects in one sentence.

3 **Select subjects that are both members of a particular group.** For example, two athletes, two jobs, and two people are all similar enough to be good subjects.

One way to compare and contrast is first to write down your two subjects as headings. Then list points on which they are the same or different. For example, here are lists that a writer made to compare and contrast some abilities of males and females:

In general, males	In general, females
speak later than girls	speak earlier
stutter more	speak more clearly
catch up by age eight	speak better from age ten
solve mazes better as teenagers	do worse on mazes as teenagers
are better at mazes as adults	are better at language as adults

EXAMPLE Here is how the writer used the lists to write a paragraph.

People wonder why men and women seem to do better at different tasks. Experts have discovered some facts about male and female development. First, girls generally learn to speak earlier and better than boys, and boys have more speech problems. Far more boys than girls stutter, for example. Boys catch up by age eight, though. From age ten on, most girls again speak better than boys, and women generally do better than men on speech and language tasks. Meanwhile, teenage boys tend to do better than teenage girls on tests with mazes. The same is true for men and women. Even after much research, no one can tell why there are these differences in males and females.

WRITE **For each topic below, write one sentence that compares and one that contrasts.**

1 Topic: two friends

compare _____

contrast _____

2 Topic: two places that you have been

compare _____

contrast _____

Using Specific and Fresh Language

It is important in all your writing to choose your words with care. In descriptive writing, you learned that precise words create an interesting word picture. In persuasive writing, specific words help you persuade your reader that your belief or opinion has value. By using specific words, you help your reader understand your way of thinking.

EXAMPLE   **Vague:** Many people work too hard.
Specific: Tool-and-die machinists may work ten hours a day, six days a week.

The first sentence may seem to give you a fact, but look closely at the words. What does "many people" mean? What does "too hard" mean? The second sentence states the same idea with specific words.

PRACTICE

Rewrite each sentence. Replace each underlined part with a more specific word or phrase. The first one is done for you.

1 **Vague:** Sabrina's new dog is great.

Specific: *Sabrina's new fox terrier is good-natured.*

2 **Vague:** My leg was hurt in the crash.

Specific: _____

3 **Vague:** Mr. Mori drives a truck part-time.

Specific: _____

4 **Vague:** The man went to the boss's office for an answer.

Specific: _____

5 **Vague:** They were eating candy in the next row and making noise.

Specific: _____

Words and phrases often become stale through overuse. Phrases such as "in the doghouse" and "cry wolf" have been used so often that readers are tired of them. The phrases no longer mean much. Replace stale phrases with fresh words that help your reader understand your meaning.

EXAMPLE   **Stale**   **Fresh**
eat humble pie   take back your words ten times over
hit the ceiling   holler until your throat hurts

A. **Underline the stale phrase in each sentence.**

  1 We stayed friends through thick and thin.

  2 Baseball is as American as Mom's apple pie.

  3 The stamps are selling like hotcakes.

  4 "This is a tried and true cure," the doctor said.

  5 It's raining cats and dogs today.

  6 "I am sick and tired of your lateness," the boss said.

  7 The old gum was as hard as nails.

  8 If you want to do well, you have to take the bull by the horns.

B. **Rewrite each sentence. Replace the underlined stale phrase with fresh words.**

  1 **Vague:** I've had my ups and downs today.

    Specific: _____

  2 **Vague:** "Now it's time to face the music," the congressman said.

    Specific: _____

  3 **Vague:** If you eat well, get enough rest, and have a good outlook, you will live to a ripe old age.

    Specific: _____

  4 **Vague:** A summer cold is no tea party.

    Specific: _____

WRITE **Write a persuasive paragraph on one of the topics below.**

Cigarettes should (should not) be declared illegal.
The space program should (should not) be ended.
There should (should not) be speed limits on highways.

Prewrite: List the reasons you believe the way you do. List specific examples to support your belief.
Write: State your position clearly. Support it with the reasons and examples you listed. Use specific and fresh language.

Grammar Link
Subject-Verb Agreement

Your essay will be more persuasive if the subjects and verbs in your sentences are in the same form. Make a singular subject agree with a singular verb, and a plural subject agree with a plural verb. For subject-verb agreement, follow these steps.

1 Find the subject in the sentence. The subject tells <u>who</u> or <u>what</u>.

2 See if the subject is singular (one) or plural (more than one).

3 If the subject is singular, add -s or -es to most verbs.

4 If the subject is plural, use the base form of most verbs.

5 *I* and *you* use the base form of the verb: *I think* (not *thinks*), *I eat* (not *eats*), *you think* (not *thinks*), *you eat* (not *eats*).

6 Use the correct forms of the irregular verbs *be* and *have*:

be: *I am; you are; he, she,* or *it is; we are; you are; they are*

have: *I have; you have; he, she,* or *it has; we have; you have; they have*

EXAMPLE

Regular Verbs		Irregular Verbs *be* and *have*	
Singular subject	**Plural subject**	**Singular subject**	**Plural subject**
The star <u>shines</u>.	The stars <u>shine</u>.	The star <u>is</u> bright.	The stars <u>are</u> bright.
He <u>dances</u>.	They <u>dance</u>.	I <u>have</u> to dance.	We <u>have</u> to dance.

Grammar Exercise A

Circle the correct verb form for each sentence.

1 I **(hope, hopes)** the store will be open late.

2 We **(takes, take)** our daughter to that child-care center.

3 The egg **(has, have)** a strange taste.

4 She **(works, work)** hard at her new job.

EXAMPLE The box of gifts contains food, clothing, and books.

The subject in this sentence is *box*, not *gifts*. The verb is *contains*. The words *of gifts* that come between the subject and the verb do not affect agreement.

Grammar Exercise B

For more practice on subject-verb agreement, turn to pages 183–184 of the Grammar Guide.

Circle the subject in each sentence. Cross out any words that come between the subject and the verb. Then underline the correct verb.

1 A salad with extra carrots **(is, are)** my usual lunch.

2 The people in the back of the crowd **(needs, need)** to be heard.

3 Ned, with his three dogs, **(run, runs)** around the block after work.

4 The leader of the union **(say, says)** dues will go up.

 Check your answers on page 240.

Compound Subjects

A **compound subject** is two or more nouns or pronouns joined by *and*, *or*, or *nor*. A compound subject joined by *and* needs a plural verb. When a compound subject is joined by *or* or *nor*, the verb must agree with the subject that is closer to the verb.

EXAMPLE   **Plural verb:** The bus <u>and</u> subway <u>stop</u> here.
Singular verb: <u>Neither</u> the bus <u>nor</u> the subway <u>stops</u> here.

Grammar Exercise A   **Write the correct form of the verb in each sentence.**

① The roof and the window _____ **(leak)** when it rains.

② Marie or Juan _____ **(give)** me a ride to work on Thursdays.

③ My boss and I _____ **(bring)** lunch to work every day.

Singular and Plural Words

A **collective noun** is one that refers to a group of people or things as a single unit. Examples of collective nouns are *class, team, staff, crew, troop, jury, public, group*. These nouns are often singular and use singular verbs.

When the subject is a pronoun, verb agreement may be more difficult. Some pronouns are always singular, some are always plural, and some can be either.

Singular	Plural	Singular or Plural	
words with *one*: someone, no one	several	all	any
words with *other*: another, other	few	some	part
words with *body*: somebody, nobody	both	none	half
words with *thing*: nothing, something	most		
other words: each, either, much, neither	many		

EXAMPLE   **Singular**   **Plural**
<u>No one gives</u> a better haircut.   A <u>few</u> of the people <u>drive</u> to work.

Grammar Exercise B   **Decide if the verb used in each sentence is correct. If so, write C. If not, write the correct form of the verb.**

_____ **①** Each of those restaurants serves fast food.

_____ **②** Some eat burgers and fries nearly every night.

_____ **③** Nobody love fast food more than I do.

_____ **④** My family take it home at least once a week, as a matter of fact.

For more practice on subject-verb agreement, turn to pages 183–184 of the Grammar Guide.

Supporting the Main Idea

In a persuasive piece, you want the reader to agree with your main point. Therefore, you support it by giving facts, opinions, and reasons.

Facts

A **fact** is a statement that is true. The writer can prove the statement is true by giving examples. Writers often use facts to support the main idea of an essay. Here is how one writer used facts in a letter to the editor.

EXAMPLE Today, as I was walking to work, I saw a newspaper in the street. I lifted a corner of the paper and found a thin cat mewing with hunger. I could not leave the cat on the street, so I took it to an animal shelter for care. The man in charge told me that was the tenth animal that had been dropped off that day. In fact, more than 500 cats and 1,000 dogs are dropped off every year at animal shelters in our town alone. The shelter does not have the money to feed and treat all these animals, so more than half must be killed. I hope that the cat I left there today will live and that others like it will not suffer from lack of care. Please give what you can to the local animal shelter.

Opinions

An **opinion** is a point or belief that cannot always be proved. Writers use opinions as well as facts to support their main ideas. Good writers back up their opinions with reasons or logic. The next example offers the opinion that child-care workers should be licensed. Look for the logic the writer uses.

EXAMPLE Taking care of children is more difficult than many people realize. That is why all child-care workers should be licensed by the state. People who mind children in day-care centers or in their homes must be trained to watch for possible dangers and know how to prevent accidents. They also need to know how to get help fast. Specific courses should be given in how to feed and handle infants and small children. Child-care workers must also know how to choose safe toys and games for children, and how to help children get along with others.

PRACTICE

Write *O* if the sentence is an opinion or *F* if the sentence is a fact.

_____ **1** Main Street is ten blocks long.

_____ **2** Main Street has the best shopping around.

_____ **3** Cigarette smoking is America's worst health problem.

_____ **4** Men should have shorter hair than women.

_____ **5** Juan's sister has three children.

_____ **6** The United States government consists of three branches.

Reasons

Your opinions should be supported with logical reasons. <u>Avoid</u> the following three kinds of false reasoning.

A. Jumping to Conclusions: Sometimes a writer reaches a decision without having enough facts. This is called jumping to a conclusion.

EXAMPLE   Our union will not support the new overtime rules. I know because I spoke to Mike.

The writer draws the conclusion that Mike speaks for the entire union. An opinion from one union member is not enough to reach this conclusion.

B. Quoting False Experts: If you rely on experts who are not qualified to support your opinions, your proof will be false.

EXAMPLE   Dr. O. Malhot, an eye doctor, says people should run five miles a day.

Dr. Malhot is an expert on eyes, not exercise. Quote a fitness expert to make your point.

C. Mistaking Cause and Effect: A **cause** is the reason things happen. The result of a cause is an **effect.** If you cannot prove that a reason (cause) results in a specific outcome (effect), your belief is not supported.

EXAMPLE   When parents do not keep their teenagers at home at night, crime increases all over the city.

The writer has mistakenly seen a cause-and-effect relationship where none may exist. There is no reason to believe that allowing teenagers out at night affects crime. Other things may cause increases in crime.

PRACTICE

Write the letter that names the kind of false reasoning: (A) jumping to conclusions, (B) quoting false experts, or (C) mistaking cause and effect.

_____ **1** The local radio station never plays good CDs. There is nothing good on the radio.

_____ **2** Shaun says that Flair makes the best slacks. He knows because he saw a hockey star wear this brand.

_____ **3** Since Marc started dating Lucy, his work has been poor. If he were to stop dating her, his work would improve.

_____ **4** I eat bran and fruit every day. That is why I never get colds.

Apply Your Writing Skills

Write a Persuasive Essay

Now you are ready to apply what you have learned by writing a persuasive essay. Remember that a persuasive essay:

- is a form of writing in which you try to show your reader why he or she should agree with your side of an issue or take a certain action.
- uses facts, opinions, and reasons to support your point about an issue.
- uses specific language to show the reader the value of your point.

ASSIGNMENT   Write a five-paragraph persuasive essay about an issue you feel strongly about, such as prayer in schools, smoking, health care, or the right to die.

Prewriting

1   List some issues that you feel strongly about.

_____

_____

2   Choose one issue. List facts, opinions, and reasons that support your position on the issue.

_____

_____

_____

_____

3   Organize your ideas in an outline or idea map like the one below. Remember that the details can be facts, opinions, or reasons.

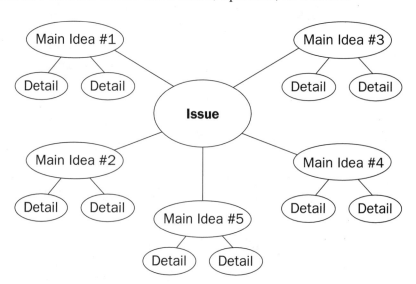

Writing the First Draft

Write a topic sentence. Your first topic sentence will state the subject you are writing about and your position on it. Write your topic sentence below.

_____

_____

On a separate piece of paper, write your first draft.

Write an introductory paragraph. Use your topic sentence and supporting sentences to introduce the subject and your position to the reader.

Write the body paragraphs. Use the ideas and details you outlined and mapped to write interesting paragraphs on your topic.

- Each sentence should support the main idea of your essay.
- Use facts, opinions, and reasons to support your position.
- Check to be sure that your writing does not jump to conclusions, quote false experts, or mistakenly see cause and effect.

Write the concluding paragraph. Write a strong ending that ties up all the points you argued. Do not bring up any new issues here. Try to save one very strong point for the end.

Editing and Revising

Review, edit, and revise. Read the entire essay to make sure you did what you set out to do. Ask yourself: "If I were reading this essay, would it persuade me?"

Then use the editing checklist on page 218 to see how you can improve your writing. Pay special attention to the points you studied in this section:

- ❑ Did you write compare and contrast sentences? _See pages 62–63._
- ❑ Did you replace vague, stale words with specific, fresh language? _See pages 64–65._
- ❑ Do all your subjects and verbs agree? _See pages 66–67._
- ❑ Did you use connecting words to link your ideas? _See page 61._
- ❑ Did you support your ideas with facts, opinions, and reasons? _See pages 68–69._

Writing the Final Draft

Write a final draft. Then proofread it one last time. If necessary, recopy or retype a final draft. Use the proofreading checklist on page 219 to review it.

Sharing the Final Draft

Publish. Let another person read your final draft. Ask if your message was clear. Also ask what else you could do to improve the essay. Make some notes that you attach to a copy of the essay. File the draft in your writing portfolio.

Writing at Work

Office: Administrative Assistant

Some Office Careers

Administrative Assistant
maintains files, writes correspondence, makes appointments, and runs office operations

Personnel Clerk
keeps and updates important, private information about a company's employees

Receptionist
represents company at entrance area, receives and routes phone calls

Stenographer
records spoken information by using shorthand and/or typing actual spoken words

Typist or Word Processor
uses computers to enter text or data, format the material, and print the final copy

Administrative assistants help keep companies running smoothly.

Office workers need to be able to write clearly. If their written work is unclear, problems or mistakes can occur. Office workers cannot follow their written work around and explain what it means to the reader. The writing must be able to stand on its own.

Administrative assistants are often called upon to use their writing skills. Administrative assistants may need to draft memos, letters, e-mail, and other types of written correspondence. Their writing must include a clear introduction, supporting details, and an effective conclusion.

Look at the chart of Some Office Careers.

- Do any of the careers interest you? If so, which ones?

- What information would you need to find out more about those careers? On a separate piece of paper, write some questions that you would like answered. You can find out more information about those careers in the *Occupational Outlook Handbook* at the library.

Administrative assistants need effective writing skills. An administrative assistant at a shelter for homeless mothers and children wrote the letter below.

Read the letter. Then answer the questions that follow.

Dear Neighbor:

Each year Judy's House gives hope to mothers and children in our town who are unable to make ends meet on their own. Our organization offers shelter, food, and clothing for our guests. Through your generous support, we are able to give services to over 400 women and children each year.

This year we hope to begin two new programs for our guests. One is a counseling program. The other is an educational program.

In the past your gifts have allowed us to buy toys and cribs, transportation services, and a washer and dryer for our residents. Won't you help us again by sending a donation to help those in the community less fortunate than yourself?

Thank you for your support.

Sincerely,

Tamara Jones

1 What is the purpose of Tamara Jones's letter?
(1) to ask for transportation services
(2) to thank past contributors
(3) to convince people to donate money
(4) to show off her writing skills
(5) to start counseling and education programs

2 Which paragraph or paragraphs should be made stronger by adding specific supporting details?
(1) Paragraph 1
(2) Paragraph 2
(3) Paragraph 3
(4) None of the paragraphs
(5) All of the paragraphs

3 On separate paper explain your answer to number 2 above. Then write two sentences for that paragraph to add specific supporting details.

UNIT
1 Unit 1 Review:
Essay and Creative Writing

Write pronouns to take the place of the underlined nouns. Choose from these pronouns: *he, she, they, her, him, them, his,* and *their.*

1 <u>Gloria and Michael</u> are planning a vacation. _____

2 <u>Michael</u> wants to go to Florida. _____

3 <u>Gloria's brother Mario</u> lives in Miami. _____

4 Gloria and Michael decide to stay with <u>Mario</u>. _____

5 <u>Mario's</u> house has a large guest room. _____

6 So, he has enough room for <u>Gloria and Michael</u> to stay there. _____

Write the correct pronoun to complete each sentence.

7 Those car keys belong to _____ (I, me).

8 Lilly and _____ (he, him) parked on the street.

9 Oscar gave Otis and _____ (she, her) a ride.

10 Rick and _____ (I, me) want to buy a used car.

11 It's hard for _____ (we, us) to decide what kind of car to buy.

12 My friends let us use _____ (their, them) car for the weekend.

For more practice with pronouns, turn to pages 171–175.

Put one line under each complete subject and two lines under each complete predicate.

13 Diana started her new job on Friday.

14 Raymond and she work at the baseball stadium.

15 They sell peanuts and ice-cream sandwiches.

16 Raymond's friends attend most of the games.

17 The employees can buy tickets for half price.

For more practice on subjects and predicates, turn to pages 183–184 and 187–188.

Check your answers on page 240.

Put an S next to each complete sentence. Put an F next to each fragment.

_____ ⑱ The groceries in the car.

_____ ⑲ Ms. Valdez wrote a check.

_____ ⑳ The clerk opened another line.

_____ ㉑ Before the end of the day.

_____ ㉒ Lost the shopping list in the parking lot.

_____ ㉓ Mr. Nio wants change for a dollar.

For more practice correcting sentence fragments, turn to pages 187–188.

Complete each sentence with an appropriate connecting word. Use one of the words below.

so	because	but	although	when
and	unless	if	even	since

㉔ I can't give you a refund _____ you have a receipt.

㉕ Ana saw Rudy, _____ he didn't see her.

㉖ Carlos gave the file to Ms. Webb, _____ she gave it to me.

㉗ Mr. Smith will get the message _____ he returns from lunch.

Make these correct compound sentences. Write each one with a comma and an appropriate coordinating conjunction—_and, or, but,_ or _so._

㉘ George filled out the form carefully he gave it to Ms. Golov when it was complete.

_____

㉙ She read his resume and liked it, it was neat and well organized.

_____

㉚ Ms. Golov offered George a job, he would have to work Saturdays.

_____

㉛ The job pays well the company also offers good benefits.

_____

For more practice with run-on sentences, turn to pages 189–190.

㉜ He likes the company, he'll probably take the job.

_____

Write the correct adjective or adverb in each sentence.

33 Our city has a _____ art museum.

large (adj.)   **largely** (adv.)

34 The museum has many _____ paintings and sculptures.

fine (adj.)   **finely** (adv.)

35 Suits of armor are _____ displayed in glass cases.

careful (adj.)   **carefully** (adv.)

36 You can get to the museum _____ on the downtown bus.

easy (adj.)   **easily** (adv.)

Write the correct form of the adjective or adverb in each sentence.

37 Of all our employees, Anita is the _____ typist.

fast   faster   fastest

38 Anita also writes _____.

well   better   good

39 Of our two new employees, Jesse works _____ than Maurice.

hard   harder   hardest

40 Anita and Jesse will be promoted _____.

quickly   more quickly   most quickly

41 Of the three employees, Anita has the _____ salary.

high   higher   highest

For more practice with adjectives and adverbs, turn to pages 176–179.

Find the verb in each sentence. Write *A* if the verb is in the active voice and *P* if it is in the passive voice.

_____ **42** Gordon locked his keys in the car.

_____ **43** The copy machine was broken by someone.

_____ **44** A wallet was found near the candy machine.

_____ **45** Tonya sprained her ankle yesterday.

_____ **46** A computer error was made on your bill.

Rewrite each sentence in the active voice.

47 The chicken soup was made by Aretha.

_____

48 The letter was written by Mr. Kingston.

_____

49 The division was won by the Chicago Cubs.

_____

For more practice with active and passive voice, turn to pages 185–186.

50 Early this morning, the pay phone was broken by someone.

_____

Write the correct form of the verb for each sentence.

51 My son and daughter _____ (**help**) me with housework every Saturday.

52 Darnell _____ (**be**) the man to see about your problem.

For more practice with subject-verb agreement, turn to pages 183–184.

53 Many applicants _____ (**write**) letters to ask for a job.

54 The shirts _____ (**cost**) $50; the tie _____ (**cost**) $10.

55 Every day Juanita _____ (**drive**) her car to work.

Write a five-paragraph expository essay on the following topic:

An old saying is "A bird in the hand is worth two in the bush." It means that it is better to hold on to what you have rather than take a risk and try to get something better. Do you agree with that saying? Or do you think taking a risk is sometimes the thing to do? Give specific facts, reasons, and examples to support your answer.

For a review of the writing process or writing an expository essay, see pages 58–59.

Writing Extension

Use your writing skills to write a narrative. The narrative can be a true story about yourself that you want to tell. Or it can be a fictional story that you want to write. Follow the Writing Process when you write your narrative.

Writing Connection: Persuasive Writing and Government

How Should We Judge Political Candidates?

LETTERS TO THE EDITOR OF *THE JOURNAL*

The Journal asks its readers . . .

What do you think of the way that politicians conduct their campaigns? Do they believe Americans respond better to negative campaigns than to a discussion of the issues?

Dear Editor:

Every election, I get worried about what is happening to politics. Candidates seem more interested in telling us about their opponents' private lives than where they stand on important issues.

Unfortunately, many candidates conduct nasty campaigns. They dig up ugly rumors about their opponents and present this information as if it is factual. Some candidates focus their *whole* campaign on negative information about their opponent. They never tell how they feel about important issues like crime control and citizens' rights.

Voters need to know a candidate's qualifications and positions on the issues. They must know if the candidates can serve the people who live in their district. The public does not need to know the intimate details about a person's life.

Negative campaigning may elect some candidates, but the main impact of this activity is to turn off many voters. Negative campaigning is the main reason why some of my friends don't vote. I don't agree with them at all. However, I do understand why negative campaigns make some people decide not to vote.

Sincerely,

Andrew Nathan

Government: Negative Campaigning vs. Talking About the Issues

Negative campaigning is a strategy used by some candidates. A candidate who uses this technique makes personal attacks on the other candidate's character or misrepresents positions. This is called **mudslinging.** Candidates who let voters know their position on matters facing the public use an **issue-oriented campaign.**

Use the material on the previous page to answer the questions.

1 Which statement best supports how Andrew Nathan feels about the question asked by *The Journal*?

(1) Political campaigns are improving.

(2) Negative campaigning has become too common.

(3) Candidates are out of touch with the public.

(4) There are not enough policies to control crime.

(5) A politician's personal life is part of his or her qualification for office.

2 Read the candidates' statements below. If the statement is more likely to be heard in a negative campaign, write *N*. If it is more likely to be heard in an issue-oriented campaign, write *I*.

_____ a. **Candidate Martinez:** I will work to make our streets safer at night.

_____ b. **Candidate Lopez:** Mr. Martinez believes that all teenagers are troublemakers.

_____ c. **Candidate Martinez:** My opponent has voiced his opposition to the construction of a new elementary school on River Road. I am in favor of this new school being built on River Road.

_____ d. **Candidate Lopez:** My opponent just wants you to pay high taxes. That's why she supports building the new school on River Road.

3 Which position represents your point of view?

Do you think people support candidates because they are convinced by negative campaigns? Or do you think voters support candidates because of their positions on the issues?

On a separate piece of paper, write your own letter to the editor about this issue. Follow these steps:

A. Take one of the two positions:

- Voters support candidates because of their negative campaigns.
- Voters support candidates because of their positions on the issues.

B. Make a list of reasons or examples to support your position.

C. Use the Letter to the Editor on page 78 as a sample to write your letter.

- Write the date and *Dear Editor,*
- Write an introductory, body, and concluding paragraph.
- End the letter with *Sincerely,* and your name.
- Review, revise, and edit the letter.
- If you would like to share your viewpoint, send the letter to your local newspaper.

UNIT 2

Workplace and Personal Writing

Writing plays an important role both in the workplace and in your personal life. Job applications, cover letters, and resumes may help you to find a job. After you are employed, you may be asked to write in your work. Improving your writing skills may also lead to a better job and higher pay. In your personal life, you may write letters or send e-mails to keep in touch with friends and relatives.

Computers have changed the way people work and write. However, a machine cannot replace good writing skills. Your ability to use the steps in the writing process can help both your workplace writing and your personal writing. In this unit, you will have an opportunity to expand your skills in both areas.

○ How can writing skills help you get a job, do a job well, and get a better job?

○ What friend or family member would you like to write a letter to? What would you write about?

SECTIONS

6 Letter Writing
Grammar Link: **capitalization and punctuation**

7 Job Search Writing
Grammar Link: **action verbs and phrases**

8 Workplace Writing
Grammar Link: **plurals, possessives, and contractions**

9 Explanatory Writing
Grammar Link: **verb tenses, misplaced and dangling modifiers, and parallel structure**

10 Report Writing
Grammar Link: **regular and irregular verbs**

Letter Writing

Personal Letters and Business Letters

At one time, people had to write letters to send a message. Today, it is easier and faster to telephone or to e-mail. However, there are times when you may want or need to write a letter. There are two main types of letters: personal letters and business letters.

Personal Letters

A **personal letter** is usually written to someone you know well. The purpose may be to keep in touch with a friend or relative in another city. It may be to say thank you for a gift or a favor, or it may be to invite someone to visit you. Other reasons for writing personal letters are to ask someone to do something or to tell someone something that has happened.

EXAMPLE

> 140 W. 116 St., Apt. 10
> New York, NY 10026
> July 25, 1999
>
> Dear Toni,
>   How are you? I hope you're enjoying the summer. The weather here has been miserable. I would love to leave the city for a few days to visit you and Vernon. I will be able to take some time off in a couple of weeks. Please write or call to let me know if that would be a good time for me to visit. I would have called you, but my phone bill last month was high. See you soon.
>
>   Love,
>   Yolanda

WRITE   Notice the parts of Yolanda's letter to her friend Toni. Yolanda began by writing her own address and the date she was writing the letter. Use Yolanda's letter as a model.

On a separate piece of paper, write a short personal letter. Assume you are writing to a friend in another town to invite him or her to visit you.

Check your answer on page 241.

Business Letters

A **business letter** is written to a company or an organization, or directly to a person who works for a company or an organization. You may be writing for yourself or as an employee. A business letter has two purposes: (1) to communicate a specific message and (2) to produce a written record. Four common types of business letters are listed below.

- **Letter of request**—written to ask for something, to get information, to place an order, to issue an invitation .
- **Letter of reply or confirmation**—written to respond to a message (written or oral) or a request, or to produce a written record of a spoken agreement
- **Follow-up letter**—written to remind someone of something, to thank someone, or to provide additional information
- **Letter to conduct business**—written to document a decision, process, or suggestion within a business

EXAMPLE Letter of Request

Overland Medical Center
39000 South Oak Drive, Overland Park, MA 02115
404-555-3200

October 6, 1999

Mr. Antonio Torres
201 Lowell Avenue
Overland Park, MA 02110

Dear Mr. Torres:

Thank you for your letter inquiring about our medical technician training program at Overland Medical Center. Please send me a copy of your resume and a cover letter stating your reason for wanting to join the program. We will review your application and get back to you as soon as possible.

Sincerely,

Joyce Hawkins

Joyce Hawkins
Human Resources Dept.

WRITE On a separate piece of paper, write a letter of reply to Ms. Hawkins.

Say that your resume is enclosed, and give two reasons you would like to be admitted to the training program for medical technicians at Overland Medical Center.

Writing Style

Your **writing style** is the way you choose your words and sentences to express yourself in a letter. Personal letters are written in an **informal style.** Your written words and sentences are like those you use when talking to your friends. Your letter "sounds" like the way you talk.

Business letters are written in a **formal style.** You may be writing to someone you do not know. The letter should state its message in a direct yet polite way.

EXAMPLE

Informal Style: Dear John,
I've been calling you for two weeks, and you haven't called me back.

Formal Style: Dear Mr. Smith:
I have called your office several times, but I have not been able to reach you.

Informal Style: Mary,
I'm busy on Friday, so we'll have to change our lunch plans. Can you make it on Monday instead? Call me.

Formal Style: Dear Mrs. Yazzie:
Thank you for your invitation to the Community Center luncheon on Friday. I am sorry that I will not be able to attend. Please keep me in mind for the next one.

PRACTICE

Practice informal and formal writing styles by writing a few sentences for each situation described below.

❶ Informal: Write to your friend Kareem, asking him to help you move a piece of furniture this weekend.

_____

_____

_____

❷ Formal: Write to the president of the large company you work for. Ask her to speak at a meeting of a group you belong to on "Success in Your Career."

_____

_____

_____

Personal Letter Format

Personal letters may be handwritten on plain paper, notepaper, or stationery, or they may be typed or written on a computer and printed. Below are the parts of a personal letter.

- **Return address**—the writer's address
- **Date**—the date on which the letter is written
- **Salutation**—an opening greeting, such as *Dear Jake,* followed by a comma
- **Body**—the contents or message of the letter
- **Closing**—a parting phrase, such as *Sincerely* or *Very truly yours,* followed by a comma
- **Signature**—the writer's signed name. In a letter written on a computer, the name is typed as well as written.

All personal letters should follow a specific format. The **format** is the way the parts of the letter are set up on the page.

EXAMPLE

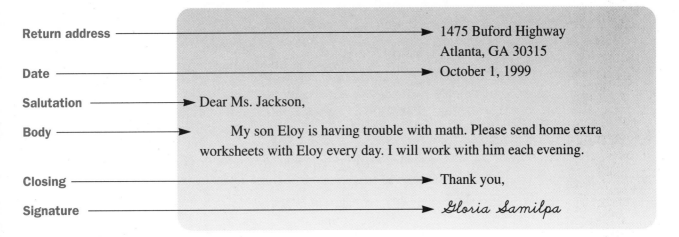

Return address → 1475 Buford Highway
Atlanta, GA 30315

Date → October 1, 1999

Salutation → Dear Ms. Jackson,

Body → My son Eloy is having trouble with math. Please send home extra worksheets with Eloy every day. I will work with him each evening.

Closing → Thank you,

Signature → *Gloria Samilpa*

PRACTICE

Below is a personal letter. Copy it on a separate piece of paper, putting it in the proper format.

P.O. Box 32 Eden Prairie, MN 55344 October 20, 1999 Dear Aunt Frances, Thanks for the beautiful sweaters! It gets really cold up here this time of year, so your timing was perfect. After living in Florida for so long, I had forgotten what cold weather feels like. Give my love to Uncle Harold. Tell him I'll visit soon. Your nephew, Danny

Business Letter Format

Business letters from a private individual are handwritten on plain paper, typed, or written on a computer and printed. Business letters from an employee are written on a computer and printed out on letterhead paper. **Letterhead** is stationery that has a company name and address printed at the top.

The parts of a business letter are similar to the parts of a personal letter. However, there are a few differences.

- **Inside address**—The name and address of the company to which the letter is written is included. If the letter is written to a specific employee of the company, the employee's name goes on a line before the inside address.
- **Salutation**—The opening greeting is followed by a colon, not a comma.
- **Signature**—The writer's signed name is always followed by the name typed.

EXAMPLE

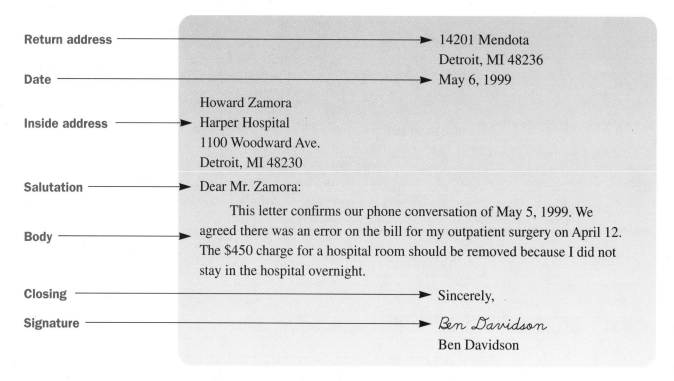

Return address	14201 Mendota
	Detroit, MI 48236
Date	May 6, 1999
Inside address	Howard Zamora
	Harper Hospital
	1100 Woodward Ave.
	Detroit, MI 48230
Salutation	Dear Mr. Zamora:
Body	This letter confirms our phone conversation of May 5, 1999. We agreed there was an error on the bill for my outpatient surgery on April 12. The $450 charge for a hospital room should be removed because I did not stay in the hospital overnight.
Closing	Sincerely,
Signature	*Ben Davidson*
	Ben Davidson

PRACTICE

Below is a business letter. Copy it on a separate piece of paper, putting it in the proper business letter format.

222 East 24th St. Philadelphia, PA 19135 June 14, 1999 Mr. Bernard Adams, Travelworld, 901 Harrison Avenue, Philadelphia, PA 19139 Dear Mr. Adams: Thank you for talking to me about the position in your word processing unit. I know my skills would fit your needs. Our meeting made me eager to work at Travelworld. I look forward to hearing from you about the job. Sincerely, Elaine Evans

Check your answer on page 242.

Grammar Link

Your business letters create an impression of you in your reader's mind. If you are writing as an employee, your business letters also create an impression of your company. Even if you are writing a personal letter to a friend, you will want it to be correct. Therefore, capitalizing and punctuating correctly are important when you write a letter.

Capitalization

1 Always capitalize the first word of a sentence.

EXAMPLE Please send me a copy of your latest catalog.

2 Capitalize each part of a person's name.

EXAMPLE Louise Guccione   Samuel C. Johnston

3 Capitalize titles and abbreviations that come before and after people's names. Do not capitalize when a title stands alone.

EXAMPLE Mr. Zell D. Moore, **Jr.**   Mrs. Barbara Westmass
Dr. Katherine Lord
No capital: The doctor has an office downtown.

4 Capitalize words showing family relationships when they are used as a title or in place of a name. Do not capitalize when the word stands alone.

EXAMPLE Aunt Jane will not be able to go.
No capital: My aunt will not be able to go.

5 Capitalize names of cities, states, and sections of the country.

EXAMPLE City and state: Chicago, Illinois   Section: Midwest

6 Capitalize names of countries, languages, nationalities, religions, and regions of the world.

EXAMPLE Country: Saudi Arabia   Language: Arabic
Nationality: Arabian   Religion: Islam
Region: Middle East

7 Capitalize names of streets, highways, bodies of water, buildings, monuments, and bridges.

EXAMPLE Street: Wall Street   Highway: New Jersey Turnpike
Monument: Statue of Liberty   Water: Atlantic Ocean
Building: Empire State Building

8 Capitalize months, days, and holidays.

EXAMPLE September   Wednesday   Thanksgiving

9 Capitalize names of companies and organizations.

EXAMPLE Company: Adams-Clarke Associates
Organization: Veterans Society

Grammar Exercise A   Rewrite each sentence with correct capital letters.

1 last year I worked on senator smith's campaign.

_____

2 the campaign office was on fifth avenue in the chrysler building.

_____

3 a debate was sponsored by a group called independent voters of america at their building on the hudson river.

_____

4 laura washington, vice president of the organization, made a speech.

_____

Grammar Exercise B   Use proofreader's marks to correct each capitalization error in the letter below. The mark to capitalize is three lines under the letter: <u><u><u>a</u></u></u> = A.

Bradley Advertising Agency
45 Capital Street
Columbus, OH 43225

may 20, 1999

supreme computer, inc.
958 alexander street
river tower
Columbus, oh 43221

dear mr. Potter:

    my supervisor, doris healy, director of sales here at bradley associates, asked me to send you the enclosed brochure detailing the services our company provides to computer stores like yours. If interested, you can take advantage of our free trial offer by calling before may 31. We are closed next Monday because of memorial day.

                    Sincerely,

                    James Hobson

                    james hobson
                    sales assistant

For more practice on capitalization, turn to pages 158–160 of the Grammar Guide.

Punctuation

1 End a sentence with a period, question mark, or exclamation point.

EXAMPLE The party was over too soon. How did you like the party?
The party was terrific!

2 Use a period after an abbreviation or an initial.

EXAMPLE Sharon A. Kaufman Co. (Company) Inc. (Incorporated)

3 Use a comma after each item before *and* in a list of three or more items.

EXAMPLE We need a new supply of red, green, and white labels.

4 Use a comma between the name of a city and state, and between the day and year in a date.

EXAMPLE New Orleans, Louisiana June 2, 2000

5 Use a comma after the salutation in a personal letter and after the closing of a personal or business letter. Use a colon after the salutation of a business letter.

EXAMPLE Dear Toni, Sincerely, Dear Ms. Thomas:

Grammar Exercise C **Place correct punctuation marks in the letter below.**

1670 Evergreen Road
Houston TX 77023
January 25 1999

Ms. Vanessa Lewis
Lewis and Evans Assoc
Houston TX 77025

Dear Ms Lewis

I attended your career planning workshop at the Valley College Library on December 15 1998 Your presentation was just what I needed to organize myself Would it be possible for you to send me copies of your resume-writing guidelines the worksheet and the sample Unfortunately, you ran out of these three handouts before you got to me

Sincerely

Joseph Wallach

Joseph Wallach

For more practice on punctuation, turn to pages 156–157 of the Grammar Guide.

Organizing Business Letters

A business letter should not be more than one page unless absolutely necessary. Two to four paragraphs are usually enough. Paragraphs should be short, usually just three or four sentences. A paragraph with only one sentence is acceptable.

EXAMPLE   Here is a sample with a few more tips to help you write business letters.

Universal Computer Company
509 Union Square
Lexington, KY 40527

January 3, 1999

Ms. Irma Salinas
Meeting Planner
Crown Plaza Hotel
1 City Plaza
Lexington, KY 40521

Dear Ms. Salinas:

Topic sentence comes first in paragraph and directly states a request. → Universal Computers wishes to reserve a meeting room in your hotel for a computer-training program. We need the space from April 9–11 or April 20–22 from 9:00 a.m. to 4:00 p.m. Below is a list of our specific needs.

- Meeting room for twenty people

Details are listed in brief statements, not complete sentences. → Table space for ten computers

- Electrical wiring and outlets to accommodate the equipment

- Refreshments for a morning and an afternoon break

Conclusion states what will happen next and thanks the reader. → Please let me know the cost of the items listed and the dates you can best serve our group. After I receive this information, I will call you to finalize the plans. Thank you for your help.

Sincerely,

Janice Adams

Janice Adams
Administrative Assistant

WRITE   Reply to the letter below. Use the tips on page 90. On the lines provided, write the body of the letter only. Do not copy the formatting.

Family Day Care Center
3300 North Beach Drive
Los Angeles, CA 90033
212-555-8899

September 23, 1999

Mr. Calvin Simpson
304 West End Blvd.
Los Angeles, CA 90011

Dear Mr. Simpson:

We are seriously considering your application for the position of administrative assistant at the Family Day Care Center.

It is our policy to screen all applicants by checking their references. Would you please send me the names of two people we can contact regarding your past work experience and personal background? I need the name, address, telephone number, and a brief description of your relationship with each person.

As soon as we have this information, we can complete processing your application.

Sincerely,

George Walker

George Walker
Director, Human Resources

_____

_____

_____

_____

_____

_____

_____

Apply Your Writing Skills

1: Write a Letter Requesting Information

Now you are ready to apply what you have learned about writing a business letter. Remember that a business letter:

- is written in a formal style
- follows a specific format
- is organized to request or give information directly and briefly

As you write, follow the steps in the writing process.

ASSIGNMENT

Imagine that you saw the following advertisement in a newspaper. Write a letter requesting information about the vacation deal.

> ### Take a Trip to Paradise!
> Save $$$. Group rates available.
> Write for details of a once-in-a-lifetime
> ### VACATION DEAL!
> Address inquiries to Vacation Deal,
> P.O. Box 25, Grand Central Station,
> NY, NY 10163

Prewriting

1 List some questions you want answered about this vacation deal. What information will you need to decide if you are interested or not?

_____   _____

_____   _____

2 On a separate piece of paper, write an outline or draw an idea map for your letter.

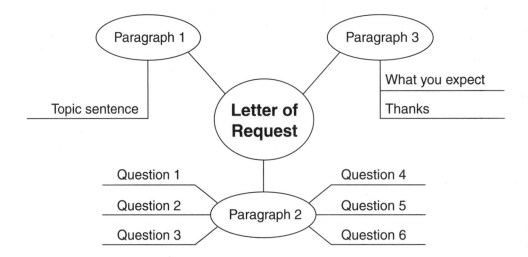

Writing the First Draft

On a separate piece of paper, write your first draft.

Format the Letter. Write your return address, the date, and your inside address. Use "Dear Sir or Madam:" for the salutation.

Write the Message. Follow the outline or map you wrote. Write the appropriate conclusion. Then write your closing, leaving space for your signature.

Editing and Revising

Review, edit, and revise. Read the entire letter to see if you accomplished what you set out to do.

Then use the editing checklist on page 218 to see how you can improve your writing. Pay special attention to the points you studied in this section.

Check the organization of your letter. *See page 90.*

❑ Is the letter brief, with short paragraphs?

❑ Does a topic sentence come first and directly state your request?

❑ Does a conclusion state what you expect to happen next and thank the reader?

Check the mechanics of your letter.

❑ Did you use correct capitalization? *See pages 87–88.*

❑ Did you use correct punctuation? *See page 89.*

Writing the Final Draft

Write a final draft. Then proofread one last time. If necessary, recopy or retype your final letter. Use the proofreading checklist on page 219 to review your final draft.

Sharing the Final Draft

Publish. Let another person read your letter. Ask if your message is clear. Show this person the ad so that he or she can judge if you requested all the information you need. Make some notes and attach them to a copy of the letter. File the letter in your writing portfolio.

2: Write Letters for a Job Interview

Now you are ready to apply what you have learned to write letters that you can use as models the next time you are job hunting.

ASSIGNMENT

On a separate piece of paper, write a letter to apply for one of the jobs in the want ads below. Or, if you wish, use an ad for a job you want and write a letter to request an interview for that job.

<table>
<tr><th>Want Ad 1</th><th>Want Ad 2</th></tr>
<tr>
<td>

**Security Guards
for Warehouse**

Day or night positions available. No experience required. Will train. Send letter of application to Mike Anderson, XYZ Packing Company, 655 Landers Avenue, Chicago, IL 60612.

</td>
<td>

**Retail Sales
Clothing Store**

Some experience preferred, but will train. Must be willing to work long hours & weekends. Send letter of application to Antonia Lucci, Rave Wear, Box 130, Sears Tower Bldg., Chicago, IL 60620.

</td>
</tr>
</table>

Prewriting

1 Select which ad you want to answer. Think about the working hours, the amount of experience wanted, and the neighborhood and transportation requirements. You cannot consider the salary since neither ad mentions the pay.

2 List some information you might need or questions you might like answered.

_____

_____

_____

3 List the main ideas you want to put in your letter. Why are you interested in applying for the job? What qualifications do you have for the job? What do you want the person reading the letter to do after he or she receives your application?

_____

_____

_____

4 On a separate piece of paper, organize your ideas in an outline or on an idea map.

Writing the First Draft

On a separate piece of paper, write your first draft.

Format the Letter. Write your return address, the date, the inside address, and the salutation.

Write the Message. Follow the idea map or outline you wrote. Then write an appropriate conclusion. Write your closing, leaving room for your signature.

Editing and Revising

Review, edit, and revise. Read the entire letter to see if you accomplished what you set out to do.

Then use the editing checklist on page 218 to see how you can improve your writing. Pay special attention to the points you studied in this section.

Check the organization of your letter. *See page 90.*

❑   Is the letter brief, with short paragraphs?

❑   Does a topic sentence come first and directly state your request?

❑   Does a conclusion state what you expect to happen next and thank the reader?

Check the mechanics of your letter.

❑   Did you use correct capitalization? *See pages 87–88.*

❑   Did you use correct punctuation? *See page 89.*

Writing the Final Draft

Write a final draft. Then proofread one last time. If necessary, recopy or retype your final letter. Use the proofreading checklist on page 219 to review your final draft.

Sharing the Final Draft

Publish. Let another person read your final letter. Ask if your message is clear. Show the person the ad you are responding to so that he or she can judge whether you asked appropriate questions and discussed appropriate skills you have. Make some notes and attach them to a copy of the letter. File the letter in your writing portfolio.

Job Search Writing

Resumes and Job Applications

When you are looking for a job, you will have many chances to use your writing skills. For some jobs, you may need to prepare a resume. For almost all jobs, you will be asked to fill out a job application form.

Resumes

A **resume** is a written summary of your qualifications for work. Your resume should have one goal: to get you interviews. It should make employers want to meet you. Employers will often spend only a few minutes looking at your resume. So, it should be carefully written to *sell* you and your skills to employers.

There are many things about you that will help you sell yourself to an employer. Write your resume to present the best possible picture of yourself. Always be honest about your background, but include only information that makes you look good. A resume usually includes the following parts:

1. **Personal data:** Your name, address, and telephone number
2. **Objective:** The position or goal you want to achieve
3. **Work experience:** Your employment record or employment skills
4. **Education:** Schools attended and courses taken
5. **Other experience, skills, activities, or interests:** Items an employer might find useful or interesting, such as a second language and volunteer or community work

Do not include this personal information on a resume:

- Your age
- Your race or ethnic origin
- Your marital status
- Your height or weight
- Your health status

An employer's request for information in some of these personal areas is not legal. However, some jobs, such as police officer or firefighter, may have special physical requirements. Find out what is required before you apply for the job, and be prepared to provide the necessary information.

Do not list personal references on your resume. Employers may request references on job application forms. If so, list them there.

PRACTICE

Look over the resumes on pages 97 and 98. What are the common categories on both resumes?

Check your answer on page 243.

EXAMPLE 1 The resume below shows how someone with a few years of work experience highlights her skills and experiences.

Resume

Juanita Diaz
1225 Pharr Road South
Los Angeles, CA 90011
213-555-3509

OBJECTIVE

To use customer service and people skills in a sales position with potential for career growth

WORK EXPERIENCE

Sales Associate, Baldwin's Department Store, Los Angeles, CA, January 1998–present. Member of a five-person sales team in a children's department for a large department store chain in Los Angeles. Responsibilities include:

- Training new sales clerks to use computer system;
- Handling return of damaged merchandise to manufacturers;
- Assisting in inventory records maintenance;
- Stocking shelves and keeping merchandise in order.

Sales Clerk, Power Video, Los Angeles, CA, June 1995 to December 1997. Worked as a sales clerk to pay for computer classes. Responsibilities included:

- Processing sales and rentals of videotapes;
- Assisting customers in finding merchandise;
- Recording merchandise inventory of incoming stock.

EDUCATION

- Southview Learning Center, Los Angeles, CA: GED Certificate, June 1998; Basic Computer Skills Certificate, September 1998
- Dover High School, Los Angeles, CA

SKILLS

Computer skills
Fluent in Spanish and English

REFERENCES

Available upon request

Comment: Juanita Diaz is looking for a sales position with potential for growth. Although she has only three years of work experience, she details her job responsibilities very specifically. She also highlights her computer and language skills, which are very important in many workplaces.

EXAMPLE 2 The resume below shows how a person with limited work experience presents his skills and background.

Resume

Jonathan Sowell
26047 Birch Road
Detroit, MI 48234
313-555-2310

OBJECTIVE

Entry-level position in data entry or computer operations

WORK EXPERIENCE

Messenger, Reed Printing Company, 19000 Jefferson Ave., Detroit, MI 48232. July 1999 to present.

EDUCATION

Attended Northern High School 1994–1997
Attended night school at J. P. Alexander Adult Learning Center; received GED Certificate June 1999
Completed courses in record keeping and accounting

SKILLS

- Keyboarding and computer literacy
- Ability to listen, follow instructions, and learn quickly
- Dependable and able to work with little supervision
- Operate photocopy and fax machines

OTHER EXPERIENCE

Worked as group leader in summer day camp program

REFERENCES

Available upon request

Comment: Jonathan Sowell does not have all of the work experience he needs, but his resume emphasizes that he is hardworking, mature, and willing to learn. The resume also lists courses he has taken that have improved the computer and math-related skills that a data-entry operator needs. It also mentions a leadership role in a day camp program, which illustrates a sense of maturity and responsibility.

Personal Data Sheet

Before you write your resume, gather and organize the information, or data, for it. One way to do this is to complete a **personal data sheet.** Even if you do not use all the information on the data sheet, completing it will help you make sure you didn't leave anything out. It may also help you discover things about yourself that you would not have thought of putting on your resume. Finally, it will help you think about questions that you may be asked when you have a job interview.

WRITE   Complete the personal data sheet on this and the next two pages.

Personal Data Sheet

Personal Data

Name _____

Address _____

City, State, Zip Code _____

Telephone _____

Objective

An *objective* is a goal or something you want. Right now your objective may be to get a job. Or perhaps you already have a job, but you would like a better one. The type of work you choose should interest you. It should make good use of your skills and talents. It should also give you a chance to learn and grow. What type of work do you want to do? Write a statement that summarizes your objective.

_____

_____

_____

_____

Education

High School _____ Years Attended _____

Address _____

Other Courses or Educational Achievement _____

_____

Work Experience

Complete a copy of this page for each job you have held.

Company _____ Telephone _____

Address _____

Dates of Employment _____

Type of Business _____

Name and Title of Supervisor _____

_____

Your Title _____

Your Job Duties _____

_____

_____

Did you receive any special training on the job, such
as using equipment, handling customer problems,
or anything not described in your job duties?

_____

_____

_____

_____

What did you like best about this job? _____

_____

_____

What did you like least? _____

_____

_____

Why did you leave? _____

_____

_____

What was your salary when you started the job? _____

What was your salary when you left? _____

Other Experiences, Skills, Activities, Interests

What personal strengths will help you achieve your objective? For instance, if you want to be a salesperson, you should enjoy working with people. Are you good at solving problems, making decisions, or organizing things? Can you draw? Can you fix things? Ask someone who knows you well to help you identify your strengths.

_____

_____

_____

What are your interests, hobbies, or accomplishments? Are you an athlete? A singer? A dancer? An artist? Have you done volunteer work?

_____

_____

_____

Do you have training in any technical skills? Do you know how to operate any kind of equipment used on the kind of job you want?

_____

_____

_____

References

Ask three people if they would recommend you for a job. If they agree, fill in the information for each of them.

1. Name _____ Title _____

    Company _____

    Address _____ Telephone _____

2. Name _____ Title _____

    Company _____

    Address _____ Telephone _____

3. Name _____ Title _____

    Company _____

    Address _____ Telephone _____

Grammar Link
Action Verbs and Phrases

Business people look for short resumes. They are busy, and long resumes take time to read. You can limit your resume and hold the attention of an employer by using phrases rather than sentences. When you state your objective, use a phrase.

Phrase: Sales position with growth potential

Sentence: I would like a position as a sales clerk and eventually hope to become a supervisor.

When you describe your experience and skills, use phrases with **action verbs.** Action verbs tell your employer what you have done or can do. They are commonly used to describe work experience and skills.

Phrase with action verb: Planned fund-raising drive

Sentence: My neighborhood had a fund-raising drive for victims of last summer's flood, and I helped plan the bake sale.

When you use the action verbs listed below, you help create an image of yourself as a capable person. In fact, some companies use computers to scan for keywords in resumes. These keywords are qualities that companies are looking for in the people they want to hire. Keywords are often action verbs.

Action Verbs			
accomplished	developed	performed	taught
achieved	directed	planned	trained
answered	handled	processed	typed
approved	input	repaired	used
assisted	led	scheduled	won
completed	managed	sold	
created	operated	solved	
designed	organized	supervised	

Grammar Exercise A

Write the best action verb to complete each phrase.

1 _____ letters and memos for department staff

  Typed   Solved   Supervised

2 _____ telephone calls for two executives

  Completed   Trained   Handled

3 _____ weekly reports on service calls

  Taught   Accomplished   Completed

4 _____ computer equipment and a fax machine

  Operated   Developed   Processed

For more practice with action verbs, turn to pages 185–186 of the Grammar Guide.

Grammar Exercise B   **Rewrite the sentences below to change them into phrases with action verbs. The first one is done for you.**

1 When the copier broke down, I was able to repair it.

Repaired equipment, such as photocopier

2 I drew all the signs we used in the window of the hardware store.

_____

3 I made up schedules for covering the reception desk.

_____

4 When the newsstand owner was out or on vacation, I took over.

_____

5 I got awards for running track when I was in high school.

_____

Grammar Exercise C   **Write phrases with action verbs to explain your work experience and skills.**

Use the information on your personal data sheet. If the verbs listed on page 102 do not fit, think of other action verbs to use.

Job Duties	Skills
_____	_____
_____	_____
_____	_____
_____	_____

Other Experience	Skills
_____	_____
_____	_____
_____	_____
_____	_____

Special Training/Equipment	Skills
_____	_____
_____	_____
_____	_____

For more practice with action verbs, turn to pages 185–186 of the Grammar Guide.

Job Application Forms

The information you put on a job application form is similar to the data on your resume. A job application usually asks for the following categories of information:

1. **Name, address, telephone.**

2. **Position wanted.** List the specific job opening or a general job category such as secretary, trainee, or supervisor. You can also write *entry-level position*.

3. **Salary required.** State the salary you are currently making or hoping to make, given your qualifications. If you do not know the salary range for a certain type of job, learn this before you apply. Check the want ads, talk with people who do similar kinds of work, or ask the interviewing company's personnel office.

4. **Social Security number.** If you don't have a Social Security number, you can apply for one at a local Social Security office. You must have a Social Security number in order to be employed.

5. **U.S. citizenship.** If you are not a U.S. citizen, the company will inform you of their requirements for hiring noncitizens. Also, U.S. citizens are required to prove citizenship after they are hired by showing a passport, birth certificate, driver's license, or other proof of identity.

6. **Other personal data.** You might be asked to list relatives who are employed in the same company, how you found out about the company or open position, or whom to contact in case of an emergency.

7. **Educational data.** Include formal schooling and any additional courses.

8. **Skills.** Although you may be applying for a particular position, there may be other jobs in the company for which you are also qualified. List all your skills here so the employer can see that.

9. **Employment history:**
   - Names and addresses of companies you worked for in the past.
   - Name and title of supervisor. If the person you worked for is no longer with the company, you should still give his or her name.
   - If asked, include the reason you left a job. Some common reasons for leaving are returning to school, seeking a better position, or staff reduction or layoffs. Do not state personal reasons for leaving a job, such as not having anyone to care for your children or not getting along with the boss. The phrase "to seek a better position" covers these kinds of reasons.
   - Your starting and ending salary for each job. Most employers consider this routine and expect an answer.

10. **References.** Most job application forms will ask whether the company can contact your present employer. If you do not want your present employer to know you are looking for a new job, ask the company not to call at this time.

Apply Your Writing Skills

1: Write Your Resume

Now you are ready to apply what you have learned about writing a resume. Remember that a resume:

- is an outline of a person's work experience, education, and training.
- is intended to get a person an interview for a job.
- describes skills in a way that presents the best possible picture of the person

As you write, follow the steps in the writing process.

ASSIGNMENT

Write a resume that presents your education and skills in the best way. Include information that will "sell" yourself to an employer.

Prewriting

① Review the personal data sheet you completed on pages 99–101. It is actually the prewriting for your resume.

② List some questions an employer might want answered about your skills or education. Think of ways you might answer those questions. Your answers may provide you with more "selling points" to put on your resume.

_____

_____

_____

_____

Writing the First Draft

On a separate piece of paper, write your first draft.

Format the Resume. Follow the format used in Example 1 on page 97 or Example 2 on page 98. Use these headings:

Personal Data
Objective
Work Experience
Education
Other Experience, Skills, Activities, or Interests

Write the Information. Include information from your personal data sheet under the appropriate headings of the resume. Use action verbs and phrases to describe your skills and experience.

Editing and Revising

Review, edit, and revise. Read the entire resume to see if you accomplished what you set out to do.

Then use the editing checklist on page 218 to see how you can improve your writing. Pay special attention to the points you studied in this section. Did you use action verbs and phrases to tell what you did on each job? *(See pages 102–103.)* Remember that on a resume you do not need to use complete sentences.

Check the formatting of your resume. Did you include the following information?

❑ Personal data

❑ Objective

❑ Work experience

❑ Education

❑ Other experience, skills, activities, or interests

Writing the Final Draft

Write a final draft. Then proofread one last time. If necessary, recopy or retype your resume. Use the proofreading checklist on page 219.

Sharing the Final Draft

Publish. Let another person read your resume. Ask if the resume presents your skills clearly. Ask what else you might include to make an employer want to interview you for a job. Make some notes and attach them to a copy of the resume. File the resume in your writing portfolio.

2: Complete a Job Application Form

Now you are ready to apply what you have learned to complete a job application form. Use the information from your personal data sheet and resume to fill in the following job application from Belvedere Hospital. Apply for a job as an orderly, nurse's aide, or receptionist at the hospital.

BELVEDERE HOSPITAL

Employment Application

An Equal Opportunity Employer

Belvedere policy and federal law forbid discrimination because of race, religion, age, sex, marital status, disability, or national origin.

Date _____

Personal Data

Applying for position as _____ Salary required _____

Name _____
       (Last)   (First)   (Middle)

Address _____
       (Street)   (City)   (State)   (Zip)

Telephone _____ Social Security Number _____

Are you a U.S. citizen? _____ Yes _____ No

If noncitizen, give Alien Registration Number _____

Person to notify in case of emergency:

Name _____ Telephone _____

Address _____

Have you ever been employed by Belvedere? _____ Yes _____ No

If yes, list department _____ Dates _____

Have you previously applied for employment with Belvedere?

_____ Yes _____ No

If yes, give date _____

How were you referred to Belvedere? _____ Agency _____ School

_____ Advertisement _____ Belvedere Employee _____ Other

Name of referral source above _____

(continue on the next page)

Military Data

Have you served in the military service of the United States?

_____ Yes _____ No

If yes, branch of service _____ From _____ To _____

Rank _____ Service duties that apply to civilian jobs _____

_____

Educational Data

List school name/address; dates attended; type course/major; graduated?; degree received.

High School _____

_____

College _____

_____

Trade, Business _____

_____

Other _____

_____

Grade Point Average: High School _____ College _____

Skills

List any special skills _____

_____

_____

Business machines you can operate _____

_____

Computer skills _____

_____

(continue on the next page)

Employment Data

List all full-time, part-time, temporary, or self-employment. Begin with current or most recent employer.

Company Name

_____

Address

_____
(Street)   (City)   (State)   (Zip)

Employed From/To   Salary or Earnings   Name/Title of Supervisor

_____

Your Title and Duties

_____

Reason for Leaving _____

....

Company Name

_____

Address

_____
(Street)   (City)   (State)   (Zip)

Employed From/To   Salary or Earnings   Name/Title of Supervisor

_____

Your Title and Duties

_____

Reason for Leaving _____

....

I confirm that all my answers to the questions in this employment application are accurate and complete. I understand that my employment will be contingent upon the accuracy, completeness, and acceptability of the information furnished to you. Permission is granted to Belvedere Hospital to verify all statements in this employment application.

_____   _____

Date   Signature of Applicant

Workplace Writing

Formats and Uses

Workplace writing is any kind of writing you do on the job. In the workplace, you may use your writing skills in a number of different ways.

Workers send and keep written information in many ways. The format you use depends on the kind of information you are writing. You may often use printed forms. Forms can also help you to take telephone messages. To write and send messages to another company, you may write a business letter. To send a message to a coworker, you may write a memo. You might also fax or e-mail your messages.

Your workplace writing begins as soon as you start a new job. New employees must fill out certain employment forms.

EXAMPLE This W-4 form gives your employer information needed to take federal income tax from your paycheck.

Form **W-4** Department of the Treasury Internal Revenue Service	**Employee's Withholding Allowance Certificate** **For Privacy Act and Paperwork Reduction Act Notice, see page 2**	DMB No. 1525INC10 19**99**

1. Type or print your first name and middle initial Frank M.	Last Name Nava	2. Your social security number 555 | 00 | 1212

Home address (number and street or rural route) 4243 Meems Avenue	3. [X] Single [ ] Married [ ] Married, but withhold at higher single rate Note: If married, but legally separated, or spouse is a nonresident alien, check the single box.
City or town, state, and zip code Chicago, IL 60601	4. If your last name differs from that on your social security card, check here and call 1-800-772-1213 for a new card . . . . . . ▶ [ ]

5.	Total number of allowances you are claiming (from line H above or from the worksheets on page 2 if they apply) .	**5.**	1
6.	Additional amount, if any, you want withheld from each paycheck.	**6.**	$ — 0 —
7.	I claim exemption from withholding for 1999, and I certify that I meet **BOTH** of the following conditions for exemption:		

• Last year I had a right to a refund of **ALL** Federal Income Tax withheld because I had **NO** tax liability **AND**
• This year I expect a refund of **ALL** Federal Income Tax withheld because I expect to have **NO** tax liability.
If you meet both conditions, enter "**EXEMPT**" here . . . . ▶ | **7.** | —

Under penalty of perjury, I certify that I am entitled to the number of withholding allowances claimed on this certificate or entitled to claim exempt status

Employee's signature ▶ *Frank M. Nava*   **Date** ▶ *August 15*   19 *99*

8.	Employee's name and address (Complete 9 and 10 only if sending to the IRS)	9. Office code (optional)	10. Employer identification number

WRITE Explain why complete and accurate information is necessary when you fill out a workplace form like the W-4 form above.

_____

_____

_____

Forms

A **form** is a printed document with spaces for filling in information. Most businesses cannot do business unless certain forms are completed. Forms help workers give and take complete, accurate information.

To fill out a form, look at it carefully to see what kinds of information it asks for and where you write each piece of information. If you are handwriting the form, print neatly so that others can read the information.

Some common business forms are order forms, invoices, and shipping forms.

Order Forms

An **order form** is a written statement of what a customer ordered from a company. It also records who ordered the item, who sold it, and how payment will be made.

EXAMPLE Here is part of an order form used by an office supply store.

CUSTOMER ORDER		DATE 10-01-99		
NAME Marlin Fisher				
ADDRESS 111 E. Main St.		ORDER NO. 23201		
CITY, STATE, ZIP Jonesville, IL 60623				
SOLD BY SM	CASH	CHECK	CHARGE	ACCT. NO. 4909

	QUAN.	DESCRIPTION	PRICE	AMOUNT
1	12	binders, imprinted	3.00	36.00
2				
3				

RECEIVED BY M. Fisher	TAX	2.00
	TOTAL	38.00

Answer these questions about the order form above. The first one is done for you.

1 Who placed the order? _____ *Marlin Fisher* _____

2 Where does he live? _____

3 What did he order? _____

4 When did he order it? _____

5 Did the customer pay in cash? _____

6 What is the total amount to be paid? _____

Invoices

An **invoice** is a form used to bill customers for what they owe. It shows what they have bought, just as an order form does. It also shows the price of each item and the number of items bought. Because order forms and invoices contain much of the same information, some companies use the same form for both.

EXAMPLE Here is a partly completed invoice used in a hardware store.

INVOICE	TAYLOR HARDWARE		INVOICE NO. 7602

SOLD TO Anne Johnson	SHIP TO same
ADDRESS	ADDRESS
CITY, STATE, ZIP	CITY, STATE, ZIP

ORDER NO. 6626	SOLD BY M. Jones	TERMS 30 days	DATE 10-3-99

ORDERED	SHIPPED	DESCRIPTION	PRICE	UNITS	AMOUNT
10-3		wood paneling, pine	30.00	8	240:00
				TAX	
				TOTAL	

WRITE Complete the invoice above. Use the following information:

In addition to 8 sheets of wood paneling at $30.00 a sheet, Anne Johnson, of 21 Ford Avenue in Detroit, MI 48011, also ordered these items on October 3: 1 package of 3″ wood nails at $5 a package and 1 decorative mirror at $75.00. The tax is $16.00, for a total of $336.00. On October 8, all the items were shipped.

Check your answers on page 244.

Shipping Forms

A **shipping form** is used to send a letter or package through a delivery service. A shipping form contains information about who is sending the package and who is receiving it. The form also shows facts about the kind of item being sent and who is paying for the shipment. Information on the form must be accurate and easy to read. Otherwise, the package may not get to the right place.

EXAMPLE Below is an example of a completed shipping form.

FedEx® USA Airbill FedEx Tracking Number **810906743968**

Form I.D. No. **0200**   Sender's Copy

1 From Please print and press hard.
Date **11-15-99** Sender's FedEx Account Number **N/A**

Sender's Name **Ben Martinez** Phone **(312) 228-1128**

Company **Martinez, Inc.**

Address **1800 W. Chicago Avenue**

City **Chicago** State **IL** ZIP **60601**

2 Your Internal Billing Reference First 24 characters will appear on invoice.

3 To
Recipient's Name **Glenn Bono** Phone **(512) 555-6111**

Company **Bono Construction**

Address **21 N. Main St.** We cannot deliver to P.O. boxes or P.O. ZIP codes.

To "HOLD" at FedEx location, print FedEx address here.

City **Austin** State **TX** ZIP **78755**

Questions? Call 1·800·Go·FedEx® (800-463-3339)
Visit our Web site at www.fedex.com

By using this Airbill you agree to the service conditions on the back of this Airbill and in our current Service Guide, including terms that limit our liability.

4a Express Package Service Packages up to 150 lbs. Delivery commitment may be later in some areas.
[X] FedEx Priority Overnight Next business morning
[ ] FedEx Standard Overnight Next business afternoon
[ ] FedEx First Overnight Earliest next business morning delivery to select locations

[ ] FedEx 2Day* Second business day
[ ] FedEx Express Saver* Third business day
* FedEx Letter Rate not available Minimum charge: One-pound rate

4b Express Freight Service Packages over 150 lbs. Delivery commitment may be later in some areas.
[ ] FedEx 1Day Freight* Next business day
[ ] FedEx 2Day Freight Second business day
[ ] FedEx 3Day Freight Third business day
* Call for Confirmation:

5 Packaging * Declared value limit $500
[X] FedEx Letter*
[ ] FedEx Pak*
[ ] Other Pkg. Includes FedEx Box, FedEx Tube, and customer pkg.

6 Special Handling
[ ] Saturday Delivery Available for FedEx Priority Overnight and FedEx 2Day to select ZIP codes
[ ] Sunday Delivery Available for FedEx Priority Overnight to select ZIP codes
[ ] HOLD Weekday at FedEx Location Not available with FedEx First Overnight
[ ] HOLD Saturday at FedEx Location Available for FedEx Priority Overnight and FedEx 2Day to select locations

Does this shipment contain dangerous goods? One box must be checked.
[X] No
[ ] Yes As per attached Shipper's Declaration
[ ] Yes Shipper's Declaration not required
[ ] Dry Ice Dry Ice, 9, UN 1845 ___ x ___ kg
Dangerous Goods cannot be shipped in FedEx packaging.
[ ] Cargo Aircraft Only

7 Payment Bill to:
Enter FedEx Acct. No. or Credit Card No. below.
[X] Sender Acct. No. in Section 1 will be billed.
[ ] Recipient
[ ] Third Party
[ ] Credit Card
[X] Cash/Check

FedEx Acct. No.
Credit Card No.
Exp. Date

Total Packages **1** Total Weight **2(oz)** Total Declared Value† **$ 12 .00**

†Our liability is limited to $100 unless you declare a higher value. See back for details. FedEx Use Only

8 Release Signature Sign to authorize delivery without obtaining signature.

By signing you authorize us to deliver this shipment without obtaining a signature and agree to indemnify and hold us harmless from any resulting claims. **360**

Rev. Date 11/98•Part #154814•©1994-98 FedEx•PRINTED IN U.S.A. GBFE 1/99

Study the form above to see where each piece of information is written. Then answer the following questions.

1 What is being sent, a letter or a package? _____

2 Who is sending the item? _____

3 To whom and where is the item being sent? _____

4 Who is paying to send this item? _____

Messages

Workers need to give and receive information all the time. Therefore, being able to write clear and accurate messages is a valuable work skill. A good message gives all the facts a reader needs. It also presents the information in a way the reader can easily understand.

EXAMPLE   Here is a phone message a worker took for his boss.

> ### While You Were Out
>
> Mr. Rice,
> Barbara Slade called at 9:00 to say she will not be able to come to work today. Her daughter is ill. Please call her when you have time. Her number is 555-4391.
> Raoul

The information is complete and clear. The message explained who called, when she called, why she called, and what Mr. Rice should do.

PRACTICE

Read the message below. Compare it with the example message above. Then answer the questions that follow.

> ### While You Were Out
>
> Ms. Luther,
> Call Jim Cowens because he won't be in.
> Terry

1   What three important facts are missing from this message?

_____

_____

_____

2   What information seems out of order in this message?

_____

Fax Messages

One way to send messages quickly is by using a fax machine. *Fax* is the shortened form of the word *facsimile.* A fax machine sends pages of written material to another fax machine over telephone lines. A fax message usually includes a cover sheet. The cover sheet is a form that has important information.

EXAMPLE   Below is a sample fax cover sheet. It is partly filled in.

FAX TRANSMITTAL SHEET		
TO: Abdel Tahiri	FROM: John Mandel	
COMPANY: Tahiri Retail	DATE: 12-5-99	
FAX NUMBER: 847-555-1212	PHONE NUMBER:	
CONTENTS: Parts information	TOTAL NUMBER OF PAGES INCLUDING COVER:	
NOTE:		

WRITE A   Complete the fax cover sheet above with the following information.

1 Mr. Mandel's phone number is 847-555-3311.

2 He is faxing four pages of catalog information about parts, along with the cover sheet.

3 He also wants to write a note to Mr. Tahiri saying that items Mr. Tahiri ordered last week are now in stock. Mr. Tahiri should call to say when he would like them delivered.

E-mail Messages

Another way to send messages quickly is by using e-mail. With e-mail, you write a message on your computer and send it electronically to another computer. Different e-mail systems use different formats. You always need to insert the receiver's e-mail address (often a form of the receiver's name). The date and your e-mail address are usually included automatically on a message.

WRITE B   On the e-mail space below, write a message to a coworker. His e-mail address has been filled in: MCox. Tell him your boss is holding a meeting in the conference room from 9:00 A.M. to 10:00 A.M. on Monday, October 1, 1999. He and his staff are expected to attend. Anyone with questions should call you at extension 7224.

TO: MCox   SUBJECT:

_____

_____

_____

Grammar Link

Your messages and other pieces of workplace writing should be free of errors. Spelling or punctuation errors can confuse your reader and make you look like a careless worker. Always edit your messages to be sure you are using plurals, possessives, and contractions correctly.

Plurals

Plural means "more than one."

1. To form the plural of most nouns, add *s* or *es*. Add *es* to nouns that end in *s, ch, sh, x,* or *z*.

   EXAMPLE   form–forms   tax–taxes   match–matches

2. Many nouns ending in *f* or *fe* form the plural by changing the *f* to *v* and adding *es*.

   EXAMPLE   half–halves   wife–wives   knife–knives

3. Nouns that end in a consonant followed by *y* form the plural by changing the *y* to *i* and adding *es*. If there is a vowel before the *y*, just add *s*.

   EXAMPLE   company–companies   baby–babies
                     boy–boys   key–keys

4. Some nouns form the plural irregularly. Many dictionaries list irregular plurals.

   EXAMPLE   child–children   man–men
                     woman–women   tooth–teeth

Grammar Exercise

Complete each sentence with the correct plural form of the noun in parentheses. The first one has been done for you.

1. **(business)** We own both painting and carpeting _____*businesses*_____.

2. **(wharf)** Oil tankers dock at the _____ in the harbor.

3. **(man)** The other four _____ in our store are clerks.

4. **(attorney)** Three _____ wrote the employee manual.

5. **(secretary)** All the _____ went to lunch together.

6. **(woman)** Several _____ applied for the welding job.

7. **(tooth)** Kari brushes her _____ after she eats lunch in the cafeteria.

8. **(roof)** Tony's company installs _____.

For more practice with plurals, turn to page 161 of the Grammar Guide.

Check your answers on page 244.

Possessives

The **possessive** form of a noun shows that something is owned and to whom it belongs. Possessive nouns can be singular or plural.

❶ Form the possessive of singular nouns and plural nouns that don't end with an *s* by adding an apostrophe (') and *s*.

EXAMPLE

Singular: The father's workday began early in the morning.
Bernard's computer was very expensive.
The business's hours are from 10 to 8.

Plural: Women's pay is sometimes less than men's.

❷ To form the possessive of plural nouns ending in *s*, add only an apostrophe (').

EXAMPLE

Plural: Both of my sisters' husbands are carpenters.
The Collins' store has been family owned for years.

Grammar Exercise

Circle the correct possessive form of the word in each sentence. The first one has been done for you.

❶ A (**secretary's,** **secretaries'**) job duties usually include typing letters and memos.

❷ A day care center in our office building provides the (**childrens'**, **children's**) breakfast and lunch.

❸ My (**friend's, friends'**) spouses take turns driving to work.

❹ He is going to work in his (**company's, companies'**) headquarters.

❺ My (**boss', boss's**) name is Hector Ramirez.

❻ All of (**Amos', Amos's**) equipment was damaged.

❼ After (**everyones', everyone's**) work is done, we can leave for the day.

❽ The (**worker's, workers'**) old desks were replaced with work stations.

❾ The softball (**player's, players'**) uniforms have the company logo on them.

❿ (**Women's, Womens'**) roles in the workplace have changed greatly.

⓫ The (**Jackson's, Jacksons'**) house was not damaged in the storm last week.

⓬ The (**machine's, machines'**) warranties all expired last year.

For more practice with possessives, turn to page 162 of the Grammar Guide.

Contractions

A **contraction** is a word formed by joining two other words. An apostrophe (') shows where a letter or letters have been left out. Many people use contractions when they speak or when they write informal letters. Do not use contractions, however, in formal business writing.

Common Contractions

Contraction	Words It Replaces
I'm	I am
he's, she's, it's	he is, she is, it is
you're, we're, they're	you are, we are, they are
isn't, aren't, wasn't	is not, are not, was not
he'll, she'll, you'll	he will, she will, you will
won't	will not
didn't	did not
I'd	I would
I've, we've	I have, we have
who's	who is, who has
let's	let us
can't	cannot

Grammar Exercise

Write the words that each underlined contraction replaces.

_____ 1 I've recently learned to use a personal computer.

_____ 2 I didn't know a computer could make my job easier.

_____ 3 There's a way to make many copies of the same letter.

_____ 4 There wasn't enough time to type every letter.

_____ 5 My co-workers weren't happy about using computers.

_____ 6 You won't be surprised to hear that most people use computers.

_____ 7 Let's agree that computers changed the way business works.

_____ 8 We didn't want to admit computers would be useful.

For more practice with contractions turn to pages 163–164 of the Grammar Guide.

Check your answers on page 244.

Memos

A **memo** (short for *memorandum*) is a short, written workplace message. Memos are written between coworkers to explain, to announce, or to inform, as well as to produce a written record of the action or information the message is about.

Memos are one page or less. They are often written less formally than a business letter, but more formally than a personal letter. Like all workplace writing, a memo should include all the facts a reader will need to understand the message.

Memos are prepared in a standard format. A memo includes the date, the sender's name, and the receiver's name. Memos also usually have a subject line to tell the topic of the message.

EXAMPLE   Below is an example of a memo written about a company policy.

Date: January 2, 2000
To: All Employees
From: Beverly Smith, Human Resources
Subject: Vacation Requests

We want to be sure that everyone enjoys a two-week vacation this year. If you have not requested a specific time for your vacation, please do so before January 15. If we receive your request by that date, you will have a better chance of receiving the vacation dates you prefer.

PRACTICE

Answer these questions about the memo above.

1   What is the memo about? _____

2   Who wrote the memo? _____

3   Who is the memo to? _____

4   Do you think the message is clear, with all of the important information included? Explain your answer.

_____

WRITE   On a separate piece of paper, write a short memo.

Ask your supervisor, Art Balsam, for permission to leave work an hour early one day next week. You have an appointment with the doctor. You can work an extra hour this week to make up the time.

Prewrite: List the important information you need to include in your memo.

Write: Write your memo, making sure you include all necessary information.

Apply Your Writing Skills

1: Completing a Form

Now you are ready to apply your writing skills to complete a form. As you complete the form, remember what a form is for and what you must do to fill one out correctly. Remember that a business form:

- has spaces in which information is entered.
- must be completed accurately and completely.
- must be completed neatly so that someone else can read it.

ASSIGNMENT   Complete the shipping form on the following page.

Prewriting

Assume the following information.

- You are sending an 8-oz. letter from your company, ABC Supplies, 100 Hudson Street, Detroit, MI 48255.
- The phone number is 313-555-0795.
- The letter is going to Mary Money at Adams Company, 1421 Wilson, Cleveland, OH 44101.
- Her phone number is 216-555-4875.
- The letter needs to arrive the next business morning but does not require special handling.
- Your company will pay the bill. Its account number is 584-906-792. The internal billing reference number is AC-34.
- Because the shipment is being charged to an account, you do not need to enter total charges.
- You do not need to enter a declared value.
- You do not want the letter left without someone at the Adams Company signing for it.

Writing

Fill in the information above in the appropriate spaces on the form on page 121. Be sure to read the form carefully so that you know where to put the information given above.

FedEx. *USA Airbill* FedEx Tracking Number **810906743968**

Form I.D. No. **0200**

Sender's Copy

1 From *Please print and press hard.*

Date _____

Sender's FedEx Account Number _____

Sender's Name _____ Phone ( ) _____

Company _____

Address _____ Dept./Floor/Suite/Room

City _____ State _____ ZIP _____

2 Your Internal Billing Reference
First 24 characters will appear on invoice.   OPTIONAL

3 To

Recipient's Name _____ Phone ( ) _____

Company _____

Address _____ Dept./Floor/Suite/Room
We cannot deliver to P.O. boxes or P.O. ZIP codes.

To "HOLD" at FedEx location,
print FedEx address here.

City _____ State _____ ZIP _____

Questions? Call 1·800·Go·FedEx® (800-463-3339)
Visit our Web site at www.fedex.com

By using this Airbill you agree to the service conditions on the back of this Airbill and in our
current Service Guide, including terms that limit our liability.

4a Express Package Service *Packages up to 150 lbs.*
Delivery commitment may be later in some areas.

☐ FedEx Priority Overnight
Next business morning

☐ FedEx Standard Overnight
Next business afternoon

☐ FedEx First Overnight
Earliest next business morning delivery to select locations

☐ FedEx 2Day*
Second business day

☐ FedEx Express Saver*
Third business day

* FedEx Letter Rate not available
Minimum charge: One-pound rate

4b Express Freight Service *Packages over 150 lbs.*
Delivery commitment may be later in some areas.

☐ FedEx 1Day Freight*
Next business day

☐ FedEx 2Day Freight
Second business day

☐ FedEx 3Day Freight
Third business day

* Call for Confirmation: _____

5 Packaging *Declared value limit $500*

☐ FedEx Letter*

☐ FedEx Pak*

☐ Other Pkg.
Includes FedEx Box, FedEx Tube, and customer pkg.

6 Special Handling

☐ Saturday Delivery
Available for FedEx Priority Overnight and FedEx 2Day to select ZIP codes

☐ Sunday Delivery
Available for FedEx Priority Overnight to select ZIP codes

☐ HOLD Weekday
at FedEx Location
Not available with FedEx First Overnight

☐ HOLD Saturday
at FedEx Location
Available for FedEx Priority Overnight and FedEx 2Day to select locations

Does this shipment contain dangerous goods?
One box must be checked.

☐ No

☐ Yes
As per attached Shipper's Declaration

☐ Yes
Shipper's Declaration not required

☐ Dry Ice
Dry Ice, 9, UN 1845 _____ x _____ kg

☐ Cargo Aircraft Only

Dangerous Goods cannot be shipped in FedEx packaging.

7 Payment *Bill to:*
Enter FedEx Acct. No. or Credit Card No. below.

☐ Sender
Acct. No. in Section 1 will be billed.

☐ Recipient

☐ Third Party

☐ Credit Card

☐ Cash/Check

FedEx Acct. No.
Credit Card No. _____

Exp. Date _____

Total Packages _____ Total Weight _____ Total Declared Value† $ _____ .00

†Our liability is limited to $100 unless you declare a higher value. See back for details.

FedEx Use Only

8 Release Signature *Sign to authorize delivery without obtaining signature.*

By signing you authorize us to deliver this shipment without obtaining a signature
and agree to indemnify and hold us harmless from any resulting claims.

360

Rev. Date 11/98•Part #154814•©1994–98 FedEx•PRINTED IN U.S.A. GBFE 1/99

Editing and Revising

After you have completed the form, check it to make sure you have filled it
out accurately and completely.

☐ Are all the spaces that need to be completed filled in?

☐ Is all the information accurate?

☐ Did you spell names correctly?

☐ Did you capitalize correctly? *See pages 87–88.*

☐ Is your writing neat enough so that someone else can read it?

Check your answer on page 245.   UNIT 2 : WORKPLACE AND PERSONAL WRITING   **121**

2: Writing a Memo

Now you are ready to apply what you have learned about writing memos by writing a memo to your coworkers. Remember that a memo:

- is a short, written workplace message.
- is less formal than a business letter, but more formal than a personal letter.
- must include all important information.
- uses a standard format.

ASSIGNMENT

Assume you are an assistant manager in a grocery store. You have noticed that some of the checkout cashiers seem to have forgotten basic store policies about how to act with customers. Some don't smile and greet the customer. Others don't count back change. You think a refresher workshop in customer relations for all checkout cashiers would be a good idea. Write a memo announcing the workshop and the reasons for it. Include a date, time, and place for the workshop.

Prewriting

❶ List the details you will need to cover in your memo. (You may make up more details if you like.)

_____

_____

_____

_____

_____

_____

_____

_____

❷ Organize your ideas in an outline or an idea map like the one below.

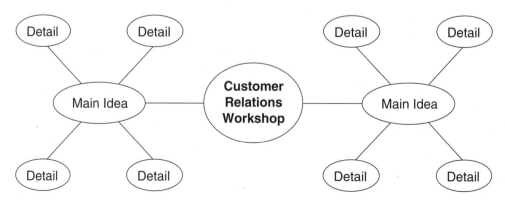

 Check your answers on page 245.

Writing the First Draft

On a separate piece of paper, write your first draft.

Write the Introduction. Briefly state the subject of your memo. Write a strong topic sentence that directly and clearly states the problem.

Develop Supporting Details. As you write your memo, remember to include all important information.

Write the Conclusion. Give the reader a person to contact and a telephone number. Do not bring up any new points here.

Editing and Revising

Review, edit, and revise. Read the entire memo to see if you accomplished what you set out to do.

Then use the editing checklist on page 218 to see how you can improve your writing. Pay special attention to the points you studied in this section. In addition to the items on the general editing checklist, check to see that you did the following:

❏ Did you use the proper memo format? *See page 119.*

❏ Did you give readers all the details employees need? *See page 119.*

❏ If you used plurals, possessives, or contractions, did you spell them correctly? *See pages 116–118.*

Writing the Final Draft

Write a final draft. Then proofread one last time. If necessary, recopy or retype your final memo. Use the proofreading checklist on page 219 to review your final draft.

Sharing the Final Draft

Publish. Let another person read your final memo. Ask if your memo is clear. Ask what you might do to improve your writing. Make some notes and attach them to a copy of the memo. File the memo in your writing portfolio.

Check your answer on page 245.

Explanatory Writing

Elements of Explanatory Writing

Explanatory writing explains, informs, or instructs. You can read explanatory writing in books, newspapers, and magazines. The writing in this textbook is explanatory.

Much of the writing that you do every day is also explanatory writing. You might write travel directions for someone or leave a note about where you are going. You might jot down your favorite recipe for someone. You might have to write down what you do to complete a certain job.

Explanatory writing contains clear and complete facts. The facts are arranged to help readers follow the point. Good explanatory writing also uses precise words so that the reader understands exactly what is being explained.

EXAMPLE Read the following paragraph. It explains how a camera works.

A camera works a little like your eye does. When you point a camera at something—say, your five-year-old daughter or the New York City skyline— light reflects from that subject and strikes the lens of your camera. The light passes through the lens and forms an upside-down image on the film at the back of the camera. You can sharpen that image by adjusting the distance between the lens and the film. To form a sharp image of a subject close to your camera, such as your daughter, adjust so that the lens is relatively far from the film. If the subject is far from your camera, such as the skyline, adjust so that the lens is closer to the film. If you have an automatic camera, the camera focuses for you.

The explanation in the example uses a spatial explanation, light moving from outside a camera to within. From that explanation, you get a basic understanding of how a camera works. You could use that explanation to know what to do when you shoot pictures.

WRITE Think of something you know about and can explain how it works.

On a separate piece of paper, write a paragraph that explains how something works to a person who knows very little about your subject.

Think of something you use. Your topic could be as simple as the table of contents in a book or as complicated as a car engine. List specific details you could include. Decide the order in which to present them. Then follow the Writing Process you learned in Section 1 to write an explanation.

Time-order Transition Words

One way to explain your ideas clearly is to include transition words in your paragraphs. **Transition words** connect ideas. They signal ways that ideas are linked. **Time-order transition words,** for example, show the order of ideas. Common time-order transition words are listed below.

first	next	before	meanwhile
second	then	soon	when
third	last	later	while
fourth	after	during	earlier

EXAMPLE **No transition words:** Go north on Main Street for two miles.
Turn left onto King Street.
Take a left by the park.

Transition words: <u>First</u>, go north on Main Street for two miles.
<u>Next</u>, turn left onto King Street.
<u>Finally</u>, take a left by the park.

PRACTICE

Write time-order transition words in the paragraph. Use each of the words below once.

when   second   last   then   first

_____ , go north to the corner. _____ ,

turn right at the food store. Look for the sign for Smith Street.

_____ you see the sign, walk a block more.

_____ turn left. _____ , stop at the dress

shop. Our apartment is on the second floor.

WRITE   On a separate piece of paper, write directions that a friend could use to go from your house or apartment to the nearest grocery store.

Prewrite: List the steps to get to the grocery store from your house.
Write: Put the steps into sentences. Link the sentences by adding time-order transition words to make the directions clearer. Begin your directions with the word *first.*

Transition Words in "How-to" Writing

Time-order transition words help link ideas in explanatory paragraphs that give directions. Time-order transition words are also used in "how-to" writing. "How-to" writing explains how things are made or done.

EXAMPLE   Read the paragraph below about how to follow the writing process. Notice that the writer uses time-order transition words to join the steps.

Writing is a step-by-step process. **First,** you decide that you want to send a written message. **Second,** you plan your message. You jot down notes about what you want to cover in your document. You organize your ideas in an outline or an idea map. **Next,** you write a first draft. **Then** you review, revise, and edit your draft to make it as clear and correct as possible. You write a final draft and proofread it. **Finally,** you share your writing with the person you wrote to.

PRACTICE

Complete the paragraph with time-order transition words. Use each of the words below once.

next   during   after   second   last   then   first

Did you ever wonder how peanut butter is made?

_____, the peanuts are shelled. _____,

they are sorted for size and value. _____, they are roasted.

_____ they are cooked, the red outer skin is removed.

_____ the nut is split, and the small piece called the

"heart" is taken off. The heart makes the peanut butter sour.

_____, the nuts are mashed. _____ the

last step of mashing, workers add honey, sugar, and salt.

WRITE   Write a paragraph to explain something simple you know how to do.

Prewrite: Think of something you can explain. It could be diapering a baby, starting a car, going grocery shopping, or shooting a basketball. List all the steps. Then number the steps in order.

Write: Use your prewriting plan to write your paragraph. Use transition words to connect the steps.

Grammar Link
Verb Tenses

Explanatory writing often deals with actions: "First, <u>do</u> this" or "Then, this <u>happens</u>." **Verbs** are words that show action. Verbs also show time, or **tense.** English has six verb tenses. There are three simple tenses and three perfect tenses. The **simple tenses** show present, past, and future time.

EXAMPLE **Present tense:** I <u>call</u> my friend daily.
She <u>is</u> my friend.

Past tense: You <u>smiled</u> at me yesterday.
They <u>gave</u> a party.

Future tense: He <u>will work</u> late tonight.
We <u>shall call</u> home.

The three **perfect tenses** show actions that have ended or that will end soon. They also can show the effect of actions.

EXAMPLE **Present perfect:** My friend <u>has offered</u> to help me.

Past perfect: The storm <u>had ended</u> when the power went off.

Future perfect: I <u>will have been</u> here three days by Tuesday.

For more practice on verb tenses, turn to pages 180–181 of the Grammar Guide.

Grammar Exercise A

Identify the tense of each underlined verb. Write *past*, *present*, or *future*.

1 We <u>will give</u> a party after work today. _____

2 Marge <u>buys</u> chips, dips, fruit, and soda. _____

3 I <u>called</u> all our friends last night. _____

4 He <u>spent</u> most of his money. _____

Grammar Exercise B

Circle the number of the best way to correct each underlined verb.

1 Your children <u>grow</u> so tall since last year!
  (1) have grown
  (2) will grow
  (3) had grown
  (4) grows

2 By the time you came home, I <u>have cleaned</u> up.
  (1) had cleaned
  (2) will clean
  (3) cleaning
  (4) cleans

3 Charles <u>did visited</u> his aunt every summer for six years.
  (1) visiting
  (2) has visited
  (3) have visited
  (4) visit

4 Steve <u>has swum</u> ten laps in the pool before you came.
  (1) swimming
  (2) swims
  (3) will be swimming
  (4) had swum

Misplaced and Dangling Modifiers

Using the wrong verb tense can make explanatory writing unclear. Placing **modifiers**—descriptive words and phrases—in the wrong place or leaving out the words they describe can also make explanations confusing.

Misplaced Modifiers

Place modifiers as close as possible to the part of the sentence they describe. Sentences are unclear when the modifiers are in the wrong place.

EXAMPLE

Wrong Place: John saw the train passing through the open window.

A train did not pass through the open window. The phrase "through the open window" should be closer to the word it describes, *saw.* Move the phrase.

Correct Place: Through the open window, John saw the train passing.

Dangling Modifiers

Don't forget to include the word that is being described in a sentence. A sentence with a dangling modifier has something missing.

EXAMPLE   **Dangling Modifier:** Coming up the stairs, the clock struck one.

A clock cannot come up the stairs. The sentence does not say <u>who</u> did the action. *Coming up the stairs* is left dangling with nothing to modify. There are two ways to correct the sentence.

Correct: Coming up the stairs, he heard the clock strike one.
Correct: As he was coming up the stairs, the clock struck one.

Grammar Exercise A

Circle the number of each sentence that has a modifier in the wrong place.

1 Save a room for the couple with a bath.

2 I found a letter in the mailbox that is not mine.

3 To get to the plant, we went nearly ten miles.

4 We bought a cat for my son we call Fluff.

Grammar Exercise B

Circle the number of the best way to correct each sentence.

1 When driving, a fatal crash was seen.
  (1) When driving a fatal crash, we saw it.
  (2) A fatal crash, when driving, was seen.
  (3) When driving, we saw a fatal crash.
  (4) A fatal crash was seen when driving.

2 While passing a large rock, a noise made me jump.
  (1) While I was passing a large rock, a noise made me jump.
  (2) While a large rock was passing, a noise made me jump.
  (3) A noise made me pass a large rock.
  (4) While a large rock was passed, a noise made me jump.

For more practice on placing modifiers correctly, turn to pages 197–198 of the Grammar Guide.

Check your answers on page 245.

Parallel Structure

Explanatory writing is clearer if all the ideas in a sentence are in the same form. When you list words or phrases in the same form, you are using **parallel structure.** The words or phrases may be used as nouns, verbs, adjectives, or adverbs.

EXAMPLE

Not parallel: TV is good for <u>news</u>, <u>movies</u>, and <u>to watch sports</u>.
Parallel: TV is good for <u>news</u>, <u>movies</u>, and <u>sports</u>. (nouns)

Not parallel: The cat likes <u>to sleep</u>, <u>scratch</u>, and <u>eating</u>.
Parallel: The cat likes to <u>sleep</u>, <u>scratch</u>, and <u>eat</u>. (verbs)

Not parallel: The room was <u>large</u>, <u>clean</u>, and <u>did not cost a lot</u>.
Parallel: The room was <u>large</u>, <u>clean</u>, and <u>low-priced</u>. (adjectives)

Not parallel: For an interview, dress <u>neatly</u>, <u>carefully</u>, and <u>plain</u>.
Parallel: For an interview, dress <u>neatly</u>, <u>carefully</u>, and <u>plainly</u>. (adverbs)

Grammar Exercise A

Circle the number of each sentence that is written in parallel structure.

1. Mr. Paul promised me a good job and a fair wage.
2. Hard workers are intense, motivated, and take care.
3. My friend is kind, generous, and interesting.
4. They like watching football, playing baseball, and to bowl.

Grammar Exercise B

Rewrite each sentence using parallel structure.

1. It is good for people to run, swim, and go jogging.

   _____

2. Running, for example, helps you stay fit and to be in good health.

   _____

3. Swimming can help in toning your muscles and to lower your blood pressure.

   _____

4. You can start by walking a block a day and to eat good food.

   _____

5. Exercise can help you look better, be stronger, and to have mental alertness.

   _____

For more practice on parallel structure, turn to pages 193–194 of the Grammar Guide.

Developing an Explanation

To write a clear explanation, you must use precise words and specific details to explain exactly what happens or what to do. You must include all the details necessary to make the explanation complete and present them in the simplest, clearest way.

Precise Words and Specific Details

Precise words and specific details help the reader to understand an explanation. As you learned in Unit 1, being precise and specific helps you create word pictures so the reader can "see" what you mean.

EXAMPLE Read the two explanations on grilling fish. The second one has precise words and specific details; the first one does not.

1. Here's a way to cook fish on a grill. First, buy a plank of wood. Clean the plank. Then soak it to prevent it from burning. Next, preheat the coals of your grill. Place the fish on the plank and some herbs on the fish. When the coals are hot, place the plank on the grill with the coals around the edges. Cook for 15 to 20 minutes, or until the fish is cooked throughout.

2. Here's a healthy, fat-free way of cooking fish that you can use on your barbecue—grilling fish on a wood plank. First, buy a cedar or fir plank at a lumberyard or home supply store. The plank should be cut to 1" by 8" by 18". Second, rinse the plank with flowing water to clean it. Then soak the plank in water for one hour to prevent it from burning on the grill. Next, preheat the coals of your grill. Place the fish on the plank and sprinkle the top of it with fresh herbs. When the coals are hot, place the plank on the grill so that the fish is in the center with coals around the edges. Cook over a medium fire for 15 to 20 minutes. Then enjoy!

Notice how the precise words (*lumberyard or home supply store, flowing, sprinkle*) and specific details (*cedar or fir, 1" by 8" by 18", for one hour*) in the second explanation help you understand much better what to do.

PRACTICE

Rewrite each sentence with precise words.

1 You can relax at night by listening to music and by taking a bath.

_____

2 You can protect yourself from crime by being careful and getting in shape.

_____

3 I can make my lifestyle healthier by watching what I eat and exercising.

_____

Check your answers on page 246.

Completeness

If an explanation is missing important details or steps, the reader will misunderstand. Look again at the two explanations on page 130. The first explanation is missing the detail "Cook over a medium fire." If you read that explanation and cooked over a hot fire, you'd have burnt, dry fish for dinner.

Write an answer for each question.

1 In the first explanation, what is missing in the step about soaking the plank?

_____

2 What might happen as a result of this missing information?

_____

Clear Presentation

Sometimes explanations are written in one or more paragraphs. Often, however, it is clearer to list the steps in an explanation. The clearest presentation depends on the topic and the number of steps involved.

EXAMPLE Here is the explanation of grilling fish given in a list of numbered steps.

1 Buy a cedar or fir plank at a lumberyard or home supply store. The plank should be cut to 1" by 8" by 18".

2 Rinse the plank with flowing water to clean it. Then soak the plank in water for one hour to prevent it from burning.

3 Preheat the coals of your grill.

4 Place the fish on the plank and sprinkle the top of it with fresh herbs.

5 When the coals are hot, place the plank on the grill so that the fish is in the center with coals around the edges.

6 Cook over a medium fire for 15 to 20 minutes, or until the fish is cooked throughout.

WRITE Choose from one of the topics below or think of a topic of your own.

| How to relax at night | How to be safe from crime | How to cook a dish |
| How to quit smoking | How to do an exercise | How to tell a joke |

On a separate piece of paper, write an explanation of the best way to accomplish a goal.

Prewrite: Picture in your mind what to do. List all the steps involved. Think of the clearest way to present the ideas: paragraph or list.

Write: Write your explanation in paragraph form or list form. Use precise words and specific details.

Apply Your Writing Skills

Write an Explanation

Now you are ready to apply what you have learned by writing an explanation. Remember that explanatory writing:

- explains, informs, or instructs.
- includes transition words to link ideas or to show the order of ideas.
- uses precise words and specific details, includes all important information, and is presented clearly.

As you write, follow the steps in the writing process.

ASSIGNMENT

Suppose you must explain to a friend or family member how to perform some skill or explain to a co-worker how to do a job at work. Write an explanation that this person could use to learn the skill or complete the job.

Prewriting

1 List several skills that you have or jobs that you perform well.

_____

_____

_____

_____

_____

2 Use the space below to organize your ideas in an outline or an idea map. Arrange your ideas in a way that will help you best explain one skill or job you listed above. If you are writing step-by-step instructions, you may want to list and number them. If you are explaining or giving information, you may want to write about related ideas in paragraph form.

_____

_____

_____

_____

_____

_____

_____

_____

Writing the First Draft

On a separate piece of paper, write your first draft.

Write the Introduction. Briefly state the subject of your "how-to" explanation. Write a strong topic sentence that states your topic best.

Develop Supporting Details. As you develop your explanation, remember to include precise words and specific details. Follow your prewriting plan.

Write the Conclusion. Write a strong ending that ties up all the points you have made. Do not bring up any new points here.

Editing and Revising

Review, edit, and revise. Read the entire explanation to see if you accomplished what you set out to do. Could someone follow your explanation to complete this job?

Then use the editing checklist on page 218 to see how you can improve your writing. Pay special attention to the points you studied in this section:

- ❏ Did you use time-order transition words? *See pages 125–126.*

- ❏ Did you use the correct verb tenses? *See page 127.*

- ❏ Did you place modifiers correctly? *See page 128.*

- ❏ Did you use parallel structure? *See page 129.*

- ❏ Did you use precise words and specific details? *See pages 130–131.*

- ❏ Did you include all necessary information? *See pages 130–131.*

- ❏ Is your presentation clear? *See pages 130–131.*

Writing the Final Draft

Write a final draft. Then proofread one last time. If necessary, recopy or retype your final explanation. Use the proofreading checklist on page 219 to review your final draft.

Sharing the Final Draft

Publish. Let another person read your final explanation. Ask if your explanation is clear. Ask what you might do to improve it. Make some notes and attach them to a copy of the essay. File the explanation in your writing portfolio.

Report Writing

Elements of Report Writing

A **report** is an organized summary of information about a topic. Some reports also include an analysis. An **analysis** is the writer's conclusions about the meaning of the information in the report. Reports may be written for school or work.

School reports include two types: book reports and research reports. In a **book report,** the writer sums up the contents of a book. In a **research report,** the writer gathers information in a subject area from many sources and sums it up. For a **business report,** the writer collects and sums up work-related information, such as monthly sales figures. The report may be used to make business decisions.

Before you can write a research or business report, you must gather information about a topic. Here are some ways to do that:

- Attend meetings of a group that has information about the topic
- Visit and observe a place where information about the topic may be learned
- Interview people
- Conduct a survey by asking several people the same oral or written questions
- Study letters or official documents
- Read books, magazine and newspaper articles, or other reference materials
- Use the Internet

EXAMPLE Below is part of a report that a government employee wrote. The writer had conducted a survey to find out what skills companies look for.

The Skills Employers Want

Generally, employers say that the most important skills for any employee are the basic skills—reading, writing, and math. Many employers say, "Give me people who can read, write, and do simple math, and we'll train them for the jobs we have available."

But checking further, one finds that employers want more than good basic skills. They also want employees who have the ability to learn new job skills quickly. They need people who can solve problems, make decisions, and come up with new ways of doing things. Employers want employees who are good listeners and who can make a good impression on their customers. They want employees who can get along well with others and who are willing to take on responsibility.

Answer the following questions about the report on page 134.

1 What other methods could you use to gather information on the topic "The Skills Employers Want"?

_____

_____

2 What questions would you ask if you were conducting a survey of employers?

_____

_____

Taking Notes

The best way to gather information for a report is to take notes in a notebook or on index cards. Index cards are 3″ × 5″ lined cards. Using index cards is a good way to take notes that can be organized later. Here are some tips for taking notes.

1 At the top of the notebook page or index card, write the subject.

2 List the source, author, and page number. If the source is a magazine, include the name of the article and the date of publication. If the source is a book, include the publisher's location and name.

3 Note the key information that you want to use in your report:
   a. Look at the title, subtitle, and captions under pictures and graphics. These items often sum up key points.
   b. Look at other material that is set apart from the main text. This might be quotations, headings, or subheadings. These are often set in italics or boldface type.
   c. Look for key points in topic sentences, concluding sentences, lists, and words in italics and boldface.

EXAMPLE   Here are notes taken on the first paragraph of the report on page 134.

Employment Skills
Dept. of Labor, "The Skills Employers Want," page 1
Basic skills are the most important—reading, writing, and math.
Employers are willing to train people who can read, write, do simple math.

The following article was published on page 35 of *Careers* magazine in April 1999. Use each set of lines below as you would an index card to take notes on the key points in one section of the article.

Communication Skills: A Key to Success
by Dorothy Warren

No other skill is more important to good human—and business—relations than knowing how to communicate. What you say to visitors in the office or what you say to coworkers makes an impression that is difficult to change. The saying "We never get a second chance to make a good first impression" is very true.

Informal and Formal Language

One major factor in the impression you make in the business world is your *use of language*. Do you ever use slang expressions? This use of informal language is all right when you are with your family and friends. For example, when a friend introduces you to someone, you may say, "Hi" or "What's happening?" In a business setting, you would use a more formal expression, such as, "How do you do?" or "I'm pleased to meet you."

Correct English

There is no substitute for *correct grammar* in the business world. Using correct Standard English creates an image of a speaker who is competent and educated. Be very aware of your grammar, including correct subject-verb agreement, verb tenses, and word usage.

Notes

1. _____
_____
_____

2. _____
_____
_____

3. _____
_____
_____

    Check your answers on page 246.

Paraphrasing

When you take notes and then write your report, put the information into your own words. This is called **paraphrasing.** Copying the information word for word as if you wrote it yourself is called **plagiarism,** and plagiarism is illegal.

EXAMPLE

Original sentence: Many employers say that the most important skills for any employee are the basic skills—reading, writing, and math.

Paraphrased sentence An employee should be able to read, write, and do math.

If you do copy some information word for word, enclose it in quotation marks. Be aware that only a small amount of information can be quoted without getting the written permission of the author or publisher of the material.

EXAMPLE   In the report "The Skills Employers Want," the government reported: "Many employers say that the most important skills for any employee are the basic skills—reading, writing, and math."

PRACTICE

Paraphrase each of the following sentences. The first one is done for you.

1. One of the biggest mistakes people make on a job interview is acting as if they need the job rather than acting as if the company could use them.

   On an interview, act as if the company could use you, not as if you really need the job.

2. Dressing appropriately for an interview will make you feel confident when you speak.

   _____

   _____

3. Sending a thank-you right after an interview shows proper manners and good job-search sense.

   _____

   _____

4. Much of your success in the business world will depend on the image that you project through the way you look and speak.

   _____

   _____

Summarizing Information

A report sums up—or summarizes—information. **Summarizing** is a way to take a large amount of material and trim it down to a few key points. To summarize information from a source, take the key points you have noted and write a brief paraphrase of them.

EXAMPLE

Original paragraph: Many job applicants do not look at want ads or go to an employment agency. They go directly to a company and request employment. If you choose this method of job hunting, make sure you find out something about the company's business and the kinds of jobs available before you go. Applicants who know what kind of job they want and who can explain how their skills match the job favorably impress employers.

Noted key points:
- some applicants go right to company to ask for job
- should first find out company's business and jobs it has
- employers impressed by applicants who know what job they want and how their skills match it

Paraphrased summary: One way to find a job is to go to a company and ask for one. If you seek a job this way, first get some information about the company and the jobs that are available. Employers look for people who know the kind of job they want and how their skills fit the job.

PRACTICE

Underline the key points in each paragraph below. On a separate piece of paper, write a paraphrased summary of each paragraph.

1   Learning is now a fact of life in the workplace. Even routine jobs are changing as the demands of business change. Often employees are moved from one job to another. They must be able to absorb information quickly. They must be able to move to another task with little supervision. The first step in adapting to this demand is losing the fear of the unknown. Most new situations are not as different as they seem at first. Learn to look at the big picture. Then you can apply what you already know to the new situation.

2   When you are faced with a problem on the job, your first reaction should be to think about it. Thinking about the problem means trying to figure out why something is going wrong. Knowing why will usually help you come up with a solution. Most problems have more than one solution. Don't always think that you have to have the right answer. Most bosses are grateful for an employee who suggests a way to solve a problem, even if they don't always think the employee's way is the best way.

Check your answers on page 247.

Organizing Information

After you have noted and summarized key points, organize all the information as you will write it in your report. Different ways of organizing were discussed in Section 1: **time order, order of importance, cause-effect,** and **compare-contrast.**

PRACTICE

How is the information organized in the government report "The Skills Employers Want" on page 134?

_____

Suppose you have gathered information on skills that employers in your area would like employees to have. In your report, you want to organize the information by comparing and contrasting what area employers said with what employers in the government report said. You could organize the information (1) one point at a time or (2) one side at a time.

EXAMPLE 1 According to a government survey, employers place reading,
Point 1 ——→ writing, and math at the top of their list of skills they want employees to have. In the East River business district, most employers agree with this. But they also want employees who speak Spanish as well as English.

In the government survey, employers want employees who learn quickly and can solve problems and make decisions. Area employers also value the
Point 2 ——→ ability to learn and solve problems. However, they did not rate decision-making as a necessary skill.

EXAMPLE 2 According to a government survey, employers place reading, writing, and math at the top of their list of skills they want employees to have.
Side 1 ——→ They also want employees who learn quickly and can solve problems and make decisions.

In the East River business district, most employers agree with the importance of the basic skills—reading, writing, and math. But they also want employees who speak Spanish as well as English. Area employers also value
Side 2 ——→ the ability to learn and solve problems, but they did not rate decision-making as a necessary skill.

WRITE **On a separate piece of paper, write a short report.**

Prewrite: Interview two employers in your area. Ask them to list the most important skills they want in their employees. Also ask why these skills are important. Take notes in a notebook or on index cards. Organize the information by comparing and contrasting it with the report on page 134.
Write: Summarize the information you gathered. Write about one point at a time or one side at a time.

Grammar Link

You will want to show your best possible work in your reports. One way to achieve this goal is to use verbs correctly.

Regular and Irregular Verbs

The basic forms of verbs are called principal parts. All verbs have four principal parts:

EXAMPLE

Present	Past	Past Participle	Present Participle
walk	walked	walked	walking

Most verbs are **regular verbs.** The past and the past participle are formed by adding *-ed.* The present participle is formed by adding *-ing.* The principal parts of **irregular verbs** do not follow this pattern. That is why they are called irregular.

The past participle and present participle of all verbs use a **helping verb.** The helping verb for the present participle is a form of the verb *be.* The helping verb for the past participle is a form of the verb *have.*

EXAMPLE

Past Participle: have, has, had   <u>have walked</u>

Present Participle: am, is, are, was, were   <u>am walking</u>

Patterns of Irregular Verbs

1 Some irregular verbs form the past in an unusual way and form the past participle by adding *-n* or *-en* to the present or past.

Present	Past	Past Participle	Present Participle
know	knew	known	knowing
speak	spoke	spoken	speaking
eat	ate	eaten	eating

2 Some irregular verbs form the past in an unusual way and have the same form for the past participle.

bring	brought	brought	bringing
find	found	found	finding

3 Some irregular verbs have the same present, past, and past participle.

cost	cost	cost	costing
shut	shut	shut	shutting

4 Some irregular verbs form both the past and the past participle in unusual ways.

drink	drank	drunk	drinking
begin	began	begun	beginning

Grammar Exercise A   Underline the correct form of the irregular verb in each sentence.

1. Many employers have **(spoke, spoken)** about what they need.

2. Employees have **(wrote, written)** articles on the subject as well.

3. Schools do not **(teach, taught)** all the skills people need to get a job.

4. Too many students have **(fell, fallen)** behind in their education.

5. Schools have **(began, begun)** to look for new ways to help students.

Grammar Exercise B   Complete each sentence with the correct form of the verb in parentheses.

1. **(see)** We _____ some great scenery on our vacation.

2. **(go)** We _____ on a fishing trip to the mountains.

3. **(drive)** We _____ two hundred miles to go camping.

4. **(sleep)** It was the first time I had _____ in a tent.

5. **(eat)** My son was almost _____ alive by mosquitoes.

6. **(catch)** The first day he _____ a large fish.

7. **(freeze)** We _____ it in the cooler.

8. **(build)** Later we _____ a fire and cooked the fish.

9. **(swim)** After a nap we _____ in the river.

10. **(take)** We _____ pictures of the sunset over the water.

Grammar Exercise C   Write a sentence using the principal part of each irregular verb below.

1. buy (past participle)

   _____

For more practice on irregular verbs, turn to page 182 of the Grammar Guide.

2. do (past participle)

   _____

3. break (past)

   _____

4. fly (past participle)

   _____

5. know (past)

   _____

The Parts of a Report

All reports have three main parts: an **introduction**, a **body**, and a **conclusion**. An **informal report**, such as a paper written for a class, may have only these three parts. A **formal report**, such as a research paper, may also have a **title page** and a **bibliography**.

1 **Title page.** In a formal report, include the title, the writer's name, the name of the person to whom the report is submitted, and the date submitted. In a business report, include job titles and departments also.

EXAMPLE

> Technical Skills for the New Century: A New Age for Workers
> Prepared by
> Sean A. Young, Secretary, Marketing Department
> Submitted to
> Beverly Johnson, Manager, Marketing Department
> April 30, 1999

2 **Introduction.** This section briefly states the main idea of the report. It may also include the methods used for the research.

EXAMPLE Within the next ten years, many people will have to learn new skills or risk losing their jobs. Bank tellers, telephone operators, and factory workers are among those whose jobs have been taken over by computers.

3 **Body.** This section presents information that supports the main idea.

EXAMPLE When computers take over jobs, workers must be retrained. In auto factories, workers are still needed to repair robots when they break down. This work requires skills that are different from those workers need to place bolts on car parts.

4 **Conclusion.** This section restates and summarizes the main idea.

EXAMPLE People who are entering the workforce now must have technical skills. They should also find companies that provide retraining for their workers.

5 **Bibliography.** In a formal report, this section lists the sources that were used to gather information for the report.

EXAMPLE **Book:** Petzinger, Jr., Thomas. *The New Pioneers: The Men and Women Who Are Transforming the Workplace and Marketplace.* New York: Simon & Schuster, 1999.

Magazine: Eisenberg, Daniel. "Offices by the Hour." *Time,* February 1, 1999, pp. 40–41.

Newspaper: "California-Based Jobs Firm Casts High-Tech Net for Prospects." *Chicago Tribune,* February 2, 1999.

WRITE A You are taking a course in American Literature. Your instructor, Carol Rivera, asked you to write a research report about the author Toni Morrison. You wrote your report about the years she lived and wrote in New York. You used the following sources to develop your report.

1 A book by Toni Morrison, entitled *Beloved,* published in New York by A. A. Knopf in 1987.

2 A book edited by Danille Taylor-Guthrie, *Conversations with Toni Morrison,* published in 1991 by UP of Mississippi in Jackson, Mississippi.

3 A journal article by Bruce Bawer, entitled "All That Jazz," published in *The New Criterion* in May 1992, on pages 10–17.

4 A magazine article by Paul Gray, entitled "Paradise Found," published in *Time* on January 19, 1999, on pages 21–25.

On a separate piece of paper, give the report a title and write the report's title page. Also write the bibliography following the models given on page 142. The bibliography should be in alphabetical order by author.

WRITE B Assume that you are a customer service assistant at Universal Electronics. Your supervisor, Shirley Jones, is on vacation. In her absence, you must prepare a report on last week's customer complaints. You must include the following information in the report.

1 How many calls were received?

2 How many calls involved equipment problems? What kind?

3 How many calls involved problems with repairers?

4 What other kinds of problems were reported?

Using the following notes your supervisor left for you, write the introduction, body, and conclusion of the report. Remember to summarize the information and organize it in a way that will make the information easy to understand.

Notes

April 4   A. Berry called—the VCR repairer did not show up.

             B. Simpson called—the channel selector on his VCR is broken.

April 5   L. Rossi returned a CD player—it was making a funny noise.

April 6   G. Jones called—the remote control for the TV was not in the delivery.

             L. Holloway called—the repairer was three hours late.

             S. Herrera returned a tape player—the record button was defective.

April 7   J. Fallon returned a CD player—Q-Mart sells the same brand for less.

April 8   R. Weiss called—repairer did not show up.

On a separate piece of paper, write a business report on the customer complaints.

Apply Your Writing Skills

Write a Report

Now you are ready to apply what you have learned about writing a report. Remember that a report:

- is a summary of information about a topic.
- may be organized in different ways so that the information is easier to understand or use.
- has three main parts: an introduction, a body, and a conclusion. Formal reports may also have a title page and a bibliography.

ASSIGNMENT

Write a report about the employment opportunities in your area. You may define the word *area* as your neighborhood, your city, or the region in which you live. The purpose of the report is to get information about jobs that might be available for you. The report should provide the following information:

- Types of businesses hiring people at the job level and type of employment that interest you
- Types of jobs available
- Past experience required for the available jobs
- Education and training needed
- Salary range for the type of work
- Any additional information that would be helpful to the reader

Prewriting

1 Think about the types of jobs you will explore for your report. List them.

_____

_____

_____

2 List some sources of information and methods you might use to gather facts for your report. Review the information on page 134 if you need help deciding on methods to use to get the information you need.

_____

_____

_____

3 Using the methods you have chosen, collect your information. Take notes on index cards or in a notebook. Review the information on page 135 before you take notes.

4 After gathering your information, organize your notes. On a separate piece of paper, write an outline or draw an idea map.

Writing the First Draft

On a separate piece of paper, write your first draft.

Write the Introduction. Briefly state the subject of the report. Write a strong topic sentence that states the main idea.

Write the Body of the Report. Present a summary of the information you have gathered. Make sure you start a new paragraph for each main point. Use your notes and outline or idea map as a guide.

Write the Conclusion. Restate and summarize the main point of the report.

Editing and Revising

Review, edit, and revise. Read the whole report to see if you accomplished what you set out to do. Is the report well organized? Does it follow your outline?

Then use the editing checklist on page 218 to see how you can improve your writing. Pay special attention to the points you studied in this section. In addition to the items on the general editing checklist, check to see that you did the following:

- ❑ Did you organize your information in a way that makes it easy to understand? *See page 139.*

- ❑ Did you include three main parts: an introduction, a body, and a conclusion? *See pages 142–143.*

- ❑ Did you use the correct form of regular verbs? *See page 140.*

- ❑ Did you use the correct form of any irregular verbs? *See pages 140–141.*

Writing the Final Draft

Write a final draft. Then proofread one last time. If necessary, recopy or retype your final report. Use the proofreading checklist on page 219 to review your final draft.

Sharing the Final Draft

Publish. Let another person read your final report. Ask if your report is clear. Ask what you might do to improve your report. Make some notes and attach them to a copy of the report. File the report in your writing portfolio.

Writing at Work

Office Services: Customer Service Representative

Some Careers in Office Services

Admitting Interviewer
obtains and records information from incoming patients in health care and nursing facilities

Interviewing Clerk
gets information from participants for use in market research studies and polls

New Accounts Clerk
obtains and records information from new customers to help them open financial accounts

Record Clerk
maintains and updates records, sometimes with the use of a computer

Do you enjoy helping people solve problems? Do you pay attention to details? Do you like to follow responsibilities through from beginning to end? If so, you may be interested in becoming a customer service representative.

Customer service representatives are often the first contact that customers have with a company. Customer service representatives receive and process customers' orders. They answer customers' questions and help them solve any problems they may have.

Much of the communication representatives have with customers is handled in phone calls and in writing. In order to perform their job effectively, customer service representatives should have excellent listening and speaking skills. They should also have strong writing and grammar skills. Representatives must be able to write clearly and logically and include relevant details in their writing.

Look at the chart on Some Careers in Office Services.

- Do any of the careers interest you? If so, which ones?

- What information would you need to find out more about those careers? On a separate piece of paper, write some questions that you would like answered. You can find out more information about those careers in the *Occupational Outlook Handbook* at your local library.

Use the material below to answer the questions that follow.

Creature Comforts Beds
1900 Sleepy Hollow Drive ◆ Wake Forest, SC

Dear Mrs. Chambers:

Thank you for ordering our Fit for a King bedroom furniture. I was sorry to receive your phone call telling me that some pieces of your furniture arrived damaged and others did not arrive at all. Please be assured that Creature Comforts Beds stands behind every piece of furniture we sell. We want our customers to be totally satisfied with their purchases.

I will send a truck to pick up your damaged dresser. Creature Comforts will cover the cost of this truck. I have also put out a tracer to find the night table you never received. If the table is not found within the next 72 hours, I will order a replacement for you.

If you have any questions or need any further assistance, please contact me at 555-7645.

Sincerely,

Lacey Curtin, Customer Service Representative

1 The purpose of customer service representative Curtin's letter is to
   (1) tell customer Chambers that her furniture is damaged.
   (2) let customer Chambers know that her table did not arrive.
   (3) apologize for the problems in customer Chambers' order.
   (4) let customer Chambers know the problems in her order will be fixed.
   (5) tell customer Chambers to call and ask for further assistance.

2 Which of the following is not a true statement about Mrs. Chambers' order?
   (1) She received a damaged dresser.
   (2) She received a damaged night table.
   (3) She ordered the Fit for a King bedroom set.
   (4) She never received a night table.
   (5) She spoke with Lacey Curtin about her order's problems.

3 In her letter, customer service representative Curtin informs Mrs. Chambers that
   (1) she will receive all pieces of furniture within 72 hours.
   (2) she will need to pay for any damages to the furniture.
   (3) Creature Comforts will find the missing table within 72 hours.
   (4) all the Fit for a King bedroom furniture did not arrive.
   (5) Creature Comforts believes in keeping their customers happy.

Unit 2 Review:
Workplace and Personal Writing

Write the best action verb to complete each phrase.

For more practice with action verbs and phrases, turn to pages 180–181 of the Grammar Guide.

1 _____ letters and memos for six people

Typed   Answered   Coordinated

2 _____ telephone calls for two attorneys

Completed   Trained   Handled

3 _____ monthly reports on service calls

Managed   Accomplished   Completed

4 _____ computer and word processing equipment

Operated   Developed   Handled

Write the plural form of each noun.

For more practice with plurals, turn to page 161 of the Grammar Guide.

5 community _____

6 desk _____

7 knife _____

8 attorney _____

9 bus _____

10 tax _____

11 thief _____

12 woman _____

Write the possessive form of each word in parentheses.

For more practice with possessives, turn to page 162 of the Grammar Guide.

13 The (**minister**) friends were invited to the party. _____

14 The ten (**workers**) paychecks were in the mail. _____

15 I went to the (**Jones**) house for lunch. _____

16 The (**bank**) hours are not convenient. _____

17 The (**people**) rights are protected by law. _____

18 All of the (**cities**) mayors attended the conference. _____

Write the contraction that could be used instead of the underlined words in each sentence.

⑲ <u>I have</u> read everything I could find about cars. _____

⑳ <u>It is</u> very difficult to find anything about electric cars. _____

㉑ Electric cars <u>will not</u> be popular for a long time. _____

㉒ There <u>has not</u> been any reason to buy one. _____

㉓ I <u>would not</u> mind buying an electric car. _____

㉔ People <u>cannot</u> buy electric cars until they become available.

_____

㉕ <u>Who is</u> going to be the first buyer of an electric car? _____

For more practice with contractions, turn to page 163 of the Grammar Guide.

Identify the tense of each underlined verb. Write *past*, *present*, or *future*.

㉖ Gina <u>started</u> her own business last year. _____

㉗ Her business <u>will earn</u> a large profit this year. _____

㉘ She <u>makes</u> custom picture frames. _____

㉙ Last week the bank <u>gave</u> her a loan. _____

㉚ Gina <u>wants</u> to rent a bigger workshop. _____

㉛ She <u>will hire</u> an assistant to help her. _____

㉜ Gina <u>has done</u> all the work herself since the business opened.

_____

Write the correct verb to complete each sentence.

㉝ I _____ before you called.

    will cook   **cook**   **had been cooking**

㉞ Hector _____ a new job next week.

    started   **has started**   **will start**

㉟ Doug _____ a mechanic for the last two years.

    will be   **has been**   **is being**

㊱ By next Friday, Lucy _____ eight hours of overtime.

    works   **has worked**   **will have worked**

㊲ Katrina _____ the news before Isaiah arrived at work.

    has told   **had told**   **will have told**

For more practice with verb tenses, turn to pages 180–181 of the Grammar Guide.

Check your answers on page 248.   UNIT 2 : WORKPLACE AND PERSONAL WRITING **149**

Write the correct verb form to complete each sentence.

(38) Mei Lei had _____ before she left.

wrote   written

(39) Mr. Lucas has _____ learning Spanish.

began   begun

(40) The TV had _____ $239 before the sale.

cost   costed

(41) Laura _____ the results of her GED Test yesterday.

knew   known

(42) He will have _____ the phone number by this time.

finded   found

(43) How many reports have you _____ this month?

wrote   written

For more practice with irregular verbs, turn to page 182 of the Grammar Guide.

Underline each letter that should be capitalized in each sentence.

(44) Her uncle was a well-known mexican doctor.

(45) He went to work for a texas company called lonestar.

(46) ms. tomkins said she was going to new york on monday.

(47) The book was written by the governor of arkansas.

(48) Your vacation begins on the fourth of july.

(49) did you see dr. jones last week?

For more practice with capitalization, turn to pages 158–160 of the Grammar Guide.

Put the correct punctuation in each sentence.

(50) Is Stan coming to the Halloween party

(51) She is serving hot dogs potato salad and baked beans

(52) Sheila was born on May 25 1965

(53) Kham's boss Charles H Garrett is from Boise Idaho

(54) Do you want red gold or blue ribbon

(55) Please call Mrs Alvarez to tell her the order is ready

For more practice with punctuation, turn to pages 156–157 of the Grammar Guide.

Check your answers on page 248.

Rewrite each sentence to correct the dangling or misplaced modifiers.

56 While passing a large rock, a clap of thunder made me scream.

_____

57 We saw many car accidents driving through the storm.

_____

58 Broken beyond repair, Juan saw his motorcycle in the front yard.

_____

For more practice with placing modifiers correctly, turn to pages 197–198 of the Grammar Guide.

59 When watching my son, he ran into the street.

_____

60 The phone rang walking into my office.

_____

Rewrite each sentence to give it parallel structure.

61 The meal was cheap, tasty, and the food was good for us.

_____

For more practice with parallel structure, turn to pages 193–194 of the Grammar Guide.

62 I should walk, jog, or go swimming to stay in shape.

_____

63 The alley cat has long hair, sharp claws, and one ear is crooked.

_____

Write a business letter.

For a review of writing a business letter, turn to pages 83–84 and page 86.

Suppose you ordered a set of three CDs, _Marco's Best Songs._ Two of the CDs were exactly what you wanted and expected. The third CD was blank. The company's address is Music-Pro, Inc., 222 Mission Street, Santiago, TX 76543. Write a letter to Music-Pro, Inc. Return the blank CD and request a new one.

Writing Extension

Use your writing skills to write a business letter to a company that makes some product. Explain why you like the product or why you don't like it. Follow the Writing Process when you write your letter. Share your final draft with your instructor or another student.

Writing Connection: Personal Writing and Life Science

1120 Bay Street
Chicago, IL 60601
November 26, 2000

Dear Editor:

In your last issue of *Healthy Children,* you asked your readers to send in ideas about what they do to make sure their kids eat a healthy, balanced diet. After lots of trial and error, here is what seems to work for my family.

First, I learned to shop more carefully. I read the nutrition facts label on all packages. I try to choose food products that have low amounts of fat, cholesterol, sodium, and sugar.

For snacks, I used to give my children cookies and chips. Now, I try to give them lots of fresh fruits and vegetables that are low in fat. Sliced apples, crunchy carrots, and juicy grapes are among our favorites.

I found that if I let the children help prepare their own snacks, they really enjoy eating them. I let them make fruit plates or vegetable faces with carrots, tomatoes, celery, and cucumbers. Sometimes I let them use salad dressing to dip the vegetables. They think this is a special treat.

While we work to maintain healthy eating habits, we also recognize the need to have an occasional treat. Yes, we still eat ice cream and cookies, but not nearly as often as we used to.

Sincerely,

Theresa Lopez
Theresa Lopez

Life Science:
Eating Healthy, Staying Healthy

To live a healthy lifestyle, scientists and doctors encourage us to eat more fruits, vegetables, natural grains and pastas. They advise us to reduce the amount of fat in our diet and limit intake of fats found in animal food products.

The Food Guide Pyramid demonstrates the daily intake an individual needs to get the necessary nutrition while maintaining a healthy weight. The range of the number of servings allows the pyramid to be adapted to a person's age, size, and other issues. For example, pregnant women and teenagers need more servings from the Milk, Yogurt, and Cheese Group than other people do.

Food Pyramid

Fats, Oils, and Sweets
Use Sparingly

Milk, Yogurt, and Cheese Group
2–3 servings

Meat, Poultry, Fish, Dry Beans, Eggs & Nuts Group
2–4 servings

Vegetable Group
3–5 servings

Fruit Group
2–4 servings

Bread, Cereal, Rice & Pasta Group
6–11 servings

Use the material on the previous page to answer the questions.

1 Theresa's main purpose in writing the letter to *Healthy Children* was to
(1) explain how her children make healthy snacks.
(2) encourage readers to shop in different grocery stores.
(3) let readers know it was okay to eat ice cream and cookies.
(4) encourage readers to check nutrition facts labels.
(5) share ideas about keeping a healthy, balanced diet.

2 The Food Guide Pyramid encourages people to eat the most servings from the following food group:
(1) Bread, Cereal, Rice, and Pasta
(2) Fruit
(3) Vegetable
(4) Milk, Yogurt, and Cheese
(5) Meat, Poultry, Fish, Dry Beans, Eggs, and Nuts

3 Theresa's letter to the magazine was in answer to a question about getting families to eat a more healthful diet. Imagine that you read the following in a magazine:

What are some things you do to lead a healthy life? What works for you? Write and tell us your tips on exercise, nutrition, hobbies, or any other lifestyle topic. We will share the best letters with our readers in a future issue.

On a separate piece of paper, write your letter.

A. Brainstorm some topics you might want to write about.

B. Then choose one and make a list of three main points you want to make about that topic.

C. Add details or examples for each point.

D. Then write your letter. Use Theresa's letter on page 152 as a model for the format, style, and content of your letter.

Grammar Guide

Very often people think of grammar when they say the word *writing*. They are thinking of things like punctuation and use of correct words and sentences. Even though good writing involves much more than these things, they are important.

For example, if you look at an uncut and unpolished gem, it may be difficult to see its color and brilliance. Yet when the stone is cut and polished by the hands of an expert, it becomes a jewel. That is what a command of good grammar does to your writing. It helps the ideas that you are presenting to shine through.

The use of good grammar is essential to success on the job. It is basic to good written communication skills. Additionally, in your own personal writing, you will want to use correct grammar so that your reader will understand your meaning and respect what you have to say. In this unit you will have the opportunity to polish your use of good grammar.

◖ What might an employer think if he or she reads a letter from a job applicant or a memo from an employee that is filled with errors in grammar?

◖ What part of grammar do you consider your strong point? Your weak point?

SECTIONS

⑪ **Mechanics**

⑫ **Usage**

⑬ **Sentence Structure**

End Punctuation

Punctuation is the set of symbols used in writing to guide the reader. A sentence always ends with a period, a question mark, or an exclamation point. Each type of punctuation signals something different to the reader.

1. Use a **period** to end a statement—a sentence that gives information or states facts. Also use a period to show the end of a command.

   I am studying right now.   Open your books to page 156.

2. Use a **question mark** to end a question.

   When are you planning to move?   Is heat included in the rent?

3. Use an **exclamation point** to end a sentence that shows strong emotion.

   That's great!   Watch out for that truck!

PRACTICE

Add the correct end punctuation to complete each sentence.

1. When do you think the first soap opera was broadcast on TV
2. The first TV soap opera was aired on October 2, 1946
3. Called *Faraway Hill*, it was the only network show on Wednesday nights
4. Amazingly, the show was done live—on a budget of less than $300 a week
5. Soap operas were originally broadcast on the radio
6. Do you know anyone who likes soap operas
7. Some people say that soap operas help them relax
8. What a ridiculous waste of time

Write three sentences about soap operas. Use correct end punctuation.

9. (statement)

   _____

10. (question)

   _____

11. (strong emotion)

   _____

Commas

Commas help to break up sentences to make them easier to read.

1.   Use commas to separate three or more items in a list.

Joe, Paul, Hector, and Luis are going to a cabin.
They plan to go fishing, take walks, and sleep late.

2.   Use a comma between the two independent clauses of a compound sentence. Join the clauses with a coordinating conjunction: *and, but, or,* or *so.* Other coordinating conjunctions are *yet, for,* and *nor.* Put the comma before the conjunction.

They saw a lot of rabbits, but they didn't see any deer.
The weather was bad the first day, so everyone stayed inside.

Do <u>not</u> use a comma between the two subjects in a compound subject or the two verbs in a compound predicate.

Compound subject: <u>Joe and Paul</u> played cards that day.

Compound predicate: Hector <u>read magazines and sorted his gear.</u>

3.   Use commas with dates and place names. Place a comma between the day and the month, and between the number of the day and the year. Also use a comma between the city and state or city and country.

Monday, May 8	January 1, 2000	Sunday, July 4, 1999
Chicago, Illinois	Paris, France	San Juan, Puerto Rico

PRACTICE

Add commas where they are needed in each sentence.

1   My aunt was born on January 13 1960.

2   She grew up in Toledo but she and her family moved to Los Angeles in 1975.

3   She is a store manager a swimmer and a mother of two.

Answer each question in a complete sentence. Use commas correctly.

4   Think of a relative. When was this person born? (Include month, day, and year.)

_____

5   Tell something about the person. Use a compound sentence.

_____

Capital Letters

1. Use a capital letter for the first word in a sentence.

   Do I smell something burning?   That paper is on fire.   Help!

2. Use a capital letter for **proper nouns.** A proper noun names a certain person, place, or thing. Do not use a capital letter for common nouns.

	Proper Nouns	**Common Nouns**
Person:	Mark Walsh	man
Place:	Kenya	country
	Elm Street	street
	North Carolina	state
Thing:	the White House	building
	Star Wars	movie
	Microsoft	company

3. Use a capital letter for **proper adjectives.** A proper adjective is an adjective that is made from a proper noun.

   the French language   African clothing   South American food

PRACTICE

Use the proofreader's mark to show where capital letters are needed (a̲ = A).

harriet quimby was the first woman to earn a pilot's license. she was a writer in new york before she flew a plane. she fell in love with airplanes in 1910 when she saw her first flying meet. harriet became a pilot and toured in mexico with a troupe of pilots. she decided she would be the first woman to cross the english channel. she took off on april 16, 1912, sitting on a wicker basket in the cockpit. after a scary flight, she landed on a french beach.

Answer each question with a complete sentence. Use capital letters correctly.

Sample: *I live in Little Rock, Arkansas.*

❶ What city (or town) and state do you live in?

_____

❷ Where do you like to shop? (use names of stores)

_____

4. Use a capital letter for each part of a person's name. Also use a capital letter for a title when it is used with a person's name.

Dr. McNally   Mr. J. S. Goldfarb   Ms. Van Slyke   Miss Chen

But: The doctor will see you now.

5. Use a capital letter for any place that can be found on a map.

Streets: Broadway   Park Place   Main Street

Towns and cities: Sioux Falls   Berlin   Baghdad

States: Texas   Kansas   Georgia

Countries: Spain   Chad   France

Islands: Guam   Cuba   Prince Edward Island

Bodies of water: Dead Sea   Great Salt Lake   Mississippi River

Natural landmarks: Mt. Ranier   Grand Canyon   Everglades

Tourist attractions: Six Flags   Yellowstone National Park
Yankee Stadium

PRACTICE

Use the proofreader's mark to show where capital letters are needed ($\underline{\underline{a}}$ = A).

1. writer ed j. smith reports that people are taking cheaper trips in the summer.

2. mr. and mrs. mott drove to orlando, florida, and went camping.

3. last year, the motts would have gone to sea world instead.

4. this year, dr. ortega and his family went hiking instead of going to mt. rushmore in south dakota.

5. ms. wills visited her friend in wisconsin rather than flying to the island of st. kitts.

6. miss e. k. link from new town, long island, spent two days in maine.

7. she went to lake mead last year.

8. busch gardens in tampa, florida, is still very busy, though.

9. mr. hunt wants to go to israel and see the dead sea.

Complete each sentence. Use capital letters correctly.

Sample: *My dentist is Dr. Thomas Duffy.*

10. My dentist is _____. (title + name)

11. I would love to go to _____. (place name)

12. I was born in _____. (country)

6. Use a capital letter for the days of the week and months of the year. Do not capitalize the names of the seasons.

    My birthday is in March.   It's hard to get up on Monday mornings.
    I've always loved summer.

7. Use a capital letter for holidays.

    Will you go to a party New Year's Eve?   My friends celebrate Kwanzaa.

PRACTICE

Use the proofreader's mark to show where capital letters are needed (a = A).

1. This year, monday, january 18, dr. martin luther king, jr. day will be a paid holiday.

2. This holiday is in the place of columbus day, which we took as a day off on october 10.

3. The plant will, of course, be closed for the usual fall and winter holidays—thanksgiving, christmas, and new year's.

4. If any of these holidays falls on a monday or a friday, you will have a long weekend.

5. This year the company's independence day picnic will be on sunday, july 7.

6. I will be back at work on tuesday, september 6, the day after labor day.

7. Some people want to have the party on flag day, june 14, instead.

8. There has also been talk of a halloween party for october 31, which is a thursday this year.

9. We could hold the party on friday, october 25, if that is a better time.

Answer each question with a complete sentence. Use capital letters correctly.

Sample: _My favorite holidays are Thanksgiving and New Year's Eve._

10. What are your favorite holidays?

    _____

11. Which is the best day of the week for you?

    _____

12. What is your favorite season of the year?

    _____

Check your answers on page 250.

Plurals

Plural means "more than one." For example, the singular word *cat* means one cat; the plural form *cats* means more than one cat.

1. To form the plural of most nouns, add -*s*. Add -*es* to nouns that end in *ch, sh, s, x,* or *z*.

> friend/friends   box/boxes   watch/watches

2. For most nouns that end in *f* or *fe*, change the *f* or *fe* to *v* and add -*es*.

> leaf/leaves   knife/knives

3. For nouns that end in a consonant followed by *y*, change the *y* to *i* and add -*es*.

> city/cities   try/tries

4. For irregular plurals, look in the dictionary. Here are some common irregular plurals.

> child/children   crisis/crises   deer/deer
> tooth/teeth   woman/women   mouse/mice

PRACTICE

Circle the correct plural form of each word in parentheses.

1. My brothers and their **(wifes, wives)** are taking a few **(daies, days)** off in August.

2. My **(nephews, nephewes)** and young **(cousines, cousins)** are coming for a visit.

3. I like to watch the **(childrens, children)** play in the yard.

4. They like to pick **(peachs, peaches)** from the trees.

5. My nephew Sam lost his two front **(teeth, tooths)** and looks cute.

6. I always have great **(memorys, memories)** of their **(visites, visits)**.

Make each word in parentheses plural and use it to complete the sentence.

7. (celebrity) My two favorite

    _____.

8. (man) In our class, there are

    _____.

9. (shelf) My refrigerator has

    _____.

Possessives

The **possessive** form of a noun shows that something is owned, and it shows who or what the owner is.

1.   Add an **apostrophe** (') and *s* to form the possessive of singular nouns and irregular plural nouns that don't end with an *s*.

   Troy drove his <u>wife's</u> car to work yesterday.

   I saw him yesterday at <u>Roberto's</u> house.

   I have already put away the <u>children's</u> toys.

2.   Add only an apostrophe (') to form the possessive of plural nouns that end in *s*.

   Both of my <u>sisters'</u> houses are on the west side.

   We left the <u>Sanchezes'</u> house at eight o'clock last night.

3.   Use an apostrophe for possessive nouns only. Do not use an apostrophe with plural nouns that are *not* possessive.

   My <u>sisters</u> and the <u>Sanchezes</u> live near each other.

PRACTICE

Circle the correct word in the story about a man named Tran.

1   (Trans, **Tran's**) workday begins very early.

2   He gets up at six o'clock to make his (**childrens'**, **children's**) breakfast.

3   At seven o'clock, he drives by his (**friend's**, **friends'**) houses to take them to work.

4   By eight o'clock, Tran and his friends are at work on the (**factories**, **factory's**) main floor.

5   Tran enjoys his work painting car (**body's**, **bodies**).

Tell about people's favorite foods or activities. Use the possessive form.

Sample: (My cousin) *My cousin's favorite sport is soccer.*

6   (My friends)

_____

7   (My boss)

_____

8   (My mother)

_____

   Check your answers on page 251.

Contractions

A **contraction** is a word formed by joining two other words. An apostrophe (') shows where a letter or letters have been left out. Many people use contractions when they speak and write informal letters. Do not use contractions in formal writing such as business letters or reports.

Common Contractions

Contraction	Words It Replaces
I'm	I am
he's, she's, it's	he is, she is, it is; he has, she has, it has
you're, we're, they're	you are, we are, they are
isn't, aren't, wasn't, weren't	is not, are not, was not, were not
he'll, she'll, you'll	he will, she will, you will
I'll, we'll, they'll	I will, we will, they will
won't	will not
doesn't, don't, didn't	does not, do not, did not
I'd	I would, I had
I've, we've, you've, they've	I have, we have, you have, they have
who's	who is, who has
there's	there is, there has
let's	let us
can't	cannot

PRACTICE

Write the words that each underlined contraction replaces.

_____ **1** I know a writer who's writing a book about baseball.

_____ **2** I've read about the first pro baseball player, Al Reach.

_____ **3** He wasn't cheered when he left Brooklyn for the Phillies.

_____ **4** Fans weren't pleased that a player wanted a salary.

_____ **5** In Reach's time, players didn't even get paid.

Write two sentences—one about something you cannot do and one about something you will not do. Change the words in parentheses to contractions.

6 (cannot) _____

7 (will not) _____

Contraction or Possessive?

Be careful not to confuse **contractions** with **possessive pronouns** or **possessive adjectives**. Pronouns with apostrophes (') are parts of contractions. Possessive pronouns and possessive adjectives do <u>not</u> use apostrophes.

Pronoun	Contraction	Possessive Pronoun/Adjective
he	he's (he is)	his
she	she's (she is)	hers
it	it's (it is)	its
you	you're (you are)	yours, your
they	they're (they are)	theirs, their
we	we're (we are)	ours, our
who	who's (who is)	whose

Note: The possessive *its* and the contraction *it's* are often confused.

Possessive: The airplane lost power in one of <u>its</u> engines.

Contraction: <u>It's</u> possible to make an emergency landing.

Note: These words are misspellings: *its'*, *his'*, *her's*, *yours'*, *theirs'*, *whos'*. Always correct them.

PRACTICE

Circle the correct word to complete each sentence.

1 People have a lot to say about **(their, they're)** jobs.

2 "**(Its, It's, Its')** hectic!" says a thirty-year-old nurses' aide.

3 "My patients are so ill that **(they're, their)** always asking for me."

4 "**(You're, Your)** always up and down helping someone."

5 "**(Who's, Whose)** going to do the job with as much care?"

6 "I know one thing about this job: **(it's, its', its)** never dull."

7 A bartender said, "What I really like is helping people solve **(their, they're)** problems."

8 A cook said, "**(They're, Their)** never going to come back for seconds if I don't put in the time!"

9 "I'm happy when **(your, you're)** at the counter at 6:00 A.M.," he said.

10 "**(Who's, Whose)** job is it to clean the griddle?"

Write *their* or *they're* to complete each sentence. Use a capital letter when necessary.

Some people are always complaining about _____

jobs. _____ always talking about the things they don't like

about _____ work.

Check your answers on page 251.

Homonyms

Homonyms are words that sound alike but are spelled differently and have different meanings. Study this list of common homonyms to help you use each word correctly.

Word	Meaning	Word	Meaning
aisle	a space between rows	forth	forward
isle	an island	fourth	number four
brake	to stop	hole	opening
break	to destroy; a short time off	whole	complete
capital	center city of government	know	to understand
capitol	building in which a legislative body meets	no	not at all
		lessen	decrease, make less
clothes	things to wear	lesson	something that is taught
close	to shut		
fair	even, just; a festival	weak	not strong
fare	money for transportation	week	seven days

Some words are not homonyms, but their sounds and spellings are close enough to cause problems.

I <u>accept</u> your apology.   Do not <u>lose</u> your bus pass.

We're all here <u>except</u> Jim.   Do you have any <u>loose</u> change?

PRACTICE

Circle the correct word to complete each sentence.

1. Last **(week, weak)** our state passed a new law allowing more dumps.

2. The government thinks the law is **(fair, fare)**, but many people don't agree.

3. Some of us gathered to meet in the state **(capital, capitol)** of Lansing.

4. The meeting was so crowded that even the **(isles, aisles)** were full.

5. I **(no, know)** we have to work out a way to deal with this problem.

6. We need to **(lessen, lesson)** our need for new dumps.

7. We should be trying to **(clothes, close)** old dumps, not open new ones.

8. We need a **(hole, whole)** new plan for taking better care of our environment.

Write a sentence with each word.

9. (accept) _____

10. (brake) _____

Spelling

One good way to improve your spelling is to study a few basic spelling rules. While some words must be memorized, many others follow these seven spelling rules.

Rule 1: *ie:* There is a rhyme to help you learn the *ie* rule: Use *i* before *e* except after *c* or when sounded as *a* as in *neighbor* and *weigh.*

i before *e*:	achieve	believe
ei after *c*:	receive	conceive
ei when sounded as *a*:	weight	reins

The following words do not fit this rule. You need to memorize them.

either	neither	heir	seize	forfeit	foreign
weird	sheik	their	height	ancient	conscience

Rule 2: *-ceed/-cede:* Only three English verbs end in *-ceed.* All the other verbs with that long *e* vowel sound end in *-cede.*

-ceed:	succeed	proceed	exceed
-cede:	secede	recede	concede

Note: There is one exception—the verb *supersede,* which ends in *-sede.*

Rule 3: *-ful:* The sound /*ful*/ at the end of a word is spelled with one *l.*

graceful   careful   helpful

PRACTICE

Circle the correct spelling of each word in parentheses.

1 Sitting Bull was **(chief, cheif)** of the Hunkpapa tribe of Sioux.

2 Sitting Bull felt he had to **(succede, succeed)** against efforts to **(sieze, seize)** his tribe's land.

3 After all, he was the **(hier, heir)** to a great nation.

4 **(Their, Thier)** culture reached back hundreds of years.

5 Sitting Bull was **(hopefull, hopeful)** that the Sioux would be a **(powerful, powerfull)** nation again.

6 However, the Sioux were not **(successful, successfull)** in remaining a great nation.

7 Sitting Bull and his people could not **(acheive, achieve)** their dream.

Rule 4: Adding prefixes and suffixes: In general, do not change the spelling of a word when you add a prefix or a suffix.

dis- + pleased = displeased   mis- + spell = misspell

joy + -ous = joyous   hope + -ful = hopeful

govern + -ment = government

But: lay/laid   pay/paid   say/said

Rule 5: Adding suffixes to words ending in *y* after a consonant: If a word ends in *y* after a *consonant,* change the *y* to *i* before adding the suffix. Exception: Keep the *y* before a suffix that begins with *i,* such as *-ing* and *-ish.*

hurry/hurried   happy/happier

But: apply/applying   baby/babyish

Rule 6: Adding suffixes to words ending in silent *e:* If a word ends in silent *e* and the suffix begins with a vowel, drop the final *e.* If the suffix begins with a consonant, do not drop the final *e.*

fascinate/fascinating   nice/niceness

But: true/truly

Rule 7: Doubling consonants before a suffix: If a short (one-syllable) word ends in *one* consonant and *one* vowel, double the consonant before a suffix that begins with a vowel, such as *ed, ing, er, est.* If a longer word ends in one vowel and one consonant, double the consonant *only* if the last part of the word is the loudest part, such as *comMIT* or *exPEL.* Never double *x, y,* or *w.*

rap/rapping   trap/trapped   big/biggest

stop/stoppable   rebel/rebelling   commit/committed

PRACTICE

Circle the correct spelling of each word in parentheses.

1 I have not been **(geting, getting)** my paychecks on time.

2 My checks have been **(delayed, delaied)** by three days or more.

3 I have not been **(payed, paid)** on time for the last month.

4 That is why I am **(submiting, submitting)** this complaint in **(writing, writting)**.

Add the suffix to each word. Write a sentence with the new word.

5 carry + -ed _____

_____

6 begin + -ing _____

_____

Words That Cause Trouble

Here are some words that are often misused.

Word	Use	Example
few, fewer, many	pieces you can count	I have very few books. I have fewer books than you do. How many books do you have?
little, less, much	amounts you can't count	I have little patience. I have less patience than you do. How much patience do you have?
good	an adjective; tells about a person, place, or thing	This is a good picture.
well	an adverb; tells about an action	You draw well.
among	three or more	The three fought among themselves.
between	two	The choice was between the two of them.
who, whom	use with people	My children, who are now grown, live close by. He is the one to whom I spoke.
which	use with things	Cigarettes, which can cause cancer, aren't cheap.

PRACTICE

Circle the correct word to complete each sentence.

1 Michael Cullen, **(who, which)** opened the first "warehouse grocery" store, did not know that he was making history back in the 1930s.

2 Times were hard then, and people were looking for **(good, well)** prices.

3 Almost at once, his store was doing **(good, well)** because it was self-service, cash-and-carry, and one-stop shopping.

4 There was a lot of competition **(among, between)** all the grocery stores.

5 Mr. Cullen's store, **(which, who)** was the first supermarket, beat all the other stores.

Complete the following sentences.

6 I don't have much _____

7 I have very few _____

Usage

Nouns

A **noun** is the name of a person, place, or thing. All nouns belong to one of two groups: common nouns or proper nouns.

Common Nouns

A **common noun** names a person, place, or thing.

Person		Place		Thing	
writer	athlete	street	country	movie	marriage
woman	actor	city	sea	car	year

Proper Nouns

A **proper noun** names a <u>specific</u> person, place, or thing. A proper noun always begins with a capital letter.

	Person	Place	Thing
Common noun:	writer	street	box
Proper noun:	Stephen King	Front Street	Zippy Cola

PRACTICE

Draw <u>one</u> line under each common noun and <u>two</u> lines under each proper noun.

1. President Bill Clinton was the only president to be impeached in the 20th century.

2. President Clinton's trial began in January 1999 and ended the next month.

3. The trial was held in the United States Senate in Washington, D.C., the capital of the nation.

4. Dale Bumpers, the retired senator from the state of Arkansas, spoke at the trial.

5. The men and women in the room listened carefully to the speech Mr. Bumpers gave.

6. The newsmagazines *Time* and *Newsweek* reported on the trial for weeks.

7. CNN and all the major networks covered the event on television.

8. The Senate decided not to remove President Clinton from office.

Collective Nouns and Mass Nouns

Collective Nouns

Collective nouns are nouns that name groups of people, places, or things.

family	team	jury
company	committee	group

A collective noun usually takes the singular form of the verb.

The team <u>begins</u> the tournament on Tuesday.

Mass Nouns

Mass nouns are nouns that name qualities and things that cannot be counted.

water	chaos	strength	anger
time	courage	hair	gold

Mass nouns do not have plural forms because the things they name cannot be counted. Use the singular form of the verb with a mass noun.

There isn't much <u>time</u> left.

<u>Water</u> flows downhill.

PRACTICE

Underline each collective noun. Circle each mass noun.

1 Our team is warming up for the race.

2 The runners are breathing in the fresh morning air.

3 The race begins, and the crowd cheers.

4 The runners are filled with energy.

5 The gravel crunches under their feet.

6 Time will soon run out.

7 My family has come to watch us win the race.

8 To celebrate, we share a bottle of fizzy grape juice.

Complete each sentence.

Sample: After I go swimming, my hair *is dry and frizzy.*

9 My favorite team _____.

10 During a game, the crowd _____.

Pronouns

A **pronoun** is a word that takes the place of a noun.

When the <u>Johnsons</u> moved, <u>they</u> hired a moving company to help <u>them</u>.

(The pronouns *they* and *them* take the place of the noun *Johnsons*.)

Just like nouns, pronouns can be singular or plural. **First-person pronouns** refer to the speaker or speakers; **second-person pronouns** refer to the person or people being spoken to; **third-person pronouns** refer to the person, people, or things being spoken about.

	Singular	Plural
First-Person:	I, me, my, mine	we, us, our, ours
Second-Person:	you, your, yours	you, your, yours
Third-Person:	he, him, his/she, her, hers/it, its	they, them, their, theirs

These personal pronouns may be divided into three basic types: subject, object, and possessive.

Subject Pronouns

A **subject pronoun** can act as the subject of a sentence. A subject tells who or what the sentence is about. The subject pronouns are *I, you, he, she, it, we,* and *they*.

<u>We</u> are going to get married. (*We* is the subject.)

<u>I</u> need to rent a truck. (*I* is the subject.)

PRACTICE

Write a subject pronoun to take the place of the underlined word or words.

_____ ❶ <u>My fiancé Mike and I</u> also have to find a band.

_____ ❷ <u>Mike</u> wants a band to play the hits.

_____ ❸ <u>He and I</u> can't agree on a band at all.

_____ ❹ <u>My mother</u> does not know much about music.

_____ ❺ <u>My parents</u> will pay for part of the wedding.

Write a sentence to go with the one that is given. Use a subject pronoun.

Sample: <u>My neighborhood</u> is very friendly. *It is a good place to live.*

❻ <u>My neighbors</u> sometimes help me out.

_____

❼ <u>My neighbors and I</u> usually get along.

_____

Object Pronouns

Object pronouns are pronouns that are used as the object of a verb or preposition. The object pronouns are *me, you, him, her, it, us,* and *them.*

1.   An object pronoun can be a **direct object.** A direct object receives the action in the sentence.

> I met my new boss today, and I like <u>her</u>. (Whom do you like? Her.)
>
> Take the glass, and put <u>it</u> in the sink. (What should you put in the sink? It.)

2.   An object pronoun can be an **indirect object.** An indirect object tells *to whom* or *for whom* an action is done.

> My sister sent <u>me</u> a gift for my birthday.

3.   An object pronoun can be the **object of a preposition.** The object of a preposition is simply the noun or pronoun that follows a preposition. Some common prepositions are *about, above, in, by, to, at, in front of, inside, into,* and *with.*

> Sit down by <u>me</u>.
>
> I have not spoken to <u>him</u> yet.

PRACTICE

Write the correct pronoun or pronouns to complete each sentence.

1   My aunt told _____ **(I, me)** that she once heard Martin Luther King, Jr. speak.

2   _____ **(She, Her)** heard _____ **(he, him)** speak when she was a little girl.

3   My brother and I were excited when she told _____ **(we, us)** about how he sounded.

4   At one point, she thought he looked directly at _____ **(she, her).**

5   He was such a good speaker that all the people in the crowd thought he was speaking directly to _____ **(they, them).**

Write a sentence using the object pronoun in parentheses.

Sample: (him) *I gave the tickets to him.* _____

6   (me) _____

7   (them) _____

8   (us) _____

Possessive Pronouns

Possessive pronouns show ownership.

1.   Use the **possessive pronouns** *my, your, his, her, its, our,* and *their* before nouns to show ownership. (These words are sometimes called **possessive adjectives.**)

> Nick left his glove in our car.   Their dog buried its bone.

2.   Use the **possessive pronouns** *my, your, his, her, its, our,* and *their* before a gerund. A **gerund,** such as the word *driving,* looks like the *-ing* form of a verb, but it acts as a noun.

> Their driving to Nashville was my idea.
>
> He did not agree with my changing jobs.

3.   Use the **possessive pronouns** *mine, yours, his, hers, its, ours,* and *theirs* alone to show ownership.

> Is this coat his?   Mine is in the closet.
>
> Are those papers ours?   No, they are theirs.

4.   A possessive pronoun is <u>never</u> written with an apostrophe. Spellings such as *their's, your's,* and *our's* are incorrect.

PRACTICE

Circle the correct word to complete each sentence.

1   Antonio seemed to have a problem with **(he's, his)** eyes.

2   **(His, He)** squinting was obvious to everyone.

3   "We are worried about **(you're, your)** vision," I told him.

4   "My eyes are **(my, mine),** not **(yours, your's),**" he growled.

5   He finally listened to **(our, ours)** concerns and went to an eye doctor.

Read each sentence about a man named Kim. Write <u>two</u> sentences comparing yourself with Kim. Use *mine* in one sentence and *my* in the other.

Sample: Kim's children are young. *Mine are grown up.*

My children are grown up.

6   Kim's home is very messy. _____

_____

7   Kim's hometown is a big city. _____

_____

Pronoun Antecedents

A pronoun gets its meaning from the noun to which it refers. This noun is called the **antecedent**. Pronouns usually have specific antecedents.

1. An **antecedent** is the word to which a pronoun refers. The antecedent usually comes before the pronoun.

> Louisa forgot to buy her weekly bus pass. She had to pay cash every day.
> (*Louisa* is the antecedent for *her* and *She*.)

> Every cat in the shelter received its shots.
> (*Cat* is the antecedent for *its*.)

> Carolyn and I left our keys on the desk. We didn't realize that until much later.
> (*Carolyn and I* is the antecedent for *our* and *We*.)

2. Sometimes the antecedent comes after the pronoun.

> Since they moved, Donna and Jim have not called us.
> (*Donna and Jim* is the antecedent for *they*.)

> Because of its climate, San Diego is my favorite city.
> (*San Diego* is the antecedent for *its*.)

PRACTICE

Circle the antecedent for the underlined word in each sentence.

1. Cities that get a lot of snow must keep their snow plows in good condition.

2. When two snowstorms hit town last January, they nearly shut down the city.

3. On its front page, the newspaper had a photo of a snow plow stuck in the snow.

4. The mayor knew she had to act fast to clear the snow.

5. Even though it was his day off, the police chief met with the mayor to make a plan.

6. My brother worked overtime. He was one of fifty city snow plowers.

Write a sentence with each pronoun. Underline its antecedent in your sentence.

Sample: *When the phone rang at 7:00 a.m., it surprised me.*

7. (it) _____

8. (he) _____

Pronoun Agreement

Pronouns and antecedents must match, or agree with one another.

1. A pronoun must **agree** with its antecedent in number, person, and gender. *Number* means that the words are either singular or plural. *Person* refers to first-person, second-person, or third-person. *Gender* refers to whether the words stand for males, females, or things.

> Lucy gave her bill to the clerk.
>
> (Both the antecedent *Lucy* and the pronoun *her* are singular, in the third-person, and used for females.)

2. Use a **plural pronoun** with two or more antecedents joined by *and*.

> My roommate and I disagree about our responsibilities.

3. Use a **singular pronoun** with two or more singular antecedents joined by *or* or *nor*.

> Either Steve or Ricardo should give up his seat for the elderly woman.

4. Be sure that the pronoun agrees with the antecedent in **person**.

> **Correct:**   When students want to get a GED, they must work hard.
> (*Students* and *they* are both third-person pronouns.)

> **Incorrect:** When students want to get a GED, you must work hard.
> (*Students* is a third-person pronoun, but *you* is second-person.)

PRACTICE

Circle the correct pronoun to complete each sentence.

1 Most of us have **(our, their)** own views on women in sports.

2 In my opinion, female athletes don't get the recognition **(you, they)** deserve.

3 If a female athlete is very talented, **(she, they)** can become famous.

4 However, male athletes are more likely to be known for **(his, their)** skills.

5 My uncle or my brother will be happy to give **(his, their)** opinion.

Write a sentence with a pronoun that agrees with the antecedent. Underline the pronoun and its antecedent.

Sample: (man) *The man brought his date to the movie.*

6 (actress) _____

7 (beef or chicken) _____

Adjectives

An **adjective** is a word that modifies, or helps describe, a person, place, or thing. Adjectives describe by answering one of these questions:

What kind?	<u>red</u> light	<u>good</u> dog	<u>hot</u> shower
How many?	<u>few</u> fish	<u>many</u> bills	<u>ten</u> cards
Which one?	<u>first</u> hit	<u>this</u> box	<u>any</u> choice
How much?	<u>more</u> tea	<u>little</u> time	<u>some</u> luck

1. An adjective can come before or after the noun or pronoun it describes.

    The <u>sick</u> dog lay by the door.
    He is <u>sick</u>.
    I saw a movie about a <u>far-off</u> land.
    Many of the workers say they are <u>underpaid</u>.

2. **Proper adjectives** are formed from proper nouns. Like proper nouns, they are capitalized.

    We like <u>Mexican</u> food.

PRACTICE

Underline all the adjectives in these sentences.

1 In long-ago times, dogs served people as skilled hunters.

2 Irish setters and Russian wolfhounds are some examples of early dogs that hunted.

3 Dogs that were strong and intelligent often worked on farms.

4 German shepherds and English collies are part of this group.

5 Dogs make good hunters because they have sharp senses.

Write each sentence about a different animal. Use at least one adjective in each sentence.

Sample: (dogs) *Dogs are friendly and loyal animals.*

6 (cats) _____

7 (birds) _____

8 (horses) _____

9 (rats) _____

10 (elephants) _____

Check your answers on page 253.

Adverbs

An **adverb** is a word that describes a verb, an adjective, or another adverb. Adverbs describe by answering one of these four questions:

How?	walked <u>slowly</u>	ate <u>well</u>	worked <u>carefully</u>
When?	left <u>today</u>	start <u>now</u>	arrived <u>early</u>
Where?	flew <u>above</u>	moves <u>aside</u>	climbs <u>up</u>
To what extent?	<u>almost</u> done	<u>fully</u> healed	<u>barely</u> open

1. When adverbs describe verbs, they can come before or after the verbs.

   We <u>often</u> eat chicken.   We eat chicken <u>often</u>.

   Chicken must be <u>cooked well</u>.   You need to <u>check</u> it <u>frequently</u>.

2. When adverbs describe adjectives, they often come right before the adjectives.

   I was <u>very happy</u> to hear about your success.

   Helene is <u>never ready</u> on time.

3. When adverbs describe other adverbs, they often come right before the adverbs they describe.

   Helene moves <u>very slowly</u> in the morning.

   She just <u>barely</u> catches her bus on time.

PRACTICE

Underline all the adverbs in this paragraph.

Are people ever really happy with their appearance? They must not be, judging by how warmly they greet each new diet. They must want to lose weight very badly. Some people hardly finish one diet before they begin another. My friend had almost finished his powdered diet drink when he quickly started a new diet.

Answer these questions using complete sentences.

Sample: What do you do well? *I play tennis well.*

1 What do you do well? _____

2 What do you do badly? _____

3 What do you do carefully? _____

Comparing with Adjectives and Adverbs

When you compare people, places, things, or actions, use either the comparative or superlative form of the adjective or adverb.

	Adjectives		Adverbs	
	big	short	highly	slowly
Comparative:	bigger	shorter	more highly	more slowly
Superlative:	biggest	shortest	most highly	most slowly

1.   Use the **comparative form** of the adjective or adverb to compare two people, places, or things. Add -*er* to one-syllable adjectives and adverbs to form the comparative. Use *more* or *less* before most adjectives and adverbs with two or more syllables to compare them.

> This box is <u>smaller</u> than the other.
>
> The turtle moves <u>more slowly</u> than the rabbit.
>
> *But:* This box is <u>heavier</u> than the other one.

2.   Use the **superlative form** of the adjective or adverb to compare three or more people, places, or things. Add -*est* to one-syllable adjectives and adverbs to form the superlative. Use *most* or *least* before most adjectives and adverbs with two or more syllables to compare them.

> Of the three brothers, Jason drives <u>fastest</u>.
>
> He is the <u>most careless</u> dresser, too.
>
> *But:* He is also the <u>funniest brother</u>.

3.   Never add both -*er* and *more* (or *less*), or both -*est* and *most* (or *least*), to an adjective or adverb.

> **Not correct:** *This is the <u>most hardest</u> thing I've ever done.*
>
> **Correct:**   *This is the <u>hardest</u> thing I've ever done.*

PRACTICE

Circle the correct word or words to complete each sentence.

1   Shopping on Saturdays is **(more hard, harder)** than shopping during the week.

2   Of all the days, Saturday is when the stores are **(most crowded, more crowded).**

3   Traffic moves **(more slowly, more slowlier)** on Saturday than it does on other days.

4   Even so, I think Saturday is the **(most best, best)** day for shopping.

Common Problems with Adjectives and Adverbs

1. Adjectives and adverbs usually have different forms. Many adverbs are formed by adding *-ly* to the end of an adjective.

<u>bright</u> light (adjective)   <u>brightly</u> lit (adverb)

To be certain whether to use an adjective or an adverb, see what kind of word it is describing. Use an adjective to describe a noun or a pronoun. Use an adverb to describe a verb, an adjective, or another adverb.

Incorrect: They took their job serious.

Correct: They took their job seriously. (*Seriously* is an adverb describing the verb *took.*)

2. Not all adjectives and adverbs have regular comparative and superlative forms. Here are some common irregular adjectives and adverbs.

Adjective/Adverb	Comparative	Superlative
good	better	best
well	better	best
bad	worse	worst
badly	worse	worst
little	less	least
many/a lot of	more	most
much/a lot of	more	most
far	farther	farthest

Tuna is <u>good</u>, shrimp is even <u>better</u>, but lobster is the <u>best</u> seafood of all.

I get very <u>little</u> time off, my brother gets <u>less</u>, and my sister gets the <u>least</u>.

PRACTICE

Circle the correct word to complete each sentence.

❶ Eric is not a good map reader, but Larry is even **(worst, worse).**

❷ However, Chris reads maps very **(careful, carefully).**

❸ Li is the **(best, better)** driver in the group.

❹ This group has **(fewer, less)** accidents than the others.

Write a sentence using each word correctly.

Sample: (worst) *Of everyone in my family, I am the worst dancer.*

❺ (farther) _____

❻ (real) _____

Verbs

Verb Tense

Verbs are words that show action or a state of being. Every verb has four different forms. The forms of a verb are used to make the different verb tenses. **Tense** is the form of a verb that shows when the action takes place.

Verb Forms

Present	Present Participle	Past	Past Participle
talk/talks	talking	talked	talked
eat/eats	eating	ate	eaten

Simple Tenses

There are three simple tenses: present, past, and future. Form the present tense by using the present form of the verb. Form the past tense by using the past form of the verb. Form the future tense by using the helping verb *will* and the present form of the verb.

Tense	Form	Use
Present	talk/talks	repeated action or habit; general truth
Past	talked	action completed in the past
Future	will talk	action not yet completed

Present: I <u>talk</u> to my children on the phone every week.

Past: I <u>talked</u> to my daughter yesterday.

Future: I <u>will talk</u> to my son next week.

PRACTICE

In each sentence write *collect, collected,* or *will collect.*

1 I _____ coins when I was a child.

2 I still _____ coins.

3 Next year, I _____ stamps for a change.

Complete each sentence. Use the correct form of the verb *like.*

Sample: When she gets older, I *think my daughter will like basketball.*

4 As a child, I _____

5 Now I _____

6 Next year I _____

Perfect Tenses

There are three perfect tenses: present perfect, past perfect, and future perfect. Use the correct form of the helping verb *to have* and the past participle to form all of the perfect tenses.

Tense	Form	Use
Present perfect	have/has worked have/has taken	A completed action or an action that continues into the present
Past perfect	had worked had taken	An action completed before another past action or event
Future perfect	will have worked will have taken	An action completed before another future action or event

Present perfect: Vernon has worked here for a long time.

Past perfect: He had worked at another job before he came here.

Future perfect: By May 1, he will have worked here for ten years.

PRACTICE

Circle the correct form of the verb to complete each sentence.

1. Shawn has asthma. He **(has suffered, had suffered)** from it since he was a child.

2. By the time he was ten years old, he **(had gone, will have gone)** to the emergency room several times.

3. Now that he is an adult, he **(had gotten, has gotten)** his asthma under control.

4. By this time next month, it **(had been, will have been)** exactly one year since his last asthma attack.

5. Shawn is glad his baby **(had not shown, has not shown)** any signs of asthma so far.

Write a sentence using each verb phrase.

Sample: (have lived) *I have lived here for two months.*

6. (will have lived) _____

7. (has been) _____

8. (had wanted) _____

9. (have seen) _____

10. (will have written) _____

Irregular Verbs

Most verbs in English are regular, but some verbs have irregular past and past participle forms. Here are some common irregular verbs.

Present	Past	Past Participle
am, is, are	was, were	been
begin	began	begun
break	broke	broken
bring	brought	brought
buy	bought	bought
choose	chose	chosen
do	did	done
drink	drank	drunk
eat	ate	eaten
get	got	gotten
give	gave	given
go	went	gone
has, have	had	had
know	knew	known
leave	left	left
lose	lost	lost
send	sent	sent
see	saw	seen
show	showed	showed/shown
speak	spoke	spoken
take	took	taken

PRACTICE

Circle the correct form of the verb for each sentence.

1 I (**leave, leaved, left**) high school when I was 16.

2 I (**lose, lost, losed**) years of education when I was a teenager.

3 I (**am, been, was**) unhappy during that time and wanted to go back to school.

4 Now that I have (**gone, went, go**) back, I have (**begin, began, begun**) to feel better.

Write a sentence using each irregular verb form.

Sample: (took) _When I was younger, I took too many risks._

5 (known) _____

6 (done) _____

7 (begun) _____

Subject-Verb Agreement

In some tenses, subjects and verbs must agree in number. A singular subject must have a singular verb. A plural subject must have a plural verb.

Singular subject and verb: A big <u>ship</u> <u>sails</u> into the harbor.

Plural subject and verb: <u>We</u> <u>are</u> waiting for the ship to arrive.

1.   Words between the subject and verb do not affect the agreement.

The <u>insects</u> on the oak tree <u>are</u> harmful.

(The subject is *insects,* not *tree*. The verb is *are*. The phrase *on the oak tree* between the subject and verb does not affect the agreement.)

2.   Use a plural verb for subjects joined by *and*.

The door <u>and</u> the window <u>are</u> both stuck.

3.   Use a singular verb for singular subjects joined by *or* or *nor*.

Each morning Julia <u>or</u> Lucy <u>buys</u> fresh rolls.

4.   If a singular subject and a plural subject are joined by *or* or *nor*, the subject that is closer to the verb must agree with the verb.

Neither the loaf of bread nor the <u>eggs</u> <u>were</u> fresh.
Neither the eggs nor the <u>loaf of bread</u> <u>was</u> fresh.

PRACTICE

Circle the correct verb to complete each sentence.

1 The sky (**appears, appear**) blue as we look up from Earth.

2 In space, both the sun and moon (**is, are**) easy to see during the day.

3 The moon and the planet Venus (**glow, glows**) at night.

4 The Big Dipper, along with many other stars, (**shines, shine**) as well.

5 Neither Pluto nor Saturn (**is, are**) easy to find, though.

6 Stars that shoot across the sky (**is, are**) a special treat.

Write a sentence with each word or phrase as the subject of the sentence.

Sample: (Tony or Leo) *Either Tony or Leo is going to help us paint.*

7 (cars) _____

8 (buses or the train) _____

9 (son or daughters) _____

Pronoun and Verb Agreement

A pronoun used as a subject must agree with the verb in number.

1. These pronouns always use singular verbs: *much, neither, anybody, no one, nothing, one, other, somebody, someone, something, another, anybody, anyone, anything, each, either, everybody, everyone, everything.*

<u>Someone</u> <u>has</u> been in the house.

<u>Everything</u> <u>is</u> fine, thanks.

2. These pronouns always use plural verbs: *both, few, many, others, several.*

<u>Both</u> of the glasses <u>have</u> been used.

<u>Several</u> of the glasses <u>are</u> broken.

3. These pronouns use singular or plural verbs, depending on what they stand for: *all, some, any, part, none, half.*

<u>All</u> of the books <u>have been</u> checked out. (*All* stands for *books.*)

<u>All</u> of the milk <u>was</u> spilled on the floor. (*All* stands for *milk.*)

PRACTICE

Circle the correct verb to complete each sentence.

1 Both of my children **(are, is)** planning to look for famous people in New York.

2 Everyone **(has, have)** told them not to be disappointed if they don't see any.

3 At 11:00 P.M. all of the actors **(take, takes)** their last bow and leave the theater.

4 Each of the actors **(gives, give)** my children a smile and an autograph.

5 Few **(is, are)** this nice.

6 Several **(has, have)** since answered letters from my children.

Complete each sentence using *is, are,* or *has/have.*

Sample: Several of my friends *have twins.*

7 Everyone in my family _____.

8 No one in my family _____.

9 All of my friends _____.

10 Several of my coworkers _____.

Check your answers on page 254.

Active and Passive Voice

Voice refers to the form of the verb that shows whether the subject of the sentence is doing the action. Only action verbs show voice. English has two voices: the active voice and the passive voice.

1.   When the subject of the sentence performs the action, the verb is in the **active voice.**

> The robbers stole my gold ring. (*The robbers* is the subject.)
>
> My sister decorated the birthday cake. (*My sister* is the subject.)

2.   When the subject of the sentence receives the action, the verb is in the **passive voice.**

> My gold ring was stolen by the robbers. (*My gold ring* is the subject.)
>
> The birthday cake was decorated by my sister. (*The birthday cake* is the subject.)

> Note that the passive voice is made up of a form of the helping verb *to be* plus the past participle of an action verb.

PRACTICE

Write *A* if the sentence is in the active voice. Write *P* if the sentence is in the passive voice.

_____   **1**   The newspaper is delivered before 6:00 A.M.

_____   **2**   Sometimes the paper boy delivers it late.

_____   **3**   I report every missing paper to the newspaper office as soon as possible.

_____   **4**   Without a doubt, many missing papers are reported every day by irritated customers.

_____   **5**   Sometimes our complaints are ignored by the newspaper office.

_____   **6**   Sometimes the newspaper office pays attention to our complaints.

Write two sentences, one with the verb in the active voice and one with it in the passive voice.

7   Active: *send* _____

Passive: *are sent* _____

8   Active: *tell* _____

Passive: *were told* _____

Using Active and Passive Voice

Because the active voice stresses the person or thing doing the action, sentences in the active voice are more direct than passive-voice sentences. Active-voice sentences also use fewer words than passive-voice sentences. Use the active voice when possible. Compare these two sentences.

Active voice: *Russ closed the door.*

Passive voice: *The door was closed by Russ.*

The active-voice sentence is clearer because it shows the action more directly. There are times, though, when you should use the passive voice.

1.   Use the passive voice when you do not know, do not care, or do not want to name who did the action.

The community center was built in 1995.
A terrible mistake has been made.

2.   Use the passive voice when you want to stress the action or the receiver of the action, not who did the action.

My coworker was struck by a car.
Three of our teachers were honored by the mayor.

PRACTICE

For each sentence, decide if it makes sense to use the passive voice. If so, underline *OK*. If not, underline *Change to active voice.*

1   The wedding party was held last Saturday. (OK/Change to active voice.)

2   The room was decorated beautifully. (OK/Change to active voice.)

3   The room was entered by me at 9:00 P.M. (OK/Change to active voice.)

4   Drinks and appetizers were served by waiters. (OK/Change to active voice.)

5   A glass of champagne was drunk by Tanya. (OK/Change to active voice.)

6   It was decided by me not to drink anything. (OK/Change to active voice.)

7   The happy bride and groom were congratulated by all. (OK/Change to active voice.)

Choose two of the sentences above that are <u>not</u> OK in the passive voice. Write them in the active voice.

_____

_____

Check your answers on page 254.

13 Sentence Structure

Sentence Fragments

A **sentence fragment** is a group of words that does not express a complete thought. Even if a fragment begins with a capital letter and ends with a period, it is not a sentence. Some information is missing from it.

Fragment: *Ran away with the bone.* (missing a subject)
Correct: *A dog ran away with the bone.*

Fragment: *Helped her get a job as a cashier.* (missing a subject)
Correct: *Her friend in the diner helped her get a job as a cashier.*

Fragment: *The rags under the sink.* (missing a verb)
Correct: *The rags under the sink are dirty.*

PRACTICE

Write *C* if the group of words is a complete sentence. Write *F* if it is a fragment.

_____ ❶ "Road rage" is an act of aggression similar to an assault.

_____ ❷ Taking place after two drivers have a disagreement.

_____ ❸ Tailgating, yelling curses, and flashing the headlights.

_____ ❹ Also fall into this category.

_____ ❺ Because driving can be very stressful.

_____ ❻ Some drivers are unable to control themselves.

_____ ❼ Often these drivers are already angry about a problem at home or work.

Turn each fragment below into a complete sentence.

Sample: One safety rule. *One safety rule is to use your seat belt.*

❽ The minimum driving age.

_____

❾ Drive too fast.

_____

There are three ways to test whether a group of words is a fragment. If you answer *no* to one of the following questions, you have a fragment.

1. **Is there a verb?** If there is no verb, the group of words is a fragment. All parts of the verb must be present for a sentence to be complete.

> **Fragment:** Mark taking a GED class.
> **Correct:** Mark is taking a GED class.

2. **Is there a subject?** If there is no subject, the group of words is a fragment. To find out if a sentence has a subject, ask who or what is doing the action.

> **Fragment:** Studied hard for the test. (Who studied?)
> **Correct:** Mark studied hard for the test.

3. **Do the subject and verb express a complete thought?** Even if the group of words has a subject and a verb, it is not a complete sentence if it does not express a complete thought.

> **Fragment:** Whoever studied a lot. (What is the complete thought?)
> **Correct:** Whoever studied a lot did well on the test.

PRACTICE

Explain why each of the following groups of words is a fragment.

1 In the last twenty years, the number of families with adult children living at home.

This is a fragment because _____.

2 Increased by four percent.

This is a fragment because _____.

3 Compared to a generation ago, fewer young adults.

This is a fragment because _____.

4 Can afford to set up their own households.

This is a fragment because _____.

Turn each fragment below into a sentence.

5 My older sister still living with our parents.

_____

6 Enjoys spending time with them in the evenings.

_____

Check your answers on page 254.

Run-on Sentences

A **run-on** sentence is two or more complete thoughts that are not correctly separated. There are two kinds of run-on sentences.

1.   One type is made up of two sentences that are not separated by punctuation.

Run-on: The storm got worse it turned toward the land.
Correct: The storm got worse. It turned toward the land.

Run-on: The Japanese subway is the fastest train it travels over 100 miles an hour.
Correct: The Japanese subway is the fastest train. It travels over 100 miles an hour.

2.   The other type is made up of two sentences joined with a comma when they should be joined with a semicolon or a comma and a connecting word. This type of run-on is sometimes called a comma splice.

Run-on: We were not hungry, we had already had lunch.
Correct: We were not hungry; we had already had lunch.

Run-on: You can visit the White House, you can tour many rooms.
Correct: You can visit the White House, and you can tour many rooms.

PRACTICE

Write *RO* if the sentence is a run-on. Write *C* if the sentence is correct.

_____   ❶   Bacteria in food can cause illness you should take care to store food properly.

_____   ❷   Don't keep cooked food that's been standing out for two or more hours, don't even taste it.

_____   ❸   Hamburgers should be eaten well-done, cooking kills bacteria.

_____   ❹   Raw eggs are not safe to eat they may contain salmonella.

_____   ❺   It's a good practice to date your leftovers and throw them out after three to five days.

_____   ❻   Dishes should be washed right away it's better to air-dry them than to use a towel.

_____   ❼   You can use soap to clean the kitchen counter, but bleach is better.

_____   ❽   It's important to store food properly and to keep food preparation areas clean.

How to Correct Run-on Sentences

1. Use an end punctuation mark to separate the two complete thoughts.

    Run-on: Do most people like crowds I don't think so.
    Correct: Do most people like crowds? I don't think so.

2. Use a semicolon to connect two complete thoughts.

    Run-on: I couldn't wait to jump in the water looked so cool.
    Correct: I couldn't wait to jump in; the water looked so cool.

3. Use a comma and a coordinating conjunction to connect the two complete thoughts. Coordinating conjunctions are *and, but, or, so, for, nor, yet.*

    Run-on: The sky got dark it started to rain.
    Correct: The sky got dark, and it started to rain.

PRACTICE

Correct each run-on sentence by using one of the three methods described above.

❶ The Special Olympics was started more than 30 years ago it is a program of sports for people with disabilities.

_____

❷ More than 7,000 athletes attend they come from 150 nations.

_____

❸ Each nation competes in nineteen sporting events athletes do not have to enter every event.

_____

❹ Everyone is a winner each athlete gets a ribbon or medal.

_____

❺ Many people come to watch the games they are impressed by the athletes.

_____

Add another complete thought to each complete thought below. Separate the thoughts with correct punctuation or punctuation and a connecting word.

❻ I enjoy watching the Olympic Games _____

_____

❼ Winning a gold medal must be a thrill _____

_____

Check your answers on page 254.

Compound Sentences

A **compound sentence** is made up of two or more complete thoughts. Each of these thoughts could stand alone as a sentence. There are two ways to create a compound sentence.

1. Join the complete sentences with a **coordinating conjunction** such as *and, but, or,* or *so.* Other coordinating conjunctions are *for, nor,* and *yet.*

> Jill wanted the job, and she knew she had the skills for it.
> She could accept the job, or she could reject it.
> The job had many good points, so she decided to accept it.

2. Join the complete sentences with a semicolon. Use this method when you do not need a connecting word to show how the thoughts are related.

> Martin read the book in two hours; he wrote his essay in three.
> Jess liked the movie; she saw it last Friday.

PRACTICE

Write *CS* in the blank before each compound sentence. If it is not a compound sentence, write *S.*

_____ **1** Soap operas have earned a bad name, and they don't always deserve it.

_____ **2** Some people watch too many TV programs; other people take the plots too seriously.

_____ **3** This does not make the programs themselves bad.

_____ **4** Some people think soap opera viewers are not smart, but people from all walks of life watch soaps.

_____ **5** Even doctors, lawyers, and other highly educated people watch soap operas.

_____ **6** Some hospitals tell patients to watch the soaps, and some doctors tell depressed people to tune in as well.

Add another complete thought to each complete thought below to create a compound sentence. Use a coordinating conjunction and a comma.

7 James watches soap operas every day _____

_____

8 Some soap stars have been on the air for many years _____

_____

3.   Use a compound sentence to join related ideas. The sentence will not make sense unless the two ideas are related.

Not related: Computers became popular in the 1970s, for they were very expensive. (The high prices did not make computers popular.)

Related: Computers became popular in the 1970s, for they had many different uses.

4.   Use a coordinating conjunction that helps show the relationship between the parts of a compound sentence. Each of these connecting words has a certain meaning. Use the word that shows a logical relationship.

Connecting Word	Meaning	Function
and	also	joins ideas
but	on the other hand	contrasts
or	a choice	shows a choice
so	thus	shows a result
for	because	shows a reason
nor	not	joins negative ideas
yet	but	contrasts

Not logical: I decided not to go to the party, or I planned to call you and apologize. (The sentence does not make sense.)

Logical: I decided not to go to the party, but I planned to call you and apologize.

PRACTICE

Combine the two sentences to create a logical compound sentence.

1 My first week on the job was a disaster. My boss told me so.

_____

_____

2 I was really upset. I knew things had to get better.

_____

_____

3 I tried as hard as I could. I really wanted to keep the job.

_____

_____

4 My coworker gave me good advice. I felt more confident.

_____

_____

Check your answers on page 255.

Parallel Structure

Your writing will be clearer if the ideas within each sentence are written in a similar way. Put them all in **parallel,** or similar, form. For example, all verbs should be in the same tense and form. To have **parallel structure,** use matching nouns, verbs, adjectives, and adverbs when you write a list.

Not parallel: The store is good for fruit, meat, and to buy cheese.
Parallel: The store is good for fruit, meat, and cheese. (nouns)

Not parallel: Doctors say I should run, swim, and go walking.
Parallel: Doctors say I should run, swim, and walk. (same verb form)

Not parallel: The meal was tasty, quick, and the food was good for you.
Parallel: The meal was tasty, quick, and healthful. (adjectives)

Not parallel: In the rain I drive slowly, carefully, and watch out for other drivers.
Parallel: In the rain I drive slowly, carefully, and defensively. (adverbs)

PRACTICE

Write *P* if the sentence has parallel structure. Write *NP* if the sentence does not have parallel structure.

_____ 1 Eating the right foods will help you feel healthier, more attractive, and strongly.

_____ 2 Fruits, vegetables, and grains are an important part of a well-balanced diet.

_____ 3 They provide vitamins, minerals, and are low in fat.

_____ 4 Meat, fish, and poultry are good sources of zinc, iron, and B vitamins.

_____ 5 Fiber, which is good for digestion, is found in plant foods like beans, peas, and whole grain cereals.

_____ 6 To lose weight, eat smaller portions and limiting second helpings.

_____ 7 Eat slowly and be careful; be sure to chew your food well.

Complete each sentence. Use parallel structure.

Sample: Three important paths to good health are diet, sleep, and exercise.

8 Three places you can buy food are a grocery store, a snack shop, and

_____.

9 When you are sick, you should stay home, drink fluids, and

_____.

In addition to using parallel words in lists, use parallel phrases in all your writing. Write each parallel idea in the same grammatical structure.

Not parallel: The members of the council read the letter, discussed its points, and the decision was to ignore it.

Parallel: The members of the council <u>read</u> the letter, <u>discussed</u> its points, and <u>decided</u> to ignore it.

Not parallel: The members of the council, the person who wrote the letter, and people at the meeting then got into a shouting match.

Parallel: The <u>council members</u>, the <u>letter writer</u>, and the <u>audience</u> then got into a shouting match.

PRACTICE

Rewrite each sentence so that it has parallel structure.

1 Writing helps people think, speak, and be learning.

_____

_____

2 Those who can write well will be leaders in the community, state, and nationally in years to come.

_____

_____

3 By writing frequently, reading often, and to seek feedback, writers can improve.

_____

_____

4 Learning to write clearly, correctly, and be effective is a goal.

_____

_____

Answer each question in a complete sentence. Use parallel structure.

5 What different things can you write?

_____

_____

6 What are three qualities of good writing?

_____

_____

Complex Sentences

1. A **clause** is a group of words with its own subject and verb. A clause that can stand alone as a sentence is called an **independent clause.**

He woke up at seven o'clock, just in time to catch the bus.

2. A clause that cannot stand alone as a complete sentence is a **dependent clause.**

He woke up at seven o'clock, just in time to catch the bus.

3. Many dependent clauses begin with a connecting word called a **subordinating conjunction.** Here are some of the most common subordinating conjunctions:

after	although	as	as if	because
before	even though	if	since	so that
though	unless	until	when	while

4. A sentence with both an independent clause and a dependent clause is a **complex sentence.** You can write a complex sentence with the dependent clause at the beginning or the end. Put it where it helps you state your point most clearly. If the dependent clause is at the beginning of the sentence, put a comma after it.

Even though his alarm didn't go off, he woke up at seven o'clock.
He woke up at seven o'clock even though his alarm didn't go off.

PRACTICE

Draw a line under the dependent clause in each complex sentence. This is the clause that cannot stand alone.

1. Although I have a car, I usually take the bus.
2. I prefer the bus because I care about the environment.
3. If we don't help to reduce pollution, the problem will only get worse.
4. Let's act before it's too late.

Write directions for walking from one place to another in your neighborhood. Include your favorite shortcuts. Use at least two dependent clauses.

Sample: Walk down Elm Road until you see a recreation center on the right. If the building is open, you can walk straight through it. After you come out on the other side, you'll see a dirt path.

_____

_____

_____

5.   Use complex sentences to link related ideas. Make sure the ideas you link make sense together.

> **Ideas that are not related:** Because Helen Keller was unable to speak and hear, her books have been in print for many years.
>
> **Ideas that are related:** Because of a serious illness in childhood, Helen Keller was later unable to speak and hear.

6.   Use a subordinating conjunction to show the relationship between the ideas in a complex sentence. Since each subordinating conjunction has a certain meaning, choose the conjunction that best links your ideas. Choose from the categories below.

Time	Reason	Contrast
after	since, as	although
before, until	because	even though
once	so that	though

> **No dependent clause:** You are late. You will not get a break.
>
> **Complex sentence:** Because you are late, you will not get a break.

PRACTICE

Combine each pair of sentences by changing one sentence to a subordinate clause. Use an appropriate subordinating conjunction to link the ideas.

Sample: I got tired. It was so late. _I got tired because it was so late._

1 I went to bed. I heard a loud crash in the kitchen.

_____

2 I pulled the blankets over my head. I was afraid.

_____

3 I finally got up. I heard the cat's meow.

_____

4 I knew what had happened. I saw the cat sitting by the broken plate.

_____

Continue the story by completing the sentences.

5 I went to get a broom so that _____

_____

6 I didn't get very much sleep that night because _____

_____

Misplaced and Dangling Modifiers

1.   Place a **modifier** (a descriptive word or phrase) as close as possible to the word or phrase it describes.

> The woman <u>who delivered the package</u> spoke to the man at the desk.
>
> The batter <u>with the red shirt</u> hit a home run.

2.   If the modifier is far from the word it describes, the sentence might not make sense. A **misplaced modifier** is a modifier in the wrong place in a sentence.

Misplaced modifier:	The woman spoke to the man at the desk <u>who delivered the package</u>. (The sentence now means that the man, not the woman, delivered the package.)
Misplaced modifier:	The batter hit a home run <u>with the red shirt</u>. (The sentence now means that the batter used the red shirt to hit the ball.)

PRACTICE

Write C if the underlined modifier is in the correct place in the sentence. Write M if the modifier is misplaced.

_____ **1** We saw many smashed houses <u>driving through the storm</u>.

_____ **2** The storm <u>even</u> wrecked the sidewalks.

_____ **3** <u>Scarcely</u> people could believe the damage.

_____ **4** The storm was <u>barely</u> over when people came to help.

_____ **5** <u>Nearly</u> everyone pitched in.

_____ **6** First, a list was given to each owner <u>with many items</u>.

_____ **7** Then, Marta picked up the clothes for the children <u>that had been left in the box</u>.

_____ **8** A neighbor bought a pie <u>with a crumb crust</u> from the store.

_____ **9** The house was rebuilt by the owners <u>destroyed by the storm</u>.

Describe a bad storm that you experienced. You can make up details if you need to. Use at least three sentences that have modifiers.

_____

_____

_____

_____

3. Every modifier must describe a specific word in a sentence.

<u>Coming up the stairs</u>, he heard the clock strike six.
(Coming up the stairs describes *he*.)

4. A sentence cannot make sense if the modified word is missing. A **dangling modifier** is a modifier that does not describe anything in the sentence. Watch for dangling modifiers and rewrite them.

Dangling modifier: Driving down the road, a bad accident happened.
(Who was driving down the road?)

Correct: While driving down the road, they saw a bad accident happen.

Correct: While they were driving down the road, a bad accident happened.

PRACTICE

Rewrite each sentence to correct the dangling modifier.

1 While passing a large rock, a clap of thunder made me scream.

_____

2 Sailing up the harbor, the boat was seen.

_____

3 Flying over the town, the cars and houses looked like toys.

_____

4 Do not sit in the chair without being fully put together.

_____

5 Opening the jar, the sauce spilled all over.

_____

6 Walking up the steps, the packages fell.

_____

Complete these sentences. Include a word that can be modified by the phrase that is already written.

Sample: Eagerly waiting for news, *I jumped at the ring of the phone* .

7 Going to my class, _____ .

8 Angry at her husband, _____ .

9 Already hungry, _____ .

10 Without thinking, _____ .

Revising Sentences

Eliminate Wordiness

After you write, revise your sentences to make your meaning as clear as possible. Remove any extra words that make it harder for your reader to grasp your point. If you are saying the same thing twice, you need to cut some words.

Too wordy: Please repeat your comment again.
Revised: Please repeat your comment.

Too wordy: Is that the real truth?
Revised: Is that the truth?

PRACTICE

Revise each of the following sentences to get rid of the extra words.

1 The baseball game took place at 3 P.M. in the afternoon on Saturday.

_____

2 When the game started to begin, the players relaxed, and the tension was over with.

_____

3 The pitcher he did not know to whom to throw the ball to.

_____

4 After each inning, they repeated their signals again.

_____

5 In the last inning, the game ended with a home run with the bases loaded.

_____

6 Up to this point, no one knows where the next game will be held at.

_____

Describe a sport or game that you know very well. Include details. When you are finished, check your writing for extra words.

_____

_____

_____

_____

_____

Correct Informal Speech

Another reason to revise your sentences is to get rid of expressions that are not correct to use in writing or in formal situations, even though they may be used in informal speech. Here is a list of some words and expressions to avoid in writing.

Avoid: What kind of a movie are you going to see?
Use: What kind of movie are you going to see?

Avoid: Being that I have been here longer, I can help you.
Use: Because I have been here longer, I can help you.

Avoid: We had ought to leave now.
Use: We ought to leave now.

Avoid: My boss, she says I am a good worker.
Use: My boss says I am a good worker.

Avoid: Try and work more.
Use: Try to work more.

Avoid: This here book will help you.
Use: This book will help you.

Avoid: The reason is because the bus was late.
Use: The reason is that the bus was late.

Avoid: Like I told you, he moved to the city.
Use: As I told you, he moved to the city.

Avoid: I saw on TV where a man was hurt.
Use: I saw on TV that a man was hurt.

PRACTICE

Write C if the sentence is correct. Write W if the sentence is wrong because of informal expressions.

_____ **1** Being that the food is good, the place is always crowded.

_____ **2** The critics say it is the best restaurant in town.

_____ **3** You had ought to get there early to get a seat.

_____ **4** The reason is that all the food is fresh.

_____ **5** Like I told you, the fish is excellent.

_____ **6** All the take-out food is listed on this here menu.

_____ **7** I heard on the radio that they are opening a new place.

_____ **8** We have to try and get there soon.

 Check your answers on page 256.

Avoid Slang

Like informal expressions, slang may sometimes be all right to use in speech with friends. However, slang is seldom appropriate in writing. For example, it is definitely not suited for a note to your boss.

Slang: My boss gave me grief for being late.

Write: My boss reprimanded me for being late.

Slang: It's a bummer when you can't get the vacation time you requested.

Write: It's a problem when you can't get the vacation time you requested.

PRACTICE

Replace each of the underlined slang words or phrases with language appropriate for writing. Write the new word or phrase on the line.

1 By the end of each week, I am flat broke. _____

2 They goofed off on the job. _____

3 I am really into my new job. _____

Replace the slang in this note with appropriate language for writing. Then revise the sentences to make them smoother. Rewrite the note on the lines below.

You really ticked me off when you yelled at me about the tools that might have been swiped. I'm not the one who waltzed off with the stuff. This whole thing stinks to high heaven. You have been treating me lousy all week over this. I know I am not the most dynamite worker in the garage, but I don't rip off stuff. Don't hassle me about it anymore.

_____

_____

_____

_____

_____

_____

_____

Writing at Work

Horticulture: Nursery Worker

Some Careers in Horticulture

Florist
sells plants, flowers and floral arrangements; selects and arranges flowers for floral designs

Garden Center Worker
tends plants in store, assists customers, stocks store with additional gardening supplies such as pots, fertilizer, and soil

Groundskeeper
may work in private or public settings caring for flowers, grass, trees, and shrubs

Landscape Worker
plants flowers, shrubs, and trees according to design plans and blueprints

Lawn Service Worker
mows, fertilizes, and aerates lawns; may also tend flower beds and shrubbery

Nursery workers work in greenhouses and in the outdoors.

Nursery workers help cultivate new trees, shrubs, and flowers, and they also tend growing and mature plants and trees. Nursery workers usually learn about their profession on the job. They gain experience with fertilizing, watering, pruning, staking, and wrapping the plants and trees. They use their knowledge of the seasons, growing schedules, local climates, and customers' buying habits to grow and sell products.

Because much of the work may be physically demanding, nursery workers should be in good shape. In addition, workers should be able to follow written directions, write directions, and make notes of their own. These writing tasks must be done clearly and accurately. Nursery workers are also called upon to apply basic math skills involving money and measurement. Nursery workers who work at landscaping companies may also have to interpret plans and blueprints.

Look at the chart on Some Careers in Horticulture.

- Do any of the careers interest you? If so, which ones?

- What information would you need to find out more about those careers? On a separate piece of paper, write some questions that you would like answered. You can find out more information about those careers in the *Occupational Outlook Handbook* at your local library.

Read the following note. Then answer the questions.

Bev,

While I'm on vacation next week, please take care of the following items. Thank you for doing this, as the plants will not survive without your care.

1. Be sure to water all the plants located indoors every two days, except for the cacti.

2. Pay close attention to the bedding plants. You can use the sprinkling system in the greenhouses. Leave the system on for 15 minutes when you first come in.

3. Do not water in the evening, as the plants may sit in the cold, damp soil too long. This can cause root damage to some plants.

4. Apply plant food fertilizer to the flowering plants. Since we are entering our heavy selling season for these plants, we want them to look really terrific. The more blooms on each plant, the better they look. The plant food will help them produce lots of blooms.

Thanks,

Joe

1 Joe has asked Bev to water all the plants except for the
- (1) trees.
- (2) shrubs.
- (3) flowering plants.
- (4) cacti.
- (5) bedding plants.

2 According to Joe's memo, plant food fertilizer will help plants
- (1) grow faster.
- (2) grow taller.
- (3) grow bigger.
- (4) soak up more water.
- (5) produce more flowers.

3 On a separate sheet of paper, write a short note asking someone to do a task for you. As the note above does, give a reason why doing the task is important. Also, include a series of steps to complete the task.

Prewrite: What is the task that you want done?
Why is it important?
What are the steps that need to be taken?

Write: Write the note.

Revise and Edit: Have your instructor or another student read the note. Ask if the instructions are clear. If they are not, find out what is not clear. Also, ask your reader if there are any grammar, spelling, capitalization, or punctuation errors. Use the feedback to revise the note.

Write the correct pronoun to take the place of each underlined noun.

1 Jeff and Melissa decided to buy a new car. _____

 They   **Their**

2 Melissa needs Melissa's own car to drive to work. _____

 her   **hers**

3 The rest of the family will use Jeff's car. _____

 him   **his**

4 Jeff's parents approved of Jeff and Melissa's buying a new car. _____

 them   **their**

5 Jeff's mother is elderly and needs to get a ride to the doctor. _____

 She   **Her**

6 Jeff does a lot of errands for his father, too. _____

 he   **him**

7 Jeff and his parents are very close. _____

 Him   **He**

8 He tells them, "You can always depend on your son." _____

 I   **me**

Put an *S* next to each complete sentence. Put an *F* next to each fragment.

_____ **9** The apartment on the fourth floor.

_____ **10** Has been empty for some time.

_____ **11** It is a studio apartment.

_____ **12** Pedro looked at it last week.

_____ **13** On his way home from work.

_____ **14** After thinking about it.

_____ **15** He decided he wanted a bigger place.

_____ **16** And too expensive anyway.

    Check your answers on page 256.

Complete each sentence with one of the connecting words listed below.

or	and	because	before	but
if	even	although	when	so that

17 Jen likes to walk her dog at night _____ it's cooler outside then.

18 It's also pleasant in the morning _____ it gets too hot out.

19 She treats her dog like a person, _____ she takes him everywhere.

20 _____ she could, she would take him to work with her.

21 She took him to dog training school _____ he could learn to behave.

22 _____ she loves her dog, she doesn't let him sit on the couch.

23 _____ people see her dog, they decide that they want to own one, too.

Correct each of the following run-on sentences by writing it as two complete sentences.

24 Craig has an unusual job he is a chef.

_____

25 He used to work in a store he was a cashier.

_____

26 Then he went to cooking school for two years, it was a long program.

_____

27 He had to take out a big loan it was a difficult time in his life.

_____

28 Now he works in a fancy French restaurant, his friends visit him there.

_____

29 There is only one problem he doesn't like working on Saturday night.

_____

Write the correct adjective or adverb to complete each sentence.

30. Weldon Jones is a _____ worker.

    fine (adj.)   **finely** (adv.)

31. He takes his work _____ .

    serious (adj.)   **seriously** (adv.)

32. He works _____ and makes few mistakes.

    quick (adj.)   **quickly** (adv.)

33. Customers like the fact that he is very _____ with their orders.

    careful (adj.)   **carefully** (adv.)

34. Weldon is a _____ young man with a good future.

    bright (adj.)   **brightly** (adv.)

35. I recommend him _____ for the position he is seeking.

    high (adj.)   **highly** (adv.)

36. I feel _____ that he will do an excellent job.

    confident (adj.)   **confidently** (adv.)

37. However, we will miss him _____ .

    great (adj.)   **greatly** (adv.)

Write the correct form of the adjective or adverb to complete each sentence.

38. Of the three gas stations in town, Sun Gas has the _____ service.

    good   **better**   **best**

39. It is also the _____ .

    expensiver   **more expensive**   **most expensive**

40. The line moves _____ at Sun than at Joe's.

    quick   **more quickly**   **most quickly**

41. Joe's Truck Stop is _____ from downtown than Sun Gas.

    farther   **more farther**   **farthest**

42. The owners of Diamond Gas are doing _____ this year than ever before.

    bad   **more badly**   **worse**

43. They will have to close if business doesn't get _____ by the end of the year.

    well   **better**   **best**

Write the correct verb to complete each sentence.

44 I _____ TV when the power went out.

watched   **am watching**   **was watching**

45 Gloria _____ a haircut last week.

got   **has gotten**   **will get**

46 Jeff _____ in the shop ever since he finished high school.

will be working   **has been working**   **was working**

47 On January 10, I _____ here for one year.

will have lived   **will live**   **am living**

48 When he finally got through, he said he _____ to reach me for several days.

was trying   **had been trying**   **is trying**

49 Does he have any idea where he _____?

is going   **will have gone**   **was gone**

50 I _____ in the next election.

vote   **had voted**   **will vote**

Rewrite each sentence with capital letters where they are needed.

51 when Bob went to new york last september, he visited the world trade center.

_____

_____

52 he arrived on tuesday, and by friday he had seen all the major sights.

_____

_____

53 on labor day, he went on a picnic in central park.

_____

_____

54 he saw dustin hoffman eating french food at the restaurant called south street seaport.

_____

_____

55 he said to him, "can I have your autograph, mr. hoffman?"

_____

_____

Add punctuation marks where they are needed in each sentence.

56 My husband and I were married on June 15 1999

57 The wedding took place in Chicago Illinois

58 His brothers Edward Hal John and Joe attended the wedding

59 You wouldn't believe the crazy toasts they made

60 The wedding was beautiful and all the guests had a good time

61 Do you know where we went on our honeymoon

62 We went to Atlantic City Niagara Falls and New York City

Write the correct verb to complete each sentence.

63 Allen had _____ the movie before it came out on video.

    saw   **seen**

64 Therefore, he already _____ how it ended.

    knew   **known**

65 The movie is about a boy who _____ his nose in a fight at school.

    broke   **broken**

66 He had _____ with almost everyone in the class at some time.

    fight   **fought**

67 He had been _____ trying to break into another student's locker.

    catch   **caught**

68 He _____ his car into a glass door.

    drove   **driven**

69 Surprisingly, the principal _____ him a second chance.

    gave   **given**

70 She _____ that he acted that way because of his troubled family life.

    think   **thought**

71 By the end, the boy had _____ to control his violent behavior.

    began   **begun**

Write the correct form of the verb in parentheses.

72 **(build)** My friends and I _____ a log cabin in the woods.

73 **(do)** You should be ashamed of what you _____ !

74 **(sleep)** I _____ in the car on the way home.

75 **(drink)** I think I've _____ too much coffee.

76 **(teach)** Who _____ you how to play the guitar so well?

Write the correct word to complete each sentence.

77 Those _____ don't fit you properly.

    clothes   **close**

78 How much is the subway _____ ?

    fair   **fare**

79 Tim's mother finds it hard to _____ his decision to move away.

    accept   **except**

80 That store is open seven days a _____ , twenty-four hours a day.

    weak   **week**

81 I've learned an important _____ from this experience.

    lessen   **lesson**

82 I don't _____ what to do about the situation.

    no   **know**

83 Albany is the _____ of New York.

    capitol   **capital**

84 Wait until you've heard the _____ story.

    hole   **whole**

85 Put this receipt in a safe place and don't _____ it.

    loose   **lose**

Writing Extension

Use your grammar skills to edit and proofread a piece of writing done by a friend, coworker, or family member. If you find any mistakes in grammar, explain to the person what each error is and how to correct it.

Check your answers on page 257.

Writing Connection: Grammar and Fiction

Choose Your Words Carefully

Homonyms, malapropisms, and misplaced modifiers are just some of the challenges writers continuously face. Even the best writers fall prey to these tricky beasts of language. Homonyms, malapropisms, and misplaced modifiers are all related to word choice and usage.

- **Homonyms** are words that are spelled differently but sound the same when spoken. One familiar example is *here* and *hear*.

- A **malapropism** is made when a word is substituted for a similar sounding word and the result is a sentence worth chuckling over. In fact, some comedians have based their careers on malapropisms. Legendary baseball catcher and manager Yogi Berra became very famous for using malapropisms. One of his most famous was, "He hits from both sides of the plate. He's amphibious." (*Amphibious* means "able to operate on both land and water." The word he meant was *ambidextrous,* which means "able to use both the right and left hand equally.")

- **Misplaced modifiers** can also result in humorous statements. Phrases or groups of words incorrectly placed in a sentence present images to the reader that the writer did not intend to create. "They went swimming with the sharks wearing their new wet suits" is an example of a sentence with a misplaced modifier. (The sharks were wearing new wet suits?)

A Dog's Tale

How I loved my Grate Ant Estelle! What a caricature she was. She was full of energy. Every time I saw her, she was in a strange predicate. But there's one tail that remains especially vivid in my mind. My Ant Estelle was always as neat as a pin–even on the hottest summer day. So the day that she burst into our house with her wild, loose hare, carrying a wounded dog in her bathing suit, I knew something was seriously wrong.

"Aunt Estelle, Aunt Estelle! What happened?" I asked, as I felt every beet of my heart practically explode in my chest.

"Oh, Ozzie! Quick! Call the vegetarian! We must get this pour beast to the animal hospital. I was driving home to fast from the beech when I hit the pour thing. Oh, how I wish I had mist him," cried Estelle. "I think I hit his tale."

You'll be happy two no that the dog totally heeled from the energy.

Use the material on the previous page to answer the questions below.

1 Explain what a malapropism is.

_____

_____

2 On the line next to each word below, write the word that should be used in the story. The numbers in parentheses tell the paragraph where the word appears.

Grate (1) _____ hare (1) _____

Ant (1) _____ beet (2) _____

tail (1) _____ vegetarian (3) _____

3 Write each of the following sentences from the story correctly.

a. I was driving home to fast from the beech when I hit the pour thing.

_____

_____

b. You'll be happy two no that the dog totally heeled from the energy.

_____

_____

4 Circle the number of the best way to rewrite this sentence from the story:

So the day that she burst into our house with her wild, loose hare, carrying a wounded dog in her bathing suit, I knew something was seriously wrong.

(1) So the day that she burst into our house with her wild, loose hair, carrying a wounded dog in her bathing suit, I knew that something was seriously wrong.

(2) So the day that she burst into our house in her bathing suit with her wild, loose hair carrying a wounded dog, I knew that something was seriously wrong.

(3) So the day that she burst into our house in her bathing suit with her hair wild and loose, carrying a wounded dog, I knew that something was seriously wrong.

(4) So the day that she burst into our house with her wild, loose hare in her bathing suit, carrying a wounded dog, I knew that something was seriously wrong.

(5) No correction to the sentence is necessary.

5 On a separate sheet of paper, rewrite "A Dog's Tale," correcting all of the errors. There are 22 homonym errors, malapropisms, and misplaced modifiers in the story.

Writing Handbook

The Writing Process

Step 1: Prewriting

Plan your writing by following these prewriting steps:

A. Define your topic. To define your topic, first define your **purpose** for writing and the **audience** for whom you are writing.

- **Identify your purpose.** Is it to narrate? To describe? To explain? To persuade? To inform?
- **Identify your audience.** Is it the general public? An instructor? A classmate? A family member? A friend? Your boss? A coworker?

B. Generate ideas. Explore your thoughts and feelings about the topic. Brainstorm. Talk to others; ask experts. Do research—consult books, magazines, newspapers, TV, the Internet.

C. Organize your ideas. Outlining and mapping are two ways of organizing.

Prewriting Model

A. Define your topic.
Purpose: To convince or persuade people
Audience: Classmates
Topic Chosen: A low-fat, low-cholesterol diet is good for the heart.

B. Generate ideas. Research. Read articles on foods, cholesterol, and fat. Take notes. List foods low in cholesterol.

Notes: Foods high in fat and cholesterol include eggs, red meat—especially organ meats and fatty meats—pork, poultry skin, and saturated fats—shortening, butter.
Foods low in fat and cholesterol include fish, beans, soybean products, vegetables, fruits.

C. Organize your ideas. Use an idea map or an outline.

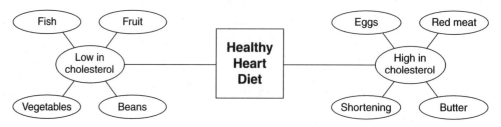

I. Main idea
- A. Subtopic
  1. Supporting detail
  2. Supporting detail
  3. Supporting detail
- B. Subtopic
  1. Supporting detail
  2. Supporting detail
  3. Supporting detail

II. Conclusion
- A. Concluding statement
  1. Supporting detail
  2. Supporting detail

I. Healthy heart diet
- A. High-fat/cholesterol foods
  1. Red meat
  2. Egg yolks
  3. Saturated fat
- B. Low-fat/cholesterol foods
  1. Fish
  2. Beans
  3. Fruits and vegetables
  4. Soy products

II. Conclusion
- A. Benefits of a healthy diet
  1. Helps the heart
  2. Controls weight

Step 2: Writing the First Draft

Write a good topic sentence stating your main idea of the entire piece. Use your outline or idea map to guide you through the main points of the piece. As you get to each main point, begin a new paragraph. Write a good topic sentence for each paragraph and include supporting details that relate to the main idea. Include details that state facts or reasons, give examples, compare and contrast, show time order, show order of importance, or show cause and effect. End with a concluding paragraph.

First Draft Model

Paragraph 1
Topic Sentence
Supporting Detail
Cause/Effect

Paragraph 2
Topic Sentence
Supporting Detail
Examples
Supporting Detail
Facts/Reasons

Paragraph 3
Supporting Detail
Facts/Reasons
Cause/Effect

Foods for a Healthy Heart

When it comes to heart disease, eating a low-fat, low-cholesterol diet is the key to staying healthy. In the past, if people were killing themselves with a poor diet they didn't know it. Today, unless you live in a cave, you cannot ignore that the choice of eating healthy foods or unhealthy foods is yours.

The biggest problem in avoiding cholesterol is to avoid eating fatty red mean and egg yolks. Unless ate in very small amounts, red meat is harmful to a healthy heart. That means avoid too much meat—especially organ meats such as liver. Other meats that are high in fat should also be avoided, such as bacon, ham hocks, and chicken skin. A large egg contains about 274 milligrams of cholesterol and saturated fat. egg whites, on the other hand, have protein, but don't add cholesterol or saturated fat to the diet.

It is also important to be aware of the different types of fat. Even without eating meat, the body creates cholesterol from foods that contain saturated fats. Coconut and palm oils are sourses of saturated fats. These types of fat are found in many prepared and processed foods. Avoid shortening and butter, because they also have high levels of saturated fat.

Paragraph 4
Topic Sentence
Supporting Detail
Facts/Reasons
Examples

Conclusion
Summary and
Final Thought

Eat plenty of loow-fat foods. Fish is low in fat and provides protein for the diet. Beans are an excellent source of protein, because they are completely free of saturated fat and cholesterol. Some authorities also consider them the cheapest source. They also provide iron, B vitamins, and vitamin A. Fresh fruit and and vegetables are another delicious source of low-fat foods.

In addition to being fit and healthy, you will look your best. One of the best things about a low-fat, low-cholesterol diet is that while helping your heart, it will also regulate your weight. All you have to is choose the right foods. Remember, you can't say you didn't know.

Step 3: Editing and Revising

Edit and revise your first draft. You can use the Editing Checklist on page 218 until you remember on your own all the items that you need to check.

Editing and Revising Model

Foods for a Healthy Heart

Paragraph 1

When it comes to heart disease, eating a low-fat, low-cholesterol diet is the key to staying healthy. In the past, if people were killing themselves with a

Idea not clear

poor diet they didn't know it. Today, ~~unless you live in a cave,~~ *with all the data available* you cannot ignore that the choice of eating healthy foods or unhealthy foods is yours.

Paragraph 2
Incorrect verb form
Incorrect verb tense

The biggest problem in avoiding cholesterol is to *having* avoid eating fatty red mean and egg yolks. Unless ~~ate~~ *eaten* in very small amounts, red meat is harmful

Language not clear

to a healthy heart. ~~That means~~ *It is necessary to* avoid too much meat—especially organ meats such as liver. Other meats that are high in fat should also be avoided, such

Detail missing
Not clear

as bacon, ham hocks, and ~~chicken skin.~~ *sausage. Poultry can be eaten in large amounts but the skin should be removed.* A large egg *yolk* contains about 274 milligrams of cholesterol and saturated fat. egg whites, on the other hand, have protein, but don't add cholesterol or saturated fat to the diet.

Paragraph 3
Detail missing

Detail missing

Cholesterol is a fat that is found in the human body and in animal fat. It is also important to be aware of the different types of fat. Even without

(solid)

eating meat, the body creates cholesterol from foods that contain saturated

fats. Coconut and palm oils are sourses of saturated fats. These types of fat are

found in many prepared and processed foods. Avoid shortening and butter,

because they also have high levels of saturated fat.

Paragraph 4

Eat plenty of loow-fat foods. Fish is low in fat and provides protein for

the diet. Beans are an excellent source of protein, because they are completely

Unnecessary detail

free of saturated fat and cholesterol. ~~Some authorities also consider them the cheapest source.~~ They also provide iron, B vitamins, and vitamin A. Fresh fruit

and and vegetables are another delicious source of low-fat foods.

Conclusion
Detail out of order

In addition to being fit and healthy, you will look your best. One of the

best things about a low-fat, low-cholesterol diet is that while helping your

heart, it will also regulate your weight. All you have to is choose the right

foods. Remember, you can't say you didn't know.

Step 4: Writing the Final Draft

Proofread and correct any errors in spelling, punctuation, or paragraph indentation. You can use the Proofreading Checklist and list of proofreader's marks shown on page 219 until you remember these items on your own. Then copy the corrected final draft carefully.

Final Draft Model	Foods for a Healthy Heart
Paragraph 1	When it comes to heart disease, eating a low-fat, low-cholesterol diet is the key to staying healthy. In the past, if people were killing themselves with a
Punctuation missing	poor dieṱ they didn't know it. Today, with all the data available, you cannot ignore that the choice of eating healthy foods or unhealthy foods is yours.
Paragraph 2	The biggest problem in avoiding cholesterol is having to avoid eating
Spelling error	fatty red ⟨mean⟩ *meat* and egg yolks. Unless eaten in very small amounts, red meat is harmful to a healthy heart. It is necessary to avoid too much meat— especially organ meats such as liver. Other meats that are high in fat should also be avoided, such as bacon, ham hocks, and sausage. Poultry can be eaten
Punctuation missing	in large amounts̭ but the skin should be removed. A large egg yolk contains
Capital letter missing	about 274 milligrams of cholesterol and saturated fat. e̲gg whites, on the other hand, have protein, but don't add cholesterol or saturated fat to the diet.
Paragraph 3	It is also important to be aware of the different types of fat. Cholesterol is a fat that is found in the human body and in animal fat. Even without eating meat, the body creates cholesterol from foods that contain saturated (solid)
Spelling error	fats. Coconut and palm oils are ⟨sourses⟩ *sources* of saturated fats. These types of fat are found in many prepared and processed foods. Avoid shortening and butter, because they also have high levels of saturated fat.

Eat plenty of loow-fat foods. Fish is low in fat and provides protein for the diet. Beans are an excellent source of protein, because they are completely free of saturated fat and cholesterol. They also provide iron, B vitamins, and

Extra word

vitamin A. Fresh fruit and and vegetables are another source of low-fat foods.

Conclusion

One of the best things about a low-fat, low-cholesterol diet is that while helping your heart, it will also regulate your weight. In addition to being fit

Word missing

and healthy, you will look your best. All you have to is choose the right foods. Remember, you can't say you didn't know.

Step 5: Publishing (Sharing the Final Draft)

Make the final corrections, and share your work with the intended audience.

Editing Checklist

	YES	NO
Content		
Does the content reflect your original purpose?	❏	❏
Is the content right for your intended audience?	❏	❏
Is the main idea stated clearly?	❏	❏
Does each paragraph have a topic sentence?	❏	❏
Are topic sentences supported by details?	❏	❏
Are details written in a logical order?	❏	❏
Is the right amount of information included?	❏	❏
(Check for details that are missing or not needed.)		
Style		
Will the writing hold the reader's interest?	❏	❏
Are thoughts and ideas expressed clearly?	❏	❏
Are any ideas repeated?	❏	❏
Are some words used too many times?	❏	❏
Grammar		
Are all sentences complete sentences?	❏	❏
Are any sentences too long and hard to understand?	❏	❏
Are any sentences too short and choppy?	❏	❏
Are nouns and pronouns used correctly?	❏	❏
Are verbs used correctly?	❏	❏
Are adjectives and adverbs used correctly?	❏	❏

Proofreading Checklist

	YES	NO
Is correct punctuation used in every sentence?	❏	❏
Is correct capitalization used in every sentence?	❏	❏
Are all words spelled correctly?	❏	❏
Are new paragraphs clearly shown?	❏	❏

(Check to see if paragraphs either are indented or
have an extra line space in between.)

	YES	NO
If handwritten, is the handwriting as neat as possible?	❏	❏
Is there enough space between words and lines?	❏	❏
If typed on a computer or word processor, are the type font and size appropriate?	❏	❏
Are the margins adequate?	❏	❏

Proofreader's Marks

Mark	Meaning
a̲	change to a capital letter
A̸	change to a lowercase letter
⊙	insert period
⋀	insert comma
word ⋀	insert word(s)
⟨sp⟩ ⟨thiir⟩	check spelling
¶	insert a paragraph indent
no ¶	no new paragraph
ℓ	delete a letter, word, group of words
ℐ	delete and close up space
#	add a space between words

Posttest

Use this Posttest to see how much you have learned. Read and answer the questions that follow. Check your answers on pages 258–260. Then enter your scores on the chart on page 230.

Capitalization and Punctuation

Read each sentence. If the underlined part is correct, write _C_ in the blank. If the part is wrong, write _W_ in the blank.

_____ 1. The Barbie doll, sold by <u>Mattel, Inc.,</u> celebrated her fortieth birthday in 1999.

_____ 2. The doll, which is made in <u>Hawthorne California,</u> is sold in over 140 countries.

_____ 3. Barbie was created by a woman named <u>ruth handler.</u>

_____ 4. Handler got the idea for Barbie on a trip to <u>Switzerland.</u>

_____ 5. She saw a <u>german</u> doll named Lilli that had an adult figure.

_____ 6. In 1959 the first Barbie was <u>manufactured, and</u> her male friend Ken was introduced in 1961.

_____ 7. Would you be surprised to learn that Handler's children were named Barbara and <u>Ken.</u>

_____ 8. Barbie was supposed to teach girls how to <u>look pretty find a man</u> and get married.

_____ 9. In the 1970s feminists <u>protested. they</u> believed Barbie taught girls to be sex objects.

_____ 10. For several years sales of Barbie were very poor; even <u>christmas</u> sales were down.

_____ 11. In 1983 a sales executive at Mattel decided to market the dolls in a different <u>way.</u>

_____ 12. She introduced dolls that were active and professional, and Barbie suddenly became a diver, a basketball player, and even a <u>Doctor.</u>

_____ 13. Sales went up again, and by 1997 the average <u>American</u> girl owned ten Barbies.

_____ 14. My own daughter was born on <u>May 3 1994,</u> and by the time she was five, she had twelve of the dolls.

_____ 15. Thank goodness my second child was a son, or we'd be up to our ears in <u>Barbies!</u>

Go on to the next page.

Plurals and Possessives

Complete each sentence by writing the correct word in the blank.

16. Sir Arthur Conan Doyle wrote many short _____ and four novels about the great detective Sherlock Holmes.

    storys   **story's**   **stories**

17. The _____ friend, Dr. John Watson, was modeled after Doyle himself, a physician and soldier.

    detectives   **detective's**   **detectives'**

18. Unlike modern detective stories, the _____ in Sherlock Holmes stories are rarely violent.

    crimes   **crime's**   **crimes'**

19. In all the stories the _____ cleverness is evident, but the outcome is never really in doubt.

    criminals   **criminal's**   **criminals'**

20. In his _____ for the solutions to crimes, Holmes displays the most entertaining use of logic and reasoning.

    searchs   **searches**   **search's**

21. On many mystery _____ lists, Holmes rates as the top detective of all time.

    lovers   **lover's**   **lovers'**

Spelling, Homonyms, and Contractions

Complete each sentence by writing the correct word in the blank.

Small children are _____ prone to bumps and falls.
(22) especialy   especially

_____ balance and coordination are just not as developed
(23) Their   They're

as an adult's. My family learned this _____ in a scary way.
(24) lessen   lesson

Right before my son's _____ birthday, he took a serious fall
(25) forth   fourth

from a slide on the _____ playground. He knocked his two
(26) neighborhood   nieghborhood

front teeth _____. Even worse, he _____
(27) lose   loose   (28) did'nt   didn't

move from the ground at first because he'd been knocked unconscious.

Thanks to the community's efforts, _____ now a thick layer
(29) theres   there's

of soft sand on the playground to help soften kids' falls.

Nouns and Pronouns

Read each sentence. If the underlined part is correct, write C in the blank.
If the part is wrong, write it correctly in the blank.

_____ 30. Ken Adams is the new <u>receptionist</u>.

_____ 31. Please help <u>he</u> learn your names and extensions.

_____ 32. The company also has a new phone system, and <u>they</u> wants to be sure everyone knows how to use it.

_____ 33. You will find instructions in <u>you're</u> boxes.

_____ 34. Every phone has <u>its</u> own extension.

_____ 35. All employees have <u>they</u> names in the new company directory.

_____ 36. Look up your name, and make sure <u>its'</u> right.

_____ 37. When our customers call, Ken will tell <u>them</u> the right extensions.

_____ 38. This morning, Mr. Campbell from the <u>nelson supply company</u> called our office.

_____ 39. He was angry because <u>him</u> was put on hold for fifteen minutes.

_____ 40. Customers on hold expect <u>their</u> calls to be answered promptly.

_____ 41. When you put customers on hold, check back with <u>they</u> often.

_____ 42. The new company directories are <u>your's</u> to keep.

Subject-Verb Agreement, Tenses, and Irregular Verbs

Complete each sentence by writing the correct verb in the blank.

43. Children between the ages of two and five _____ an average of 33 hours of television a week.

    watches   watch

44. They _____ little time to do anything else.

    has   have

45. From age two on up, the average child _____ more than 13,000 deaths on television.

    saw   will see   has seen

46. Parents and teachers alike _____ concerned about the amount of violence on television.

    is   are

47. Recently, the government _____ studying whether television promotes violence.

    is   has been

48. Of course, television _____ also popular with adults.

    is   are

49. *TV Guide,* which can be _____ at supermarkets, had a higher circulation than any other magazine in the United States last year.

    buyed   bought

50. February and November _____ two months when people usually watch many hours of television.

    are   were

51. Every year, the TV networks _____ to show their best programs during those months.

    chose   choose

52. If a TV show is popular this year, companies _____ more money next year for commercials during that show.

    paid   will pay

53. It is well _____ that shows with low ratings are sometimes canceled.

    knowed   known

54. A TV show with low ratings _____ less money for its network.

    earns   earn

Adjectives and Adverbs

Complete each sentence by writing the correct word in the blank.

55. Low-income families find buying a computer much
    _____ than middle-income families.

    difficult   more difficult   difficulter

56. However, the job market is changing _____ , and in
    the future, many people will need computer skills.

    quick   quicker   quickly

57. With more knowledge of computers, people will have a
    _____ chance of getting a job.

    better   well   best

58. Recently, there have been efforts to make it _____ for
    people in low-income neighborhoods to get computers.

    easily   easier   more easy

59. One of these projects is designed to sell computers to families at
    _____ prices.

    low   lowly   less

60. A company in Maryland sells used computers for as
    _____ as $25.

    little   littler   littlest

61. Sometimes, parents want the computers for their children who are doing
    _____ in school.

    bad   badly   worst

62. Some people think it would be _____ to buy
    computers for libraries and learning centers.

    more sensible   sensibler   sensibly

63. That way, the _____ number of people would be able
    to use them.

    largely   largest   larger

Sentences, Fragments, and Run-Ons

Below are five complete sentences, six fragments, and five run-on sentences. Put an *S* next to each complete sentence. Put an *F* next to each fragment. Put an *R* next to each run-on.

_____ 64. Many children get motion sickness in cars.

_____ 65. They feel dizzy or tired, they feel that they may vomit.

_____ 66. Strong smells may make the child feel worse.

_____ 67. You should open a window there will be more air.

_____ 68. Reading or playing with small toys.

_____ 69. A sick child can eat soda crackers, this food calms the stomach.

_____ 70. In the front seat or behind the driver.

_____ 71. A cool cloth on the forehead, which makes the child feel better.

_____ 72. In addition, young children often get ear infections.

_____ 73. Children under four years old.

_____ 74. Small babies may get a high fever, this can be serious.

_____ 75. An ear infection is painful make sure your child sees a doctor.

_____ 76. Crying and refusing to eat.

_____ 77. To prevent ear infections, keep the ears clean.

_____ 78. Needs medicine for one week to ten days.

_____ 79. The doctor will prescribe medicine.

Compound and Complex Sentences

In each blank write the correct word from the list below.

Word List						
80. and	but	or	**83.** because	so that	although
81. and	or	yet	**84.** unless	since	if
82. before	while	when	**85.** and	or	but

Every year people lose their lives in fires, _____ 80 _____ many

fatal fires can be prevented. Everyone should know how to prevent fires,

_____ 81 _____ they should know what to do if a fire starts. Many

fires start in the kitchen _____ 82 _____ someone gets careless.

Never put water on a grease fire _____ 83 _____ the fire will spread.

Cover a burning pan with an airtight lid _____ 84 _____ fires go out

when the air is cut off. Keep a fire extinguisher handy,

_____ 85 _____ know how to use it.

Combine each pair of sentences to make a compound sentence. Use the connecting word in parentheses.

86. **(for)** Do not store papers and old clothes. These items catch fire easily.

_____

87. **(and)** Always throw away oily rags. Keep flammable liquids safely stored in metal containers.

_____

Combine each pair of sentences to make a complex sentence. Make the second sentence a dependent thought. Use the connecting word in parentheses.

88. **(if)** Electrical fires are easily avoided. You take a few precautions.

_____

89. **(because)** Never plug more than two appliances into one outlet. You may overload the circuit.

_____

90. **(when)** A fuse may blow. A circuit becomes overloaded.

_____

Go on to the next page.

Parallelism, Modifiers, and Clarity

Underline the word or phrase that best completes each sentence.

91. Movies have changed as technology added more elements: first motion, then sound, and finally ———.

    color   they added color   color was added

92. Motion pictures have changed the way we think, talk, and ———.

    to dress   dress   are dressing

93. ——— motion pictures start out as an idea written in two or three pages.

    In this day and age,   In recent times,   Modern

94. A screenwriter ———.

    with a good background writes the screenplay
    having a good background writes the screenplay
    writes the screenplay who has a good background

95. The producers study the screenplay ——— a budget for the movie.

    to plan   in order to plan   as a way of planning

96. When making a movie, ———.

    many specialized workers need to be hired
    producers must hire many specialized workers
    it's necessary to hire many specialized workers

97. Lighting technicians, production assistants, and ——— are hired to work on the movie.

    sound technicians   people to do sound
    someone who knows about sound

98. The director ——— the shooting of the movie.

    tells everyone what to do during   supervises
    is the boss of everyone during

99. ——— the editor combines the pictures, voices, and sound effects to make the movie.

    The next step is   Then   After the previous step,

100. ——— the long list of titles at the end of a movie, it is clear that many people are needed to make a film.

    Watching   Seeing   From

Essay Writing

This part of the Writing Skills Posttest will help you determine how well you write. You will write about your opinion on an issue. To write clearly, follow these steps.

❏ 1. Read the topic carefully.

❏ 2. Get your thoughts flowing. On a separate sheet of paper, write down all your ideas that relate to the topic.

❏ 3. Plan what you will say before you start to write. Choose the ideas that are the most relevant. Add details and examples to support your ideas.

❏ 4. Write your first draft on a separate sheet of paper.

❏ 5. Review what you have written, and make any changes that will improve your work.

❏ 6. Read over your essay for correct sentence structure, spelling, punctuation, capitalization, and usage.

❏ 7. Copy your final draft on a separate sheet of paper.

TOPIC

A famous writer, Henry David Thoreau, once said, "We do not ride upon the railroad; it rides upon us." Thoreau meant that modern technology hurts us more than helps us. Do you mainly agree or disagree with Thoreau? What are some of the effects of technology such as phones and cell phones, computers, and TV on our lives? Are these effects mainly negative, positive, or both?

Explain your position in an essay of five paragraphs. Use specific examples to support your view.

When you have finished your essay, give it to your instructor or a person you know with good writing skills. You may also give the person the checklist on page 229 to help him or her evaluate your essay.

Posttest

Essay Evaluation Guide

	YES	NO

Content

Is the main idea stated clearly? ❏ ❏
Does each paragraph have a topic sentence? ❏ ❏
Are topic sentences supported by details? ❏ ❏
Are details written in a logical order? ❏ ❏
Is the right amount of information included? ❏ ❏
   (Check for details that are missing or not needed.)

Style

Did the writing hold your interest? ❏ ❏
Are thoughts and ideas expressed clearly? ❏ ❏
Are any ideas repeated? ❏ ❏
Are some words used too many times? ❏ ❏

Grammar

Are all sentences complete sentences? ❏ ❏
Are any sentences too long and hard to understand? ❏ ❏
Are any sentences too short and choppy? ❏ ❏
Are nouns and pronouns used correctly? ❏ ❏
Are verbs used correctly? ❏ ❏
Are adjectives and adverbs used correctly? ❏ ❏
Is correct punctuation used in every sentence? ❏ ❏
Is correct capitalization used in every sentence? ❏ ❏
Are all words spelled correctly? ❏ ❏

Overall, on a scale of 1 to 6, how would you rate this essay?

_____

If an area is checked *NO,* turn to these pages for review: 17–23, 27, 32–33, 49, 61, 68–69;

pages 22–23, 45, 50, 51–52, 55, 64–65, 140–141, 193–194, 197–201;

pages 22–25.

See also the Correlation Chart on page 230 for pages to review specific topics.

Posttest Correlation Chart

The chart below will help you determine your strengths and weaknesses in grammar and writing skills.

Directions

Circle the number of each item you answered correctly on the Posttest. Count the number of items you answered correctly in each row. Write the amount in the Total Correct space in each row. (For example, in the Capitalization and Punctuation row, write the number correct in the blank before *out of 15*.) Complete this process for the remaining rows. Then add the nine totals to get your TOTAL CORRECT for the Posttest.

Skill Areas	Item Numbers	Total Correct	Pages
Capitalization and Punctuation	1, 2, 3, 4, 5, 6, 7, 8, 9, 10, 11, 12, 13, 14, 15	_____ out of 15	50, 87–89, 156–160
Plurals and Possessives	16, 17, 18, 19, 20, 21	_____ out of 6	116–117, 161–162
Spelling, Homonyms, and Contractions	22, 23, 24, 25, 26, 27, 28, 29	_____ out of 8	118, 163–167
Nouns and Pronouns	30, 31, 32, 33, 34, 35, 36, 37, 38, 39, 40, 41, 42	_____ out of 13	28, 169–175
Subject-Verb Agreement, Tenses, and Irregular Verbs	43, 44, 45, 46, 47, 48, 49, 50, 51, 52, 53, 54	_____ out of 12	30, 66–67, 140–141, 180–184
Adjectives and Adverbs	55, 56, 57, 58, 59, 60, 61, 62, 63	_____ out of 9	38–39, 176–179
Sentences, Fragments, and Run-ons	64, 65, 66, 67, 68, 69, 70, 71, 72, 73, 74, 75, 76, 77, 78, 79	_____ out of 16	30–31, 187–190
Compound and Complex Sentences	80, 81, 82, 83, 84, 85, 86, 87, 88, 89, 90	_____ out of 11	42–44, 191–192, 195–196
Parallelism, Modifiers, and Clarity	91, 92, 93, 94, 95, 96, 97, 98, 99, 100	_____ out of 10	45, 55, 128–129, 193–194, 197–201

TOTAL CORRECT FOR POSTTEST _____ out of 100

If you answered fewer than 95 items correctly, determine which of the skill areas you need to study further. Page numbers to refer to for practice are given in the right-hand column above.

Answers and Explanations

INVENTORY

PAGE 1

1. W. Use a comma to separate the name of a city and state.
2. C. Use a period after a statement.
3. W. Capitalize names of teams.
4. C. Capitalize nationalities.
5. W. Use commas to separate the items in a list.
6. W. Use a comma to separate a phrase and a complete thought, not a semicolon.
7. W. Use a period after a statement, not a question mark.
8. C. Capitalize the name of important historical events.
9. W. Do not capitalize the names of seasons.
10. W. Use a comma to separate two independent clauses joined by a coordinating conjunction.
11. C. Use a semicolon to connect two complete sentences that are not joined by a coordinating conjunction.
12. W. Capitalize the first word of a sentence.
13. C. Capitalize names of companies.
14. W. Capitalize months of the year.

PAGE 2

15. parents. Use the plural form of the noun.
16. expert's. Use an apostrophe to show ownership (the advice of one expert).
17. children. Use the plural form of the noun.
18. lives. Use the plural form of the noun. Drop the *fe* and add *ves* when a word ends in *fe.*
19. family's. Use an apostrophe to show ownership (the rules of one family).
20. friend's. Use an apostrophe to show ownership (the house of a friend).
21. know. *Know* means to have knowledge of; *no* is a negative.
22. break. *Break* means to split apart; *brake* means to stop.
23. producing. *Producing* is the correct spelling. (Drop the final *e* before adding *-ing.*)
24. weight. *Weight* is the correct spelling.
25. beautiful. *Beautiful* is the correct spelling.

26. hole. *Hole* means a space or cavity; *whole* means the complete thing.
27. they're. *They're* is the contraction for *they are; their* is the possessive pronoun meaning *belonging to them.*
28. it's. *It's* is the contraction for *it is; its* is the possessive pronoun meaning *belonging to it.*
29. can't. *Can't* is the correct spelling of the contraction for *cannot.*

PAGE 3

30. C. Capitalize a proper noun—the name of an ethnic group.
31. them. Use the objective pronoun *them* as the object of the verb *conquered. They* is the subjective form of the pronoun.
32. strength. Do not add an *s* to a mass noun.
33. Ivan. Capitalize a proper noun—a person's name.
34. Moscow. Capitalize a proper noun—the name of a city.
35. centuries. Do not capitalize a common noun.
36. C. Use the subjective pronoun *they* as the subject of the verb *spoke.*
37. theirs. Never use an apostrophe with a possessive pronoun. It is already in possessive form.
38. he. Use the subjective pronoun *he* as the first part of the compound subject of the second independent clause.
39. its. Use the singular possessive pronoun *its* to agree with the singular *each republic.*
40. the. Do not use an objective pronoun to modify a subject.
41. government. Do not capitalize a common noun.
42. C. Use the objective pronoun *them* as the object of the preposition *to.*
43. C. Use the objective pronoun *them* as the object of the verb *govern.*

PAGE 4

44. was. Use the past tense verb *was* to show that the action happened in the past.
45. was. Use the singular verb *was* with the singular subject *no one.*

46. taught. Use the participle *taught* with the helping verb *are* to form the present perfect tense. *Teached* is not a word.

47. go. Use the present tense verb *go* to show that the action happens regularly.

48. begin. Use the present tense verb *begin* to show that the action is happening now.

49. reduce. Use the plural verb *reduce* with the plural subject *medicines*.

50. heal. Use the present tense verb *heal* to show that the action takes place regularly.

51. prevent. Use the plural verb *prevent* with the plural subject *drugs*.

52. found. Use the participle *found* with the helping verb *have* to form the present perfect tense. *Finded* is not a word.

53. seen. Use the past participle *seen* with the helping verb *have* to form the past perfect tense.

54. repair. Use the plural verb *repair* with the plural subject *doctors*.

55. are. Use the plural verb *are* with the plural subject *plastics*.

PAGE 5

56. well. Use an adverb to describe the verb *live*.

57. worse. Use the comparative form to compare two things.

58. slowly. Use an adverb to describe the verb *recover*. Do not use a word ending in *-er* when it is preceded by *more*.

59. sooner. Use the comparative form to compare two things.

60. badly. Use an adverb to describe the verb *do*.

61. higher. Use the comparative form to compare two things.

62. better. Use the comparative form to compare two things.

63. most difficult. Use the superlative form to compare three or more things. Use *most*, not *-est*, with long words.

64. hardest. Use the superlative form to compare three or more conditions. Do not use a word ending in *-est* when it is preceded by *most*.

PAGE 6

65. F. The thought is incomplete.

66. F. The subject is missing.

67. S

68. R. The two complete thoughts are not joined by correct punctuation.

69. F. The thought is incomplete.

70. R. The two complete thoughts are not joined by correct punctuation. A semicolon rather than a comma is needed.

71. S

72. F. The thought is incomplete.

73. S

74. R. The two complete thoughts are not joined by correct punctuation.

75. S

76. R. The two complete thoughts are not joined by correct punctuation. A semicolon rather than a comma is needed.

77. S

78. S

79. F. The thought is incomplete.

PAGE 7

80. because

81. or

82. and

83. yet

84. and

85. even though

86. The sun dries out your skin, and it affects the growth of skin cells.

87. The sun feels good, but it's not good for you.

88. You should see your doctor if a mole changes shape or color.

89. Changes in a mole can be dangerous because they can be a warning sign of skin cancer.

PAGE 8

90. plays. The verb *plays* is parallel in structure with the verb *recites*.

91. Developed by. The other choices are too wordy.

92. adding. The word *adding* is parallel in structure with the word *mixing*.

93. Today. The other choices are too wordy.

94. to make. The other choices are too wordy.
95. hear it only. The modifier *only* must be placed next to the phrase it modifies—*in nightclubs*.
96. you can hear rap. This choice includes the word—*you*—that *by listening* modifies.
97. who like the music use rap slang. This choice places the modifying words *who like the music* next to the word they modify—*teenagers*.
98. drugs. The word *drugs* is parallel in structure with the words *gangs* and *crime*.
99. some male rappers opened themselves to criticism. This choice uses as the subject of the sentence the term—*male rappers*—that is modified by the opening phrase *by showing …*
100. successful. The adjective *successful* is parallel in structure with the adjectives *talented* and *popular*.

ESSAY WRITING
PAGE 9
Give your essay to your instructor or a person you know who has good writing skills. You may also give the person the checklist on page 10 to help him or her evaluate your essay.

UNIT 1: ESSAY AND CREATIVE WRITING

SECTION 1
PAGE 15, PRACTICE
Sample answers:
1. Sports Topic 1: How to Play Soccer; Topic 2: Keeping Score in Bowling
2. Jobs Topic 1: My Dream Job; Topic 2: Good Bosses and Bad Bosses
3. Movies Topic 1: My Favorite Movie of All Time; Topic 2: My Favorite Movie Character
4. Animals Topic 1: Adopt an Animal; Topic 2: Hunting Should Be Outlawed

PAGE 16, PRACTICE
Sample idea for essay topic: Advantages of a large family: never lonely, learn to get along with others, support one another.

Sample outline:
Topic: Advantages of a Large Family
  I. Never lonely
     A. When young you have someone to play with
     B. When older you have someone to go out with
 II. Learn to get along with others
     A. Learn to share
     B. Learn to solve arguments
     C. Learn to compromise
III. Support one another
     A. Have people to call on when you need help
     B. Have people to borrow money from
     C. Have people to talk to about your problems

Sample idea map:

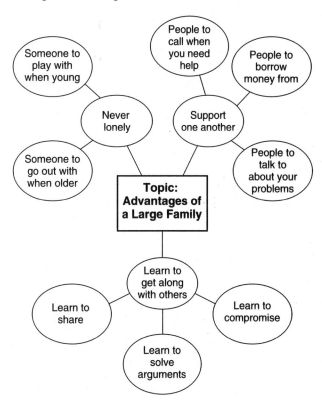

PAGE 18, PRACTICE

1. Sentence A is the best opening statement. Sentence B is not clear about which view the writer is taking. Sentence C is too general.
2. Sentence A is the best answer. It makes a strong statement about the main idea. Both Sentences B and C are vague statements that do not clearly support the topic.
3. Sentence B is the best answer. It clearly introduces the author's topic. Sentence A does not clearly support the topic. Sentence C is a supporting detail.

PAGE 19, PRACTICE
Paragraph 1
1. fact/reason
2. compare/contrast
3. examples

Paragraph 2
1. fact/reason
2. compare/contrast
3. order of importance

PAGE 20, PRACTICE A
Paragraph 1: 1, 5, 3, 2, 4
Paragraph 2: 4, 5, 1, 3, 2 or 3, 2, 1, 5, 4

PAGE 20, PRACTICE B
Paragraph 1: time order
Paragraph 2: facts/reasons

PAGE 20, WRITE
Sample paragraphs:

1.   Morning people and night people are very different. Morning people wake up with the sun, smile, and start talking. When night people have to get up early, they grumble and refuse to talk. Night people come alive at the end of the day. They are ready to party just as morning people are about to turn in for the night.

2.   Learning to organize your time will change your life. You can begin by writing down how you spend every hour of the day. Do this for one week and you will begin to see where your time is going. Next, make a list of the time wasters you can avoid. Then figure out how much time you have left for the things you have been putting off.

3.   Friendship is one of the most important things in life. If you know how to be a good friend, then you know how to be loyal. Friendship also teaches you how to keep secrets and how to make sacrifices for someone else. Friendship is supposed to be a two-way street. If this is true, then all the good you give will come back to you.

PAGE 21, PRACTICE
1. question
2. prediction
3. recommendation

PAGE 23, PRACTICE
1. a. The first sentence logically belongs directly in front of sentence (6).
2. c. Sentence (2) is the sentence that states the main idea of the paragraph.
3. f. No error.
4. e. The sentence is missing a subject.
5. d. The idea in this sentence is vague and unclear. The same idea is stated clearly in sentence (6).
6. b. *Nonsmokers* is plural, so the plural verb *are* should replace the singular verb *is*.

PAGE 23, WRITE
Edited version:

(1) There are far fewer smokers today than there were in the past. (2) The time has come to outlaw smoking in all public places. (3) Smoke is a hazard to the healthy nonsmoker. (4) In public places it pollutes the air and irritates the eyes. (5) Nonsmokers should stand up and be counted. (6) Since nonsmokers are the majority, they must push for laws that protect their rights.

Revised version:

The time has come to outlaw smoking in all public places. Smoke is a hazard to the healthy nonsmoker. In public places it pollutes the air and irritates the eyes. There are far fewer smokers today than there were in the past. Since nonsmokers are the majority, they must push for laws that protect their rights.

PAGE 25, PRACTICE

Proofread version:

I am enclosing *a* copy of my resume in respo*p*nse *sp* to your ad in the *Boston Journal* on June 26, 1999. I hope you will find ~~my~~ my (exereience) *experience* and skills *sp* inline with the qualifications for the telemarketing sales position. I *am* available to come to your office for a job interview please call me at 555-6242.

PAGE 25, WRITE

Final version:

I am enclosing a copy of my resume in response to your ad in the *Boston Journal* on June 26, 1999. I hope you will find my experience and skills in line with the qualifications for the telemarketing sales position.

I am available to come to your office for a job interview. Please call me at 555-6242.

SECTION 2

PAGE 27, PRACTICE
1. a. 3
   b. 4
   c. 5
   d. 1
   e. 2
2. a. 5
   b. 1
   c. 3
   d. 4
   e. 2

PAGE 27, WRITE
Edit and revise your paragraph. Use the Editing Checklist on page 218. Be sure that the order of events makes sense. Write a final draft. Use the Proofreading Checklist on page 219. Share your paragraph with a partner.

PAGE 28, GRAMMAR EXERCISE A
1. he, her. (Sam is the subject; Alice is the object.)
2. He, their. (Paolo is the subject; Sam and Alice's are possessive nouns.)
3. them. (Sally, Keisha, and Corinne are objects of the preposition *to*.)
4. him. (Diego is the object of the preposition *to*.)
5. They. (Sam and Alice are subjects.)

PAGE 28, GRAMMAR EXERCISE B
1. me. (*Me* is the object of the preposition *to*.)
2. We. (*We* is the subject.)
3. mine. (*Mine* is a possessive pronoun taking the place of a possessive noun.)
4. us. (*Us* is the object of the preposition *to*.)
5. I. (*I* is the subject.)
6. we. (*We* is the subject.)
7. Our. (*Our* is a possessive pronoun telling whose goal.)

PAGE 29, PRACTICE A
1. I. (*I* is the subject.)
2. my. (*My* is a possessive pronoun.)
3. my. (*My* is a possessive pronoun.)
4. me. (*Me* is the object of *telling*.)
5. I. (*I* tells who the proud father is.)

PAGE 29, PRACTICE B
Ray left in September for overseas duty knowing that his wife was going to have twins. Imagine his surprise when the telegram came telling him that he was the proud father of triplets!

PAGE 29, WRITE
Edit and revise your paragraph. Use the Editing Checklist on page 218. Be sure that your pronouns show the correct point of view. Write a final draft. Use the Proofreading Checklist on page 219. Share your paragraph with a partner.

PAGE 30, GRAMMAR EXERCISE

1. My niece Alicia plans to be a track star.
2. She runs and exercises every day.
3. Her father trains and coaches her for track meets.
4. My sister and I attend and give our support.
5. Alicia runs for the high school track team.
6. The team won a meet against the state champs last week.
7. My niece competed in three events.
8. She got first place in two events.

PAGE 31, GRAMMAR EXERCISE A

1. S
2. F. The sentence needs a subject.
3. F. The sentence needs a subject.
4. F. The sentence needs a subject and a predicate.
5. S

PAGE 31, GRAMMAR EXERCISE B

1. subject
2. predicate
3. predicate
4. subject

Sample complete sentences:

2. The host and hostess asked us to hide from Li Ling in the living room.
3. At seven o'clock, Li Ling surprised the guests by coming in the back door.
4. The look on the host's face was the funniest thing ever.

PAGE 32, PRACTICE

1. c.
2. e.
3. a.
4. d.
5. b.

PAGE 33, WRITE A

1. Sample fictional narrative paragraph:
   Carlos came to the United States to improve his life, but he never dreamed he would become such a success. He immigrated to New York City in 1990. He was 25 years old. After working for two years as a chef's assistant, he decided to go to school to learn to become a chef. When he got his degree, he found a great job in New Orleans, Louisiana. Now he is a chef at a five-star restaurant!

2. Sample fictional narrative paragraph:
   Patricia has learned that hard times can make you stronger. Last year, she lost her job because her company went bankrupt. Then her husband, Jon, had a stroke. Patricia had to get a new job and take care of Jon and the children. The stress was almost too much. But now Patricia realizes that the stress had one benefit. She has learned that she can do much more than she ever imagined she could.

PAGE 33, WRITE B

Edit and revise your personal narrative. Use the Editing Checklist on page 218. Be sure you support your topic sentence with details that answer questions such as *What happened?* and *Where?* Write a final draft. Use the Proofreading Checklist on page 219. Share your paragraph with a partner.

SECTION 3

PAGE 37, PRACTICE A

Sample answers:

2. My birthday cake had pink icing.
3. The old oak tree was over six feet tall.
4. A stooped-over man wobbled down the street with a cane in his hand.

PAGE 37, PRACTICE B

1. d.
2. b.
3. c.
4. a.
5. f.
6. e.

PAGE 37, WRITE

Edit and revise your description. Use the Editing Checklist on page 218. Be sure you include descriptive details and precise words. Write a final draft. Use the Proofreading Checklist on page 219. Share your paragraph with a partner.

PAGE 38, GRAMMAR EXERCISE

1. fine
2. fresh
3. brightly

4. beautifully
5. regularly

PAGE 39, GRAMMAR EXERCISE
1. hottest
2. new *or* newest
3. more quickly
4. most important
5. easy

PAGE 40, PRACTICE A
1. sight
2. touch
3. hearing
4. smell
5. taste

PAGE 40, PRACTICE B
Sample answers:
1. The blazing red sun sunk slowly behind the jagged trees.
2. The rhythms of beating drums came from the open window at the factory.
3. The smell of my newly powdered baby is like perfume to me.
4. My hamburgers are always spicy because I add extra onions and hot mustard.
5. Her handshake was sweaty and cold.

PAGE 40, WRITE
Edit and revise your descriptive paragraph. Use the Editing Checklist on page 218. Be sure you include sensory details. Write a final draft. Use the Proofreading Checklist on page 219. Share your paragraph with a partner.

PAGE 41, PRACTICE
Sample answers:
2. Scott has hair that is softer than a kitten's fur.
3. The wind howled like a mad dog all night long.
4. The lemonade tasted sour because it needed more sugar.
5. The smell of her perfume came through the door ten minutes before she did.

PAGE 41, WRITE
Edit and revise your descriptive paragraph. Use the Editing Checklist on page 218. Be sure you include sensory details and figurative language. Write a final draft. Use the Proofreading Checklist on page 219. Share your paragraph with a partner.

PAGE 43, GRAMMAR EXERCISE A
1. The skies opened up, and lightning streaked across the clouds.
2. Last year we had floods, but this year was not as bad.
3. The storm caused severe damage, and several people were injured.
4. Windows were shattered by the wind, so we went into the basement.
5. We read books, or sometimes we played cards.

PAGE 43, GRAMMAR EXERCISE B
Sample answers:
2. The street was deserted, and I was afraid to go out alone.
3. The couch was new, so we tried not to get it dirty.
4. The soldiers marched bravely, but their mission failed.
5. The sky looked threatening, so we left the beach early.
6. The fruit was ripe, and we picked as much as we could.
7. I should get gas soon, or I will run out.
8. We could see this movie, or we could see a different one.

PAGE 44, GRAMMAR EXERCISE
Sample answers:
1. If
2. when
3. When
4. If
5. as though or as if
6. because
7. Even if
8. Unless
9. Whichever
10. After

PAGE 45, GRAMMAR EXERCISE
1. The bus driver signaled, turned into the traffic, and slowly made her way along the street.
2. Jose's red car has bucket seats and chrome trim.
3. The sofa was old, plaid, and worn-out.

SECTION 4

PAGE 49, PRACTICE

Sample answers:

2. Then
3. As a result
4. In addition
5. However
6. Therefore
7. As a result

PAGE 50, PRACTICE

There are many ways to make this paragraph flow more smoothly. Here is one sample:

People who win big prizes in the lottery often find that the money does not make them happy. First, they have to deal with many people trying to get a piece of the pie. What is more, winners find that their friends expect them to hand over some of the winnings. Because of this, they have to be on guard all the time. After a while, lottery winners find that they cannot trust anyone. All this pressure takes the fun out of winning. They can no longer relax and enjoy life. Nonetheless, I am willing to give it a try!

PAGE 50, WRITE

Edit and revise your expository paragraphs. Use the Editing Checklist on page 218. Be sure you use connecting words and phrases to link your ideas. Write a final draft. Use the Proofreading Checklist on page 219. Share your paragraphs with a partner.

PAGE 51, PRACTICE

Sample answers:

1. maroon, scarlet, wine, ruby, crimson, cherry, rose, flame, communist.
2. succeed, master, conquer, overcome, earn, gain, attain.
3. stroll, amble, trek, march, hike, saunter.
4. cash, funds, coins, bucks, riches, income, bills.

PAGE 51, WRITE

Edit and revise your expository paragraph. Use the Editing Checklist on page 218. Be sure you use synonyms for the word *money*. Write a final draft. Use the Proofreading Checklist on page 219. Share your paragraph with a partner.

PAGE 52, PRACTICE A

1. neat
2. racket
3. mansion
4. decrease
5. gentle
6. scorn

PAGE 52, PRACTICE B

1. (A)
2. (C)
3. (B)
4. (A)
5. (C)

PAGE 52, WRITE

Edit and revise your expository paragraph. Use the Editing Checklist on page 218. Be sure you use synonyms for the word *laugh* and include details to help a reader picture and hear someone laugh in various ways. Write a final draft. Use the Proofreading Checklist on page 219. Share your paragraph with a partner.

PAGE 53, GRAMMAR EXERCISE A

1. passive. (action done to the subject, *pill*)
2. active. (subject, *We*, performs action)
3. active. (action done by the subject, *I*)
4. passive. (action done to the subject, *New York*)

PAGE 53, GRAMMAR EXERCISE B

1. 1
2. 3
3. 2
4. 3

PAGE 54, GRAMMAR EXERCISE A

1. With great force, the thief broke the lock. (The subject, *thief*, did the action, *broke*.)
2. The crew of *Apollo 11* landed on the moon. (The subject, *crew*, did the action, *landed*.)
3. They left a plaque on the moon. (The subject, *they*, did the action, *left*.)

PAGE 54, GRAMMAR EXERCISE B

1. (B)
2. (A)
3. (A)

PAGE 55, GRAMMAR EXERCISE

Sample answers:

1. He drove a taxi and also worked as a gardener.
2. Today, many people do not vote.

3. The large dog growled at anyone who walked by the yard.
4. Sam quit his job because it took too long to get to work.
5. In the distance, we could see the small ships.
6. Modern cars can be driven faster than older cars.
7. I asked the speaker to repeat what he had said.

PAGE 56, PRACTICE
Sample answers:
1. I like to read forecasts of the future, but I have to wonder if any of them are true.
2. When people are treated with respect at work, they feel better about their work.
3. Correct.
4. When you look for a loan, you find who has the best rate. *or* When one looks for a loan, one finds who has the best rate.

PAGE 56, WRITE
Edit and revise your expository paragraph. Use the Editing Checklist on page 218. Be sure you give examples of happiness and use the same point of view throughout the paragraph. Write a final draft. Use the Proofreading Checklist on page 219. Share your paragraph with a partner.

PAGE 57, PRACTICE
1. (1) The word *backgrounds* was misspelled without the letter *g*.
2. (3) The word *they*, the first word in the sentence, was not capitalized.
3. (3) The word *language* was misspelled; the letters *a* and *u* were switched.

SECTION 5
PAGE 61, PRACTICE
1. Therefore
2. so
3. In brief
4. In addition
5. as a result

PAGE 61, WRITE
Edit and revise your persuasive letter. Use the Editing Checklist on page 218. Be sure you use connecting words to make your points easier to follow. Write a final draft. Use the Proofreading Checklist on page 219. Share your letter with a partner.

PAGE 62, PRACTICE A
1. contrast (shows the difference between people who walk and those who drive to work).
2. compare (shows one way that peanuts and ice cream are the same).
3. contrast (tells one way Japan is different from France).
4. contrast (tells one way Lake Superior is different from the other Great Lakes).

PAGE 62, PRACTICE B
Sample answers:
2. The movie told the ending in the first scene, in contrast to the movie I saw last week.
3. I like him as an actor; however, he does not sing very well.

PAGE 63, WRITE
Sample answers:
1. compare: Marie is like Helen because they both enjoy watching movies, dancing, and bowling.
   contrast: Unlike Helen, Marie does not like jogging.
2. compare: My apartment and my sister's apartment are both cold in the winter and hot in the summer.
   contrast: My apartment is much smaller than my sister's, and I can clean it in one hour.

PAGE 64, PRACTICE
Sample answers:
2. My leg was broken in the crash.
3. Mr. Mori drives a moving van from 4:00 P.M. until 8:00 P.M.
4. The shop steward stormed to the boss's office for an answer.
5. They were gobbling candy in the next row and grunting like pigs.

PAGE 65, PRACTICE A
1. through thick and thin
2. as American as Mom's apple pie
3. selling like hotcakes
4. tried and true
5. raining cats and dogs
6. sick and tired
7. as hard as nails
8. take the bull by the horns

PAGE 65, PRACTICE B

Sample answers:

1. I've had both good and bad experiences today.
2. "Now it's time to suffer the results of our actions," the congressman said.
3. If you eat well, get enough rest, and have a good outlook, you will live a long life.
4. A summer cold is horrible.

PAGE 65, WRITE

Edit and revise your persuasive paragraph. Use the Editing Checklist on page 218. Be sure you support your belief with reasons and examples. Also be sure you use specific and fresh language. Write a final draft. Use the Proofreading Checklist on page 219. Share your paragraph with a partner.

PAGE 66, GRAMMAR EXERCISE A

1. hope
2. take
3. has
4. works

PAGE 66, GRAMMAR EXERCISE B

1. A salad with extra carrots is my usual lunch.
2. The people in the back of the crowd need to be heard.
3. Ned, with his three dogs, runs around the block after work.
4. The leader of the union says dues will go up.

PAGE 67, GRAMMAR EXERCISE A

1. leak (plural subject with *and*)
2. gives (singular subject with *or*)
3. bring (plural subject with *and*)

PAGE 67, GRAMMAR EXERCISE B

1. C
2. C
3. loves
4. takes

PAGE 68, PRACTICE

1. F
2. O
3. O
4. O
5. F
6. F

PAGE 69, PRACTICE

1. (A)
2. (B)
3. (C)
4. (C)

PAGE 73, WRITING AT WORK

1. (3)
2. (2)
3. Answers may vary.
   a. Both Paragraphs 1 and 3 offer specific examples. Paragraph 1 talks about shelter, food, and clothing. Paragraph 3 talks about specific items that donations were used to purchase: toys; cribs; transportation services; washer and dryer. While Paragraph 2 talks about two specific programs Judy's House would like to start, it does not offer any specific supporting details to describe the programs.
   b. Answers may vary.
      Sentence 1: A counseling program is needed to help residents understand and deal with chemical dependency and mental health.
      Sentence 2: An educational program is needed to help residents learn life skills and get their GEDs.

PAGES 74-77, UNIT 1 REVIEW

1. They. (plural subject)
2. He. (subject)
3. Her. (possessive pronoun)
4. him. (object of preposition)
5. His. (possessive pronoun)
6. them. (object of preposition)
7. me. (object of preposition)
8. he. (subject)
9. her. (object of verb)
10. I. (subject)
11. us. (object of preposition)
12. their. (possessive pronoun)
13. Diana started her new job on Friday.
14. Raymond and she work at the baseball stadium.
15. They sell peanuts and ice-cream sandwiches.
16. Raymond's friends attend most of the games.
17. The employees can buy tickets for half price.
18. F. (no verb)
19. S

20. S
21. F. (no subject or verb)
22. F. (no subject)
23. S
24. unless
25. *Either of these*: but *or* although
26. *Any of these*: and, so, *or* but
27. *Either of these*: when *or* if
28. George filled out the form carefully. He gave it to Ms. Golov when it was complete.
29. She read his resume and liked it. It was neat and well organized.
30. Ms. Golov offered George a job. He would have to work Saturdays.
31. The job pays well. The company also offers good benefits.
32. He likes the company. He'll probably take the job.
33. large. (adjective, describes museum)
34. fine. (adjective, describes paintings)
35. carefully. (adverb, tells how displayed)
36. easily. (adverb, tells how to get there)
37. fastest. (compares three or more)
38. well. (no comparison; adverb describes the verb)
39. harder. (compares two people)
40. quickly. (no comparison; adverb describes the verb
41. highest. (compares three people)
42. A
43. P
44. P
45. A
46. P
47. Aretha made the chicken soup.
48. Mr. Kingston wrote the letter.
49. The Chicago Cubs won the division.
50. Early this morning, someone broke the pay phone.
51. help. (compound subject connected by *and*)
52. is. (singular subject)
53. write. (plural subject)
54. cost. (plural subject); costs (singular subject)
55. drives. (singular subject)

Write the first draft of your essay. Then edit and revise it using the Editing Checklist on page 218. Be sure you use connecting words to make your points easier to follow. Use the Proofreading Checklist on page 219 to write the final version. Share your essay with your instructor or a partner.

PAGE 79, WRITING CONNECTION

1. (2)
2. a. I
   b. N
   c. I
   d. N
3. Edit and revise your letter. Use the Editing Checklist on page 218. Be sure you use connecting words to make your points easier to follow. Write a final draft. Use the Proofreading Checklist on page 219. Share your letter with a partner.

UNIT 2: WORKPLACE AND PERSONAL WRITING

SECTION 6

PAGE 82, WRITE
Sample answer:

> 111 West Street
> Chicago, IL 60606
> February 1, 1999

Dear Aaron,

How are you? I've been thinking about you lately and wondering when you might be able to come for a visit. It's only a two-hour ride by train, and I could meet you at the station. I'm free almost every weekend. Just let me know in advance so I can plan some interesting things for us to do.

I hope to hear from you soon.

Sincerely,
Sandra

PAGE 83, WRITE
Sample answer:

201 Lowell Avenue
Overland Park, MA 02110
October 10, 1999

Ms. Joyce Hawkins
Overland Medical Center
39000 South Oak Drive
Overland Park, MA 02115

Dear Ms. Hawkins:

I received your letter about the winter training program at Overland Medical Center. Thank you for getting in touch with me.

A copy of my resume is enclosed. As you can see, I worked as a clerk/typist at the Lenox Hill Hospital for the past two summers. Working at the hospital helped me decide that I want to pursue a career in the health field. I believe your program offers the kind of training I need to achieve my goal of becoming a medical professional.

I am pleased that you are considering me for entry into the program. If there is anything else I can do, please let me know.

Sincerely,

Antonio Torres

Antonio Torres

PAGE 84, PRACTICE

Sample answers:

1. Dear Kareem,

I've been calling you but haven't gotten an answer. Do you think you could help me move my grandmother's sofa this weekend? She's willing to pay us. Give me a call when you get the chance.

2. Dear Ms. Bowman:

I belong to a community group that is holding a jobfest for young people on Saturday, August 21. We are seeking the help of local business people who are willing to share their expert knowledge and experience. We would be extremely pleased if you could find time in your busy schedule to speak to the group on the topic of "Success in Your Career."

PAGE 85, PRACTICE

P. O. Box 32
Eden Prairie, MN 55344
October 20, 1999

Dear Aunt Frances,

Thanks for the beautiful sweaters! It gets really cold up here this time of year, so your timing was perfect. After living in Florida for so long, I had forgotten what cold weather feels like.

Give my love to Uncle Harold. Tell him I'll visit soon.

Your nephew,
Danny

PAGE 86, PRACTICE

222 East 24th St.
Philadelphia, PA 19135
June 14, 1999

Mr. Bernard Adams
Travelworld
901 Harrison Avenue
Philadelphia, PA 19139

Dear Mr. Adams:

Thank you for talking to me about the position in your word processing unit. I know my skills would fit your needs. Our meeting made me eager to work at Travelworld.

I look forward to hearing from you about the job.

Sincerely,
Elaine Evans

PAGE 88, GRAMMAR EXERCISE A

1. Last year I worked on Senator Smith's campaign.
2. The campaign office was on Fifth Avenue in the Chrysler Building.
3. A debate was sponsored by a group called Independent Voters of America at their building on the Hudson River.
4. Laura Washington, vice president of the organization, made a speech.

PAGE 88, GRAMMAR EXERCISE B

<u>m</u>ay 20, 1999

<u>s</u>upreme <u>c</u>omputer, <u>i</u>nc.
958 <u>a</u>lexander <u>s</u>treet
<u>r</u>iver <u>t</u>ower
Columbus, <u>oh</u> 43221

<u>d</u>ear <u>m</u>r. Potter:

<u>m</u>y supervisor, <u>d</u>oris <u>h</u>ealy, director of sales here at <u>b</u>radley <u>a</u>ssociates, asked me to send you the enclosed brochure detailing the services our company provides to computer stores like yours. If interested, you can take advantage of our free trial offer by calling before <u>m</u>ay 31. We are closed next Monday because of <u>m</u>emorial <u>d</u>ay.

Sincerely,

James Hobson

<u>j</u>ames <u>h</u>obson
<u>s</u>ales <u>a</u>ssistant

PAGE 89, GRAMMAR EXERCISE

1670 Evergreen Road
Houston, TX 77023
January 25, 1999

Ms. Vanessa Lewis
Lewis and Evans Assoc.
Houston, TX 77025

Dear Ms. Lewis:

I attended your career planning workshop at the Valley College library on December 15, 1998. Your presentation was just what I needed to organize myself. Would it be possible for you to send me copies of your resume-writing guidelines, the worksheet, and the sample? Unfortunately, you ran out of these three handouts before you got to me.

Sincerely,

Joseph Wallach
Joseph Wallach

PAGE 91, WRITE

Sample answer:

It was a pleasure meeting you during my interview at the day care center last week. Thank you for considering me for the position of administrative assistant.

Following are the names, addresses, and telephone numbers of two people you can contact for references:

1. Mr. Henry Banks, 1800 Doheny Drive, Los Angeles, CA 90003 (212-555-7390)

2. Mrs. Mary Kirby, 1600 Maple Avenue, Long Beach, CA 90821 (212-555-0079)

Mr. Banks was my basketball coach, and Mrs. Kirby is a family friend.

I look forward to hearing from you, and I hope your decision will be positive.

Sincerely,

Calvin Simpson
Calvin Simpson

SECTION 7

PAGE 96, PRACTICE

Objective, Work Experience, Education, Skills, References

PAGES 99–101, WRITE

Your personal data sheet should include the information requested. Share it with your instructor or a friend who can review it with you.

PAGE 102, GRAMMAR EXERCISE A

1. Typed
2. Handled
3. Completed
4. Operated

PAGE 103, GRAMMAR EXERCISE B

Sample answers:

2. Created signs for window displays
3. Scheduled coverage for reception desk
4. Managed newsstand in owner's absence
5. Won awards for running track

PAGE 103, GRAMMAR EXERCISE C

Share your lists with your instructor or a partner. Ask the reviewer to evaluate your use of action verbs and phrases.

SECTION 8

PAGE 110, WRITE

Forms like the W-4 should be filled out completely and accurately because incorrect information can cause errors in an employee's records. Such errors can cost both time and money.

PAGE 111, PRACTICE

2. 111 E. Main St., Jonesville, IL 60623
3. 12 imprinted binders
4. October 1, 1999
5. No, he put it on his account.
6. $38.00

PAGE 112, WRITE

INVOICE	TAYLOR HARDWARE				INVOICE NO. 7602	

SOLD TO	Anne Johnson		SHIP TO	same		
ADDRESS	21 Ford Avenue		ADDRESS	same		
CITY, STATE, ZIP	Detroit, MI 48011		CITY, STATE, ZIP	same		

ORDER NO. 6626	SOLD BY M. Jones	TERMS 30 days		DATE 10-3-99		

ORDERED	SHIPPED	DESCRIPTION	PRICE	UNITS	AMOUNT	
10-3	10-8	wood paneling, pine	30.00	8	240	00
10-3	10-8	3" wood nails, pkg.	5.00	1	5	00
10-3	10-8	decorative mirror	75.00	1	75	00
				TAX	16	00
				TOTAL	336	00

PAGE 113, PRACTICE

1. letter
2. Ben Martinez of Martinez, Inc.
3. Glenn Bono, 21 N. Main St., Austin, TX 78755
4. Sender

PAGE 114, PRACTICE

1. when Jim Cowens called, why he won't be in, and what his telephone number is
2. First Tony should explain that Jim won't be in. Then, it makes sense to say "Call Jim Cowens."

PAGE 115, WRITE A

FAX TRANSMITTAL SHEET		
TO: Abdel Tahiri	FROM: John Mandel	
COMPANY: Tahiri Retail	DATE: 12-5-99	
FAX NUMBER: 847-555-1212	PHONE NUMBER: 847-555-3311	
CONTENTS: Parts information	TOTAL NUMBER OF PAGES INCLUDING COVER: 5	
NOTE: The items you ordered last week are now in stock. Please call to tell us when you would like them delivered.		

PAGE 115, WRITE B

Sample e-mail message:

FAX TRANSMITTAL SHEET	
TO: MCox	SUBJECT: Meeting
My supervisor, Dan Gertz, is holding a meeting in the conference room from 9:00 A.M. to 10 A.M. on Monday, October 1, 1999. You and your staff are expected to attend. If anyone has questions, they can call me at extension 7224. Thanks.	

PAGE 116, GRAMMAR EXERCISE

2. wharves
3. men
4. attorneys
5. secretaries
6. women
7. teeth
8. roofs

PAGE 117, GRAMMAR EXERCISE

2. children's
3. friends'
4. company's
5. boss's
6. Amos's
7. everyone's
8. workers'
9. players'
10. Women's
11. Jackson's
12. machines'

PAGE 118, GRAMMAR EXERCISE

1. I have
2. did not
3. There is
4. was not
5. were not
6. will not
7. Let us
8. did not

PAGE 119, PRACTICE

1. vacation requests
2. Beverly Smith
3. all employees
4. A more thorough message would have included how to request vacation time.

PAGE 119, WRITE

Sample answer:

Date: 09/22/99
To: Art Balsam, Supervisor
From: (your name)
Subject: Time Off Request

I would like to leave work at 4:00 P.M. on September 27 for a doctor's appointment. I can work an extra hour any day this week to make up the lost time. Please let me know if this is OK. Thank you.

PAGE 121, COMPLETING A FORM

Part 1.   (the date)   584-906-792
          (your name)   313-555-0795
          ABC Supplies
          100 Hudson St.
          Detroit   MI 48255

Part 2.   AC-34

Part 3.   Mary Money   216-555-4875
          Adams Company
          1421 Wilson
          Cleveland   OH 44101

Part 4a.   ☒ FedEx Priority Overnight

Part 5.   ☒ FedEx Letter

Part 6.   ☒ No

Part 7.   ☒ Sender

         _/_ Total Packages

         _8 oz_ Total Weight

PAGE 122, WRITING A MEMO

Sample memo:

Date: (today's date)
To: All Cashiers
From: (your name)
Subject: Customer Relations Workshop

I have been noticing that some of our cashiers are not following basic store policies about how to act with customers. For example, some cashiers don't smile and greet the customer. Others don't count back change. Some even make the customers bag their own food.

Customer relations are essential to our store's success. For that reason, a refresher workshop in customer relations will be held in the staff break room on Wednesday, May 9, at 8:00 A.M. before the store opens. All checkout cashiers are required to attend. If you cannot, please let me know, and we will schedule a second workshop.

Thank you.

SECTION 9

PAGE 125, PRACTICE

<u>First</u>, go north to the corner. <u>Second</u>, turn right at the food store. Look for the sign for Smith Street. <u>When</u> you see the sign, walk a block more. <u>Then</u> turn left. <u>Last</u>, stop at the dress shop. Our apartment is on the second floor.

PAGE 125, WRITE

Sample answer:

First, walk one block to Price Street. When you pass the gas station, turn left. Next, turn right at the train tracks. After you see the post office, pass the bank and walk four more blocks. We are the third house on the right.

PAGE 126, PRACTICE

Did you ever wonder how peanut butter is made? <u>First</u>, the peanuts are shelled. <u>Second</u>, they are sorted for size and value. <u>Next</u> (or <u>Then</u>), they are roasted. <u>After</u> they are cooked, the red outer skin is removed. <u>Then</u> (or <u>Next</u>) the nut is split and the small piece called the "heart" is taken off. The heart makes the peanut butter sour. <u>Last</u>, the nuts are mashed. <u>During</u> the last step of mashing, workers add honey, sugar, and salt.

PAGE 126, WRITE

Edit and revise your explanation. Use the Editing Checklist on page 218. Be sure that the steps are in the correct order and that you have used transition words. Write a final draft. Use the Proofreading Checklist on page 219. Share your explanation with a partner.

PAGE 127, GRAMMAR EXERCISE A

1. future
2. present
3. past
4. past

PAGE 127, GRAMMAR EXERCISE B

1. (1)
2. (1)
3. (2)
4. (4)

PAGE 128, GRAMMAR EXERCISE A

1. Circle sentence 1: Save a room with a bath for the couple.
2. Circle sentence 2: I found a letter that is not mine in the mailbox.
3. Correct
4. Circle sentence 4: We bought a cat we call Fluff for my son.

PAGE 128, GRAMMAR EXERCISE B

1. (3)
2. (1)

PAGE 129, GRAMMAR EXERCISE A

1. Circle sentence 1: Parallel
2. Not parallel. The sentence should say: *Hard workers are intense, motivated, and careful.*
3. Circle sentence 2: Parallel
4. Not parallel. The sentence should say: *They like watching football, playing baseball, and bowling.*

PAGE 129, GRAMMAR EXERCISE B

1. It is good for people to run, swim, and jog.
2. Running, for example, helps you stay fit and healthy.
3. Swimming can help in toning your muscles and lowering your blood pressure.
4. You can start by walking a block a day and eating good food.
5. Exercise can help you look better, be stronger, and become more alert.

PAGE 130, PRACTICE

Sample answers:
1. You can relax at night by listening to soft jazz and taking a warm bath.
2. You can protect yourself from crime by not walking alone after dark and learning some simple self-defense.
3. I can make my lifestyle healthier by eating low-fat foods and exercising 30 minutes, three times a week.

PAGE 131, PRACTICE

1. how long to soak it.
2. It might catch on fire if you don't soak it long enough.

PAGE 131, WRITE

Edit and revise your explanation. Use the Editing Checklist on page 218. Be sure that you used precise words and specific details. Write a final draft. Use the Proofreading Checklist on page 219. Share your explanation with a partner.

SECTION 10

PAGE 135 PRACTICE

Sample answers:
1. Interview employers at local companies; research books, magazines, and newspapers that contain information about the topic; use the Internet to explore the subject
2. Possible questions are: What do you think are the most important skills for employees to have? Do you think reading, writing, and math are the most important? What skills must employees have to be hired? How important is the ability to make decisions? To solve problems? To get along with coworkers?

PAGE 136, PRACTICE

Sample answers:
1. Communication skills
   Warren, Dorothy. "Communication Skills: A Key to Success." *Careers*, April 1999, p. 35. Getting along with others is key to success on any job. Knowing how to communicate is most important skill. First impressions are important.
2. Communication skills
   Warren, Dorothy. "Communication Skills: A Key to Success." *Careers*, April 1999, p. 35. Informal language—slang—is all right with family and friends. Formal language is appropriate in a business setting.
3. Communication skills
   Warren, Dorothy. "Communication Skills: A Key to Success." *Careers*, April 1999, p. 35. Correct grammar is essential in business world. Correct Standard English creates an image of competence. Be aware of grammar—correct subject-verb agreement, verb tenses, and word usage.

PAGE 137, PRACTICE

2. If you dress well, you will have more confidence in yourself, which will show when you speak.
3. A post-interview thank-you note can help you get a job as well as show you have good manners.
4. Image is very important in business.

PAGE 138, PRACTICE

1. <u>Learning is now a fact of life in the workplace.</u> Even routine jobs are changing as the demands of <u>business change.</u> Often <u>employees are moved</u> from one job to another. <u>They must be able to absorb information quickly.</u> <u>They must be able to move to another task with little supervision.</u> The first step in <u>adapting</u> to this demand is <u>losing the fear of the unknown.</u> Most new situations are not as different as they seem at first. Learn to <u>look at the big picture.</u> Then you can <u>apply what you already know</u> to the new situation.

   Summary of paragraph 1: Learning is necessary because jobs and businesses are changing. Employees are often moved from one job to another and must absorb new information and tasks quickly with little supervision. Adapting involves being unafraid of new ideas. Look at the big picture, and apply what you already know.

2. <u>When you are faced with a problem on the job, your first reaction should be to think about it.</u> Thinking about the problem means trying to <u>figure out</u> why something is going wrong. Knowing why will usually help you <u>come up with a solution.</u> <u>Most problems have more than one solution.</u> Don't always think that you have to have the right answer. Most <u>bosses are grateful for</u> an employee who suggests <u>a way to solve a problem,</u> even if they don't always think the employee's way is the best way.

   Summary of paragraph 2: When you have a problem on the job, figure out why something is going wrong and come up with a solution. Problems usually have more than one solution. Bosses prefer employees who look for solutions, whether or not the employee has the right answer.

PAGE 139, PRACTICE

The information is organized using the compare-contrast method.

PAGE 139, WRITE

Write the first draft of your report. Then, edit and revise it using the Editing Checklist on page 218. Be sure the report's content is well-organized. Use the Proofreading Checklist on page 219 to write the final version. Share your explanation with your instructor or a partner.

PAGE 141, GRAMMAR EXERCISE A

1. spoken
2. written
3. teach
4. fallen
5. begun

PAGE 141, GRAMMAR EXERCISE B

1. saw
2. went
3. drove
4. slept
5. eaten
6. caught
7. froze
8. built
9. swam
10. took

PAGE 141, GRAMMAR EXERCISE C

Sample answers:

1. I have bought a new car.
2. John has done all his work.
3. Sue broke her engagement to Paul.
4. The pilot had flown many missions in poor weather.
5. They knew they couldn't pass the test without studying for many hours.

PAGE 143, WRITE A

Sample title page:

> Toni Morrison: Life in New York
>
> Prepared by
> (Your Name)
>
> Submitted to
> Carol Rivera
> American Literature
>
> (Current Date)

Sample bibliography:

Bawer, Bruce. "All That Jazz." *The New Criterion*, May 1992, pp. 10–17.

Gray, Paul. "Paradise Found." *Time*, January 19, 1999, pp. 21–25.

Morrison, Toni. *Beloved.* New York: A.A. Knopf, 1987.

Taylor-Guthrie, Danille, ed. *Conversations with Toni Morrison.* Jackson: UP of Mississippi, 1991.

PAGE 143, WRITE B

Sample answer:

Introduction

My supervisor, Shirley Jones, asked me to prepare the weekly report on service complaints during the week of April 4–8.

Body

The customer service department received a total of eight complaints. Five customers requested repairs—two for VCRs; two for CD players; and one for a tape player.

Two customers reported problems with repairers—one did not show up and another was late.

We received one other call about a remote control that was missing from a TV delivery.

Conclusion

A total of eight calls were received and processed. Please let me know if you need any additional information.

PAGE 147, WRITING AT WORK

1. (4)
2. (2)
3. (5)

PAGES 148–151, UNIT 2 REVIEW

1. Typed
2. Handled
3. Completed
4. Operated
5. communities
6. desks
7. knives
8. attorneys
9. buses
10. taxes
11. thieves
12. women
13. minister's
14. workers'
15. Jones's
16. bank's
17. people's
18. cities'
19. I've
20. It's
21. won't
22. hasn't
23. wouldn't
24. can't
25. Who's
26. past
27. future
28. present
29. past
30. present
31. future
32. past
33. had been cooking
34. will start
35. has been
36. will have worked
37. had told
38. written
39. begun
40. cost
41. knew
42. found
43. written
44. Her uncle was a well-known Mexican doctor.
45. He went to work for a Texas company called Lonestar.
46. Ms. Tomkins said she was going to New York on Monday.
47. The book was written by the governor of Arkansas.
48. Your vacation begins on the Fourth of July.
49. Did you see Dr. Jones last week?
50. Is Stan coming to the Halloween party?

51. She is serving hot dogs, potato salad, and baked beans.
52. Sheila was born on May 25, 1965.
53. Kham's boss, Charles H. Garrett, is from Boise, Idaho.
54. Do you want red, gold, or blue ribbon?
55. Please call Mrs. Alvarez to tell her the order is ready.
56. A clap of thunder made me scream while I was passing a large rock.
57. While we were driving through the storm, we saw many car accidents.
58. Juan saw his motorcycle, broken beyond repair, in the front yard.
59. When I was watching my son, he ran into the street.
60. As I was walking into my office, the phone rang.
61. The meal was cheap, tasty, and healthy.
62. I should walk, jog, or swim to stay in shape.
63. The alley cat has long hair, sharp claws, and one crooked ear.

Write the first draft of your business letter. Then, edit and revise it using the Editing Checklist on page 218. Be sure to state your request clearly. Use the Proofreading Checklist on page 219 to write the final version. Share your business letter with your instructor or a partner.

PAGE 153, WRITING CONNECTION

1. (5)
2. (1)
3. Sample letter:

Dear Dr. Banks,

I know I really need to lose about twenty pounds and get in shape, but I just don't have time. I work every day and then I go to school two nights a week to get my GED. I can't afford to join a gym, and I'm not usually a joiner, but Pound Losers has worked for me. I have tried fad diets, but the weight just didn't stay off. Pound Losers helps me learn about healthful food and ways to work exercise into my life. It also provides a lot of encouragement. I recommend it to everyone who needs help like I do.

Sincerely,

Sandy Lister

UNIT 3: GRAMMAR GUIDE

SECTION 11
PAGE 156, PRACTICE

1. ?
2. .
3. .
4. !
5. .
6. ?
7. .
8. !

Sample sentences:

9. My boyfriend never watches soap operas.
10. Did you ever watch the soap opera *All My Children*?
11. I just love it!

PAGE 157, PRACTICE

1. My aunt was born on January 13, 1960.
2. She grew up in Toledo, but she and her family moved to Los Angeles in 1975.
3. She is a store manager, a swimmer, and a mother of two.

Sample sentences:

4. My son was born on June 15, 1998.
5. My son's eyes are dark brown, and his hair is shiny black.

PAGE 158, PRACTICE

harriet quimby was the first woman to earn a pilot's license. she was a writer in new york before she flew a plane. she fell in love with airplanes in 1910 when she saw her first flying meet. harriet became a pilot and toured in mexico with a troupe of pilots. she decided she would be the first woman to cross the english channel. she took off on april 16, 1912, sitting on a wicker basket in the cockpit. after a scary flight, she landed on a french beach.

Sample sentences:
1. I live in (name of city capitalized), (name of state capitalized).
2. I like to shop at (store name capitalized), (store name capitalized), and (store name capitalized).

PAGE 159, PRACTICE

1. writer ed j. smith reports that people are taking cheaper trips in the summer.

2. mr. and mrs. mott drove to orlando, florida, and went camping.

3. last year, the motts would have gone to sea world instead.

4. this year, dr. ortega and his family went hiking instead of going to mt. rushmore in south dakota.

5. ms. wills visited her friend in wisconsin rather than flying to the island of st. kitts.

6. miss e. k. link from new town, long island, spent two days in maine.

7. she went to lake mead last year.

8. busch gardens in tampa, florida, is still very busy, though.

9. mr. hunt wants to go to israel and see the dead sea.

Sample sentences:
10. My dentist is Dr. Lou Graham.
11. I would love to go to Jamaica.
12. I was born in Mexico.

PAGE 160, PRACTICE

1. This year, monday, january 18, dr. martin luther king, jr., day, will be a paid holiday.

2. This holiday is in the place of columbus day, which we took as a day off on october 10.

3. The plant will, of course, be closed for the usual fall and winter holidays— thanksgiving, christmas, and new year's.

4. If any of these holidays falls on a monday or a friday, you will have a long weekend.

5. This year the company's independence day picnic will be on sunday, july 7.

6. I will be back at work on tuesday, september 6, the day after labor day.

7. Some people want to have the party on flag day, june 14, instead.

8. There has also been talk of a halloween party for october 31, which is a thursday this year.

9. We could hold the party on friday, october 25, if that is a better time.

Sample sentences:
10. My favorite holidays are Thanksgiving and Valentine's Day.
11. The best day of the week for me is Sunday.
12. My favorite season is spring.

PAGE 161, PRACTICE

1. wives, days
2. nephews, cousins
3. children
4. peaches
5. teeth
6. memories, visits

Sample sentences (compare your spelling of the plurals with the underlined words):

7. My two favorite celebrities are (names of two famous people).
8. In our class, there are seven men.
9. My refrigerator has three shelves.

PAGE 162, PRACTICE

1. Tran's
2. children's
3. friends'
4. factory's
5. bodies

Sample sentences:

6. My friends' favorite activity is to bowl on their league team.
7. My boss's favorite activity is work!
8. My mother's favorite activity is reading.

PAGE 163, PRACTICE

1. who is
2. I have
3. was not
4. were not
5. did not

Sample sentences:

6. I can't dance the tango.
7. I won't answer the phone at night.

PAGE 164, PRACTICE

1. their
2. It's
3. they're
4. You're
5. Who's
6. it's
7. their
8. They're
9. you're
10. Whose

Some people are always complaining about their jobs. They're always talking about the things they don't like about their work.

PAGE 165, PRACTICE

1. week
2. fair
3. capital
4. aisles

5. know
6. lessen
7. close
8. whole

Sample sentences:

9. I accept your apology.
10. He tried to brake the car in time, but couldn't.

PAGE 166, PRACTICE

1. chief
2. succeed, seize
3. heir
4. Their
5. hopeful, powerful
6. successful
7. achieve

PAGE 167, PRACTICE

1. getting
2. delayed
3. paid
4. submitting, writing

Sample sentences:

5. My husband carried the groceries into the house.
6. I am just beginning to study for the GED test.

PAGE 168, PRACTICE

1. who
2. good
3. well
4. among
5. which

Sample sentences:

6. I don't have much money.
7. I have very few pictures of myself.

SECTION 12

PAGE 169, PRACTICE

1. President Bill Clinton was the only president to be impeached in the 20th century.
2. President Clinton's trial began in January 1999 and ended the next month.

3. The trial was held in the United States Senate in Washington, D.C., the capital of the nation.

4. Dale Bumpers, the retired senator from the state of Arkansas, spoke at the trial.

5. The men and women in the room listened carefully to the speech Mr. Bumpers gave.

6. The newsmagazines *Time* and *Newsweek* reported on the trial for weeks.

7. CNN and all the major networks covered the event on television.

8. The Senate decided not to remove President Clinton from office.

PAGE 170, PRACTICE

1. team
2. air
3. crowd
4. energy
5. gravel
6. Time
7. family
8. juice

Sample sentences:

9. My favorite team is the Bears.
10. During a game, the crowd always cheers loudly.

PAGE 171, PRACTICE

1. We
2. He
3. We
4. She
5. They

Sample sentences:

6. They sometimes help me out.
7. We usually get along.

PAGE 172, PRACTICE

1. me
2. She, him
3. us
4. her
5. them

Sample sentences:

6. Please listen to me.
7. I don't want the tickets, so I am giving them to you.
8. Our boss gave the tickets to us.

PAGE 173, PRACTICE

1. his
2. His
3. your
4. mine, yours
5. our

Sample sentences:

6. Mine is neat. *or* My home is neat.
7. Mine is small. *or* My hometown is small.

PAGE 174, PRACTICE

Circled words:

1. Cities
2. snowstorms
3. newspaper
4. mayor
5. police chief
6. brother

Sample sentences:

7. My car had been sitting in the snow for three days, and **it** was dead.
8. Although **he** was already late for work, Joe offered to jump-start the car.

PAGE 175, PRACTICE

1. our
2. they
3. she
4. their
5. his

Sample sentences:

6. That actress is good in her first movie role.
7. Take the beef or chicken out of the freezer and thaw it.

PAGE 176, PRACTICE
Underlined words:
1. long-ago, skilled
2. Irish, Russian, some, early
3. strong, intelligent
4. German, English, this
5. good, sharp
Sample sentences:
6. Cats are independent.
7. Birds can be beautiful but messy.
8. Horses are fast and powerful animals.
9. Rats can be wonderful, clean pets.
10. Elephants have long trunks and curved tusks.

PAGE 177, PRACTICE

Are people ever really happy with their appearance? They must not be, judging by how warmly they greet each new diet. They must want to lose weight very badly. Some people hardly finish one diet before they begin another. My friend had almost finished his powdered diet drink when he quickly started a new diet.

Sample sentences:
1. I take care of my children well.
2. I sing badly.
3. I drive carefully.

PAGE 178, PRACTICE
1. harder
2. most crowded
3. more slowly
4. best

PAGE 179, PRACTICE
1. worse
2. carefully
3. best
4. fewer
Sample sentences:
5. My new apartment is far from the laundromat, but my old apartment was farther.
6. My dream last night seemed so real.

PAGE 180, PRACTICE
1. collected
2. collect
3. will collect
Sample sentences:
4. As I child, I liked to play checkers.
5. Now I like to play bingo.
6. Next year I will like seeing movies at the new theater that is being built.

PAGE 181, PRACTICE
1. has suffered
2. had gone
3. has gotten
4. will have been
5. has not shown
Sample sentences:
6. By next month, I will have lived in this state for ten years.
7. My life has been fairly happy so far.
8. Until last year, I had wanted to get a new job.
9. I have seen that movie three times.
10. When I finish, I will have written a twenty-page report.

PAGE 182, PRACTICE
1. left
2. lost
3. was
4. gone, begun
Sample sentences:
5. I have always known that I would go back to school.
6. During the last year, I have done some things to change my life.
7. Recently, I have begun to learn to drive.

PAGE 183, PRACTICE
1. appears
2. are
3. glow
4. shines
5. is
6. are
Sample sentences:
7. Cars clog the roads in my town.
8. The city buses or the train is a better way to go to work.
9. His son or daughters help in the store every Saturday.

PAGE 184, PRACTICE

1. are
2. has
3. take
4. gives
5. are
6. have

Sample sentences:

7. Everyone in my family is going to the reunion.
8. No one in my family has a van.
9. All of my friends are wonderful people.
10. Several of my coworkers have the flu.

PAGE 185, PRACTICE

1. P
2. A
3. A
4. P
5. P
6. A

Sample sentences:

7. Companies send a lot of junk mail. Many letters are sent by people, too.
8. I tell my children to study hard. My brothers and I were told the same thing by our parents.

PAGE 186, PRACTICE

1. OK
2. OK
3. Change to active voice
4. OK
5. Change to active voice
6. Change to active voice
7. OK
8. I entered the room at 9:00 P.M.; Tanya drank a glass of champagne; I decided not to drink anything.

SECTION 13

PAGE 187, PRACTICE

1. C
2. F
3. F
4. F
5. F
6. C
7. C

Sample sentences:

8. The minimum driving age in this state is 16.
9. Many drivers simply drive too fast.

PAGE 188, PRACTICE

1. the verb is missing
2. the subject is missing
3. the verb is missing
4. the subject is missing

Sample sentences:

5. My older sister is still living with our parents.
6. She enjoys spending time with them in the evenings.

PAGE 189, PRACTICE

1. RO
2. RO
3. RO
4. RO
5. C
6. RO
7. C
8. C

PAGE 190, PRACTICE

Sample sentences:

1. The Special Olympics was started more than 30 years ago; it is a program of sports for people with disabilities. *Or* The Special Olympics was started more than 30 years ago. It is a program of sports for people with disabilities.
2. More than 7,000 athletes attend, and they come from 150 nations.
3. Each state competes in nineteen sporting events, but athletes do not have to enter every event.
4. Everyone is a winner, for each athlete gets a ribbon or a medal.
5. Many people come to watch the games, and they are impressed by the athletes.

Sample sentences:

6. I enjoy watching the Olympic Games, and I'm looking forward to seeing the next games on TV.
7. Winning a gold medal must be a thrill. The athletes work so hard for it.

PAGE 191, PRACTICE

1. CS
2. CS

3. S
4. CS
5. S
6. CS

Sample sentences:
7. James watches soap operas every day, but his roommate watches only the news.
8. Some soap stars have been on the air for many years, yet others have just started their careers.

PAGE 192, PRACTICE
Sample sentences:
1. My first week on the job was a disaster, and my boss told me so.
2. I was really upset, yet I knew things had to get better. *Or* I was really upset, but I knew things had to get better.
3. I tried as hard as I could, for I really wanted to keep the job.
4. My coworkers gave me good advice, so I felt more confident.

PAGE 193, PRACTICE
1. NP
2. P
3. NP
4. P
5. P
6. NP
7. NP

Sample sentences:
8. Three places you can buy food are a grocery store, a snack shop, and a restaurant.
9. When you are sick, you should stay home, drink fluids, and rest.

PAGE 194, PRACTICE
1. Writing helps people think, speak, and learn.
2. Those who can write well will be leaders in the community, state, and nation in years to come.
3. By writing frequently, reading often, and seeking feedback, writers can improve.
4. Learning to write clearly, correctly, and effectively is a goal.

Sample sentences:
5. I can write letters, messages, and lists.
6. Three qualities of good writing are precise words, vivid details, and correct grammar.

PAGE 195, PRACTICE
Underlined clauses:
1. Although I have a car.
2. because I care about the environment.
3. If we don't help to reduce pollution.
4. before it's too late.

Sample paragraph:
Walk one block south on Andrews until you get to Anchor Lane. Turn right on Anchor. Continue west on Anchor, crossing Hyridge and Mesa. Keep walking until you get to the first parking lot on your right. Cut through the parking lot, and you'll see the community swimming pool. You can't miss it!

PAGE 196, PRACTICE
Sample sentences:
1. After I went to bed, I heard a loud crash in the kitchen.
2. Because I was afraid, I pulled the blankets over my head.
3. When I heard the cat's meow, I finally got up.
4. When I saw the cat sitting by the broken plate, I knew what had happened.

Sample sentences:
5. I went to get a broom so that I could clean up the mess.
6. I didn't get very much sleep that night because my nerves were still on edge.

PAGE 197, PRACTICE
1. M
2. C
3. M
4. C
5. C
6. M
7. M
8. C
9. M

Sample answer:
One night a tremendous windstorm ripped through our town. All night long the wind howled around our house. At one point I heard a crunching sound, followed by a loud snap. The next morning we found our small pussy willow tree uprooted, lying across our garden.

PAGE 198, PRACTICE

Sample answers:

1. While I was passing a large rock, a clap of thunder made me scream.
2. Sailing up the harbor, we saw the boat. *Or* We saw the boat sailing into the harbor.
3. As we flew over the town, the cars and houses looked like toys.
4. Do not sit in the chair without putting it together fully.
5. When I opened the jar, the sauce spilled all over.
6. As he was walking up the steps, the packages fell.

Sample sentences:

7. Going to my class, I met an old friend.
8. Angry at her husband, the woman stormed out of the house.
9. Already hungry, the dog sat by his empty food bowl.
10. Without thinking, I left the garage door up.

PAGE 199, PRACTICE

Sample sentences:

1. The baseball game took place on Saturday at 3 P.M.
2. When the game started, the players relaxed.
3. The pitcher did not know who to throw the ball to. *Or, more formal language:* The pitcher did not know to whom to throw the ball.
4. After each inning, they repeated their signals.
5. The game ended with a home run with the bases loaded. *Or* The game ended with a grand slam home run.
6. No one knows where the next game will be held.

Sample paragraph:

Solitaire is a card game I can happily spend hours playing. This game has two advantages over the other games I play. First, solitaire is played by one person, so I don't need partners to play. Also solitaire has many versions. Some are simple games using only one deck of cards. Other versions are complicated and require two decks. The more complex games can continue for a long time. Maybe that's why solitaire is also called "Patience."

PAGE 200, PRACTICE

1. W
2. C
3. W
4. C
5. W
6. W
7. C
8. W

PAGE 201, PRACTICE

1. out of money
2. did not do their work *or* wasted time
3. interested in *or* involved with

Sample revision:

I became upset when you yelled at me about the tools that were apparently stolen. I'm not the one who took them. This whole situation is very unfair. I feel as if you have been treating me poorly all week over this matter. I know I am not the best worker in the garage, but I am not a thief. Please do not blame me for this anymore; let's let the matter rest.

PAGE 203, WRITING AT WORK

1. (4)
2. (5)
3. Sample answer:

Kevin,

I need you to take the car to Sam's Garage before you go to work. Since we are going on our family vacation next week, I want to be sure that the car is in good shape for the drive.
1. Get the oil changed.
2. Get the tires' pressure and tread checked. If Sam says we need to replace one or more tires, go ahead and have him do it.
3. Check radiator fluid. If it is low, have Sam put more in.
Thanks,
Dad

PAGES 204–209, UNIT 3 REVIEW

1. They
2. her
3. his
4. their
5. She
6. him
7. He
8. me

9. F
10. F
11. S
12. S
13. F
14. F
15. S
16. F
17. because
18. before
19. and
20. If
21. so that
22. Although
23. When
24. Craig has an unusual job. He is a chef.
25. He used to work in a store. He was a cashier.
26. Then he went to cooking school for two years. It was a long program.
27. He had to take out a big loan. It was a difficult time in his life.
28. Now he works in a fancy French restaurant. His friends visit him there.
29. There is only one problem. He doesn't like working on Saturday night.
30. fine
31. seriously
32. quickly
33. careful
34. bright
35. highly
36. confident
37. greatly
38. best
39. most expensive
40. more quickly
41. farther
42. worse
43. better
44. was watching
45. got
46. has been working
47. will have lived
48. had been trying
49. is going
50. will vote
51. When Bob went to New York last September, he visited the World Trade Center.

52. He arrived on Tuesday, and by Friday he had seen all the major sights.
53. On Labor Day, he went on a picnic in Central Park.
54. He saw Dustin Hoffman eating French food at the restaurant called South Street Seaport.
55. He said to him, "Can I have your autograph, Mr. Hoffman?"
56. My husband and I were married on June 15, 1999.
57. The wedding took place in Chicago, Illinois.
58. His brothers Edward, Hal, John, and Joe attended the wedding.
59. You wouldn't believe the crazy toasts they made!
60. The wedding was beautiful, and all the guests had a good time.
61. Do you know where we went on our honeymoon?
62. We went to Atlantic City, Niagara Falls, and New York City.
63. seen
64. knew
65. broke
66. fought
67. caught
68. drove
69. gave
70. thought
71. begun
72. built
73. did
74. slept
75. drunk
76. taught
77. clothes
78. fare
79. accept
80. week
81. lesson
82. know
83. capital
84. whole
85. lose

PAGE 211, WRITING CONNECTION

1. A malapropism is the incorrect use of a similar sounding word.
2. great, hair, Aunt, beat, tale, veterinarian
3. a. I was driving home too fast from the beach when I hit the poor thing.
   b. You'll be happy to know that the dog totally healed from the injury.
4. (3)
5.   How I loved my Great Aunt Estelle! What a character she was. She was full of energy. Every time I saw her, she was in a strange predicament. But there's one tale that remains especially vivid in my mind. My Aunt Estelle was always as neat as a pin—even on the hottest summer day. So the day that she burst into our house in her bathing suit with her hair wild and loose, carrying a wounded dog, I knew that something was seriously wrong.

   "Aunt Estelle, Aunt Estelle! What happened?" I asked, as I felt every beat of my heart practically explode in my chest.

   "Oh, Ozzie! Quick! Call the veterinarian! We must get this poor beast to the animal hospital. I was driving home too fast from the beach when I hit the poor thing. Oh, how I wish I had missed him," cried Estelle "I think I hit his tail."

   You'll be happy to know that the dog totally healed from the injury.

POSTTEST

PAGE 220

1. C. Capitalize the name of a company.
2. W. Use a comma to separate the name of a city and state.
3. W. Capitalize the names of people.
4. C. Capitalize the name of a country.
5. W. Capitalize a proper adjective.
6. C. Use a comma between two independent clauses joined by a coordinating conjunction.
7. W. Use a question mark after a question.
8. W. Use commas to separate the items in a list.
9. W. Capitalize the first word of a sentence. (Another way to correct the sentence is by changing the period to a semicolon: *protested; they*).
10. W. Capitalize the name of a holiday.
11. C. Use a period after a statement.
12. W. Do not capitalize a title unless it appears immediately before the person's name.
13. C. Capitalize a proper adjective.
14. W. Place a comma between the day and year in a date.
15. C. Use an exclamation point after a strong statement.

PAGE 221

16. stories. Use the plural form. Change the *y* to *i* and add *-es*.
17. detective's. Use the singular possessive to show ownership (the friend of the detective).
18. crimes. Use the plural form.
19. criminals'. Use the plural possessive form.
20. searches. Use the plural form. Add *-es*, not *-s*, when a word ends in *ch*.
21. lovers'. Use the plural possessive form.
22. especially
23. Their
24. lesson
25. fourth
26. neighborhood
27. loose
28. didn't
29. there's

30. C. *Receptionist* is a common noun and should not be capitalized in the sentence.
31. him. Use the objective pronoun *him* as the object of the verb *help*.
32. it. Be sure the pronoun agrees with its antecedent in number. *It* agrees with *company*—a singular noun.
33. your. Use the possessive pronoun *your* to show ownership. The contraction *you're* means *you are*.
34. C. Use the singular possessive pronoun *its* as the object of the verb *phone*.
35. their. Use the possessive pronoun *their* to show ownership.
36. it's. The contraction *it's* means *it is* or *it has; its'* is not a word.
37. C. Use the objective pronoun *them* as the object of the verb *tell*.
38. Nelson Supply Company. Capitalize a proper noun—in this case, the name of a specific company.
39. he. Use the subjective pronoun *he* as the subject of the verb *was put*.
40. C. Use the possessive pronoun *their* to show ownership.
41. them. Use the objective pronoun *them* as the object of the preposition *with*.
42. yours. Never use an apostrophe with possessive pronouns because they are already in the possessive form.

43. watch. Use the plural verb *watch* with the plural subject *children*.
44. have. Use the plural verb *have* with the plural subject t*hey*.
45. will see. Use the future tense to show what will happen in the future.
46. are. Use the plural verb *are* with the compound subject *parents and teachers*.
47. has been. Use the present perfect tense to describe an action that started in the past and is still going on.
48. is. Use the singular verb *is* with the singular subject *television*.
49. bought. Use the past tense form (*bought*) of the irregular verb *buy. Buyed* is not a word.

50. are. Use the present tense verb *are* to describe something that happens regularly.
51. choose. Use the present tense verb *choose* to describe something that happens regularly.
52. will pay. Use the future tense.
53. known. Use the past tense form (*known*) of the irregular verb *known. Knowed* is not a word.
54. earns. Use the singular verb *earns* with the singular subject *show*.

55. more difficult. Use the comparative form to compare two things. Do not add *-er* to long words; place the word *more* before the adjective.
56. quickly. Use an adverb to describe the verb *changing*.
57. better. Use an adjective to describe the noun *chance*. Use the comparative form to compare two things.
58. easier. Use the comparative form to compare two things. Use *-er*, not *more*, with short words.
59. low. Use an adjective to describe the noun *prices*.
60. little. Use an adjective to describe the price. Do not use *littler* or *littlest* because the sentence does not compare two or more things.
61. badly. Use an adverb to describe the verb *are doing*.
62. more sensible. Use the comparative form to compare two things. Do not add *-er* to long words; place the word *more* before the adjective.
63. largest. Use the superlative form to compare three or more things. Add *-est* to a short word.

64. S
65. R. The two sentences should be joined by a semicolon or by the coordinating conjunction *and*.
66. S

67. R. The two sentences should be joined by a semicolon. Another way to correct the sentence is to place a period after *window* and capitalize *There*.
68. F. The thought is incomplete.
69. R. The two sentences should be joined only by a semicolon.
70. F. The subject and verb are missing.
71. F. The verb is missing.
72. S
73. F. The verb is missing.
74. R. The two sentences should be joined by a semicolon or by the coordinating conjunction *and*.
75. R. The two sentences are not joined by correct punctuation.
76. F. The thought is incomplete.
77. S
78. F. The subject is missing.
79. S

PAGE 226
80. but
81. and
82. when
83. because
84. since
85. and
86. Do not store papers, boxes, and old clothes, for these items can catch fire easily.
87. Always throw away oily rags, and keep flammable liquids safely stored in metal containers.
88. Electrical fires are easily avoided if you take a few precautions.
89. Never plug more than two appliances into one outlet because you may overload the circuit.
90. A fuse may blow when a circuit becomes overloaded.

PAGE 227
91. color. The noun *color* is parallel in structure with *motion* and *sound*.
92. dress. The verb *dress* is parallel in structure with *think* and *talk*.
93. Modern. The other choices are too wordy.
94. with a good background writes the screenplay. The modifiers in the other choices are misplaced, so the meaning is unclear.
95. to plan. The other choices are too wordy.
96. producers must hire many specialized workers. The subject of this choice—*producers*—is modified by the opening phrase.
97. sound technicians. The phrase *sound technicians* is parallel in structure with *lighting technicians* and *production assistants*.
98. supervises. The other choices are too wordy and unclear.
99. Then. The other choices are too wordy and unclear.
100. From. The other choices are unclear and would create dangling modifiers.

ESSAY WRITING

PAGE 228
Give your essay to your instructor or a person you know who has good writing skills. You may also give the person the checklist on page 218 to help him or her evaluate your essay.

Glossary

adjective a word that modifies, or helps describe, a noun or a pronoun. A **proper adjective** is made from a proper noun.

adverb a word that modifies a verb, an adjective, or another adverb

analysis the part of a report that gives the writer's conclusions about the meaning of the information in the report

antecedent the noun to which a pronoun refers

antonym a word that has the opposite meaning of another word

audience the person or persons for whom you are writing

bibliography a list of sources that were used to gather information for a report

brainstorm to generate ideas about a topic by listing everything you can think of about it

business letter a formal letter written to a company, an organization, or a person who works for a company or organization

cause and effect a way of organizing details showing how one thing (the **cause**) makes another thing (the **effect**) happen

clause a group of words with its own subject and predicate. An **independent clause** can stand alone as a sentence; it is a complete thought. A **dependent clause** cannot stand alone as a sentence because it is not a complete thought.

comparative form the form of an adjective or adverb when comparing two things

compare-contrast a way of organizing ideas showing how two things are alike and different

complex sentence a sentence with an independent clause and a dependent clause

compound sentence a sentence with two or more independent clauses, or complete thoughts

compound subject the subject of a sentence consisting of two or more nouns or pronouns joined by *and, or,* or *nor*

conclusion the last paragraph of an essay, which signals the end and highlights the points the reader should remember

contraction a word formed by joining two other words, using an apostrophe (') to show where a letter or letters have been left out

coordinating conjunction a connecting word that may be used with a comma to join two independent clauses, or complete thoughts, in a compound sentence

descriptive writing writing that describes a person, place, or thing

edit to check the content, style, and grammar of a piece of writing

explanatory writing writing that explains or instructs, such as how to do something

expository writing writing that informs or explains a complicated idea to make it easier to understand

fact a statement that can be proved true

figurative language words that describe one thing by comparing it to something very different; language that is not meant to be literal

final draft the final version of a piece of writing, prepared after editing and revising

first draft the first version of a piece of writing

form a printed document with spaces for filling in information. Common forms are **order forms, invoices, shipping forms,** and **job application forms**.

format the way the parts of a letter or any type of written material are set up on the page

homonym a word that sounds like another word but is spelled differently and has a different meaning

idea map a way of organizing ideas by putting them in groups that are related

letterhead stationery, or writing paper, that has a company name and address printed at the top

literal language words that describe exactly how something looks, tastes, feels, smells, and sounds

main idea the main point of a piece of writing

malapropism a funny expression that results when a word is mistakenly used for a similar-sounding word

memo a memorandum; a short, written workplace message

modifier a descriptive word or phrase. A **misplaced modifier** is in the wrong place in a sentence. A **dangling modifier** is one that does not modify a word in the sentence.

narrative writing a form of writing in which you tell a story about yourself or someone else

noun a word that names a person, place, or thing. A **common noun** names a person, place, or thing. A **proper noun** names a specific person, place, or thing. A **collective noun** refers to a group of people or things as a single unit. A **mass noun** names a quality or thing that cannot be counted.

opinion a belief that cannot always be proved

order of importance a way of organizing ideas from the most important to the least important or from the least important to the most important

outline a way of organizing ideas by putting them in numbered and lettered lists

parallel structure words or phrases that are in the same form

paraphrase to put information from a source into your own words

personal letter an informal letter written to someone you know well

personal narrative narrative writing about yourself

persuasive writing writing that shows readers why they should agree with a certain side of an issue or why they should take a certain action

plagiarism illegal copying of information word for word as if you wrote it yourself

plural a form of a word that shows more than one

point of view the perspective from which a piece of writing is written. The point of view may be **first person, second person,** or **third person.**

possessive the form of a noun or pronoun that shows something is owned and to whom it belongs

predicate the part of a sentence that tells what the subject does or is, or what is being done to the subject. The **complete predicate** may be one or more words.

prewriting planning before you begin to write. It includes defining your topic, generating ideas about it, and organizing those ideas.

pronoun a word that can take the place of a noun in a sentence. A **subject pronoun** can act as the subject of a sentence. An **object pronoun** is used as the object of a verb or preposition.

proofread to look at each word and punctuation mark to make sure it is correct

publishing sharing your final draft with your audience

punctuation the set of symbols used in writing to guide the reader

purpose your reason for writing—for example, to tell a story, to describe, to explain, or to persuade

report an organized summary of information about a topic. Three types of reports are **book reports, research reports,** and **business reports**. All reports have three main parts: an introduction, a body, and a conclusion. Formal reports may also have a title page and a bibliography.

resume a written summary of your qualifications for work

revise to change writing in order to improve or correct it

run-on sentence two or more independent clauses, or complete thoughts, that are not correctly separated by punctuation

sensory detail words that help the reader see, hear, smell, taste, or feel

sentence a group of words that expresses a complete thought

sentence fragment a group of words that does not express a complete thought

subject the person or thing that a sentence is about. The **complete subject** may be one or more words.

subordinating conjunction a connecting word used before a dependent clause to connect it to an independent clause

summarizing taking a large amount of material and trimming it down to a few key points

superlative form the form of an adjective or adverb when comparing three or more things

supporting detail a sentence in a paragraph or essay that tells something about the main idea

synonym a word that has nearly the same meaning as another word

tense the form of a verb that shows time, or when an action takes place. **Simple tenses** show past, present, and future actions. **Perfect tenses** show actions that have ended or that will end soon.

time order a way of organizing events in the order in which they happened; sequence

topic sentence a statement of the main idea that will be developed in a paragraph

transition word a connecting word that signals the way ideas are related

verb a word that shows action or state of being. Verbs have four basic forms, or **principal parts**. A **regular verb** forms the past and past participle by adding -*ed*. An **irregular verb** does not follow this pattern. A **helping verb** is a form of the verb *be* or *have* that is used with another verb to form its present or past participle.

voice the form of a verb that helps show how an action happens. With the **active voice,** the subject of the sentence does the action. With the **passive voice,** the subject of the sentence is acted upon.

writing portfolio a special folder or notebook that contains your best pieces of writing

writing style the way you choose words and sentences to express yourself. You may use a formal or informal style depending on your purpose and audience.

Index

A

abbreviations
  capitalizing, 87
  punctuating, 89
active voice, 53–54, 76–77, 185–186
adjectives, 38, 176
  and adverbs, 38, 76, 179, 206
  comparing with, 39, 76, 178, 179, 206
  inventory, 5
  irregular, 76, 179
  possessive, 164, 173
  posttest, 224
  proper, 158, 176
adverbs, 38, 177
  and adjectives, 38, 76, 179, 206
  comparing with, 39, 76, 178, 179, 206
  inventory, 5
  irregular, 76, 179
  posttest, 224
among/between, 168
antecedents, 175
antonyms, 51
apostrophes, 117, 118, 162, 163, 164, 173
audience, identifying, 14, 212
autobiography, 26

B

be, 66, 140
between/among, 168
bibliography, 142
brainstorming, 15, 212
business letters, 83, 84, 86, 90–91
  assignment, 92–95, 151
business report, 134

C

capitalization, 87–88, 150, 158–160, 207
  inventory, 1
  posttest, 220
cause and effect, 18–20, 69, 139, 213–214

clauses, 44, 195–196
collective nouns, 67, 170
commas, 42, 45, 50, 89, 157, 189, 190, 195
common nouns, 158, 169
comparative form, 39, 76, 178, 179, 206
compare and contrast, 18–20, 62–63, 139
complex sentences, 42, 44, 195–196
compound sentences, 42–43, 157, 191–192
conclusions, writing, 21, 142, 213–214
conjunctions
  coordinating, 42, 49, 157, 190, 191–192
  subordinating, 44, 49, 195–196
connecting words, 50, 61–62, 75, 205. *See also* conjunctions
content, editing and revising for, 22–23, 214–215, 218
contractions, 118, 149, 163–164
  inventory, 2
  posttest, 221
coordinating conjunctions, 42, 49, 157, 190, 191–192
creative writing, 12

D

dates, and commas, 157
days of week, capitalization of, 87, 160
dependent clauses, 44, 195–196
descriptive writing, 36–47
details
  descriptive, 37, 40, 41
  organizing, 20
  sensory, 40, 41
  specific, 130
  supporting, 17, 18–20, 32–33, 37, 40, 68–69, 213–214
  types of, 18–20, 68–69, 213–214
direct object, object pronoun as, 172

E

editing, 22–23, 57, 214–215, 218
e-mail messages, 115
essay writing, 12
  assignments, 34–35, 36–47, 58–59, 70–71, 77
examples, used as details, 18–20, 213–214
exclamation points, 89, 156
explanatory writing, 124–133
expository writing, 48–59, 77

F

facts, used as details, 18–20, 68, 213–214
fax messages, 115
few/fewer/many, 168
figurative language, 41
final draft, 24–25, 216–217
first draft, 17–18, 213–214
first-person pronouns, 29, 171, 175
formal writing style, 84, 118
forms, 111–113
  invoices, 112
  order forms, 111
  shipping forms, 113, 120–121
  writing assignment, 120–121
fragments, sentence, 31, 75, 187–188, 204
future tense, 127, 180

G

good/well, 168
grammar, 154
  editing and revising for, 22–23, 214–215, 218. *See also* individual topics

H

have, 66, 140, 181
helping verbs, 140, 180, 181
holidays, capitalization of, 87, 160
homonyms, 165, 209, 210
  inventory, 2
  posttest, 221
how-to writing, 126

ideas
   generating, 15, 212
   mapping, 16, 18, 212
   organizing, 16, 27, 212
   outlining, 16, 18, 212–213
independent clauses, 44, 195
indirect object, object pronoun
      as, 172
informal speech, correcting,
      200
informal writing style, 84, 118
information
   methods of getting, 134
   organizing, 139
introductions, writing, 142
inventory, 1–11
invoices, 112
irregular adjectives and
      adverbs, 39, 76, 179
irregular plurals, 116, 161
irregular verbs, 66, 140, 182,
      208–209

job application form, 104,
      107–109
job search writing, 96–109

language
   figurative, 41
   informal, and slang, 136,
      200–210
   literal, 41
   specific versus vague, 64–65
less, little, much, 168
letter writing, 82–95
   business, 83, 84, 86, 90–95
   formal and informal style, 84
   formatting letter parts,
      85–86
   for job interview, 94–95
   letter to the editor, 78–79
   personal, 82, 84, 85
little, less, much, 168

main idea, 17, 32, 68, 142,
      213
malapropisms, 210
many, few, fewer, 168
mapping ideas, 16, 18, 212
mass nouns, 170

mechanics, 156–168
memos, 119
   writing assignment, 122–123
messages, 114–115
   e-mail, 115
   fax, 115
   phone, 114
modifiers
   dangling and misplaced,
      128, 151, 197–198, 210
months, capitalization of, 87,
      160
much, little, less, 168

names, capitalization of, 87,
      159
narrative writing, 26–35, 77
notetaking, 135–136, 137
nouns, 30, 158, 169–170
   collective, 67, 170
   inventory, 3
   mass, 170
   plurals of, 116, 161
   possessives, 117, 162
   posttest, 222
   as subjects, 30

object of a preposition, object
      pronoun as, 172
object pronouns, 28, 172
opening statements, writing,
      17–18
order forms, 111
order of importance, 18–19,
      139
organizing details/ideas/
      information, 16, 20, 27,
      139, 212–213
outlines, 16, 18, 212–213

paragraphs, 18–19, 213–214
parallel structure, 129, 151,
      193–194
paraphrasing, 137, 138
passive voice, 53–54, 76–77,
      185–186
past tense, 127, 180
perfect tenses, 127, 181
periods, 89, 156
personal data sheet, 99–101
personal letters, 82, 84, 85

personal narrative, 26, 29
personal pronouns, 28, 29,
      171–173, 175
persuasive writing, 60–71
place names
   capitalization of, 87, 159
   and commas, 157
plagiarism, 137
plurals, 116, 148, 161
   inventory, 2
   possessive, 117, 162
   posttest, 221
point of view, 29, 56
possessives, 28, 29, 117, 148,
      162, 164, 173
   inventory, 2
   posttest, 221
posttest, 220–230
precise words, 37, 130
predicates, 30, 31, 74
   compound, 157
prefixes, 167
prepositions, 172
present tense, 127, 180
prewriting, 14–16, 212–213
principal parts, of verbs, 140,
      180, 182
pronouns, 28, 29, 74,
      171–175, 204
   agreement with verbs, 67,
      175, 184
   antecedents, 174–175
   inventory, 3
   object, 28, 29, 172
   possessive, 28, 29, 164, 173
   posttest, 222
   subject, 28, 29, 30, 171
proofreading, 24–25, 216–217,
      219
proper adjectives, 158, 176
proper nouns, 158, 169
publishing final drafts, 25, 217
punctuation, 50, 89, 150,
      156–157, 190, 208
   inventory, 1
   posttest, 220. *See also*
      individual marks of
      punctuation
purpose, identifying, 14, 212

question marks, 89, 156
questions, about a writing
      topic, 15, 32